American Administrative Capacity

M. Ernita Joaquin • Thomas J. Greitens

American Administrative Capacity

Decline, Decay, and Resilience

 Springer

M. Ernita Joaquin
San Francisco State University
San Francisco, CA, USA

Thomas J. Greitens
Central Michigan University
Mount Pleasant, MI, USA

ISBN 978-3-030-80563-0   ISBN 978-3-030-80564-7   (eBook)
https://doi.org/10.1007/978-3-030-80564-7

This Springer imprint is published by the registered company Springer Nature Switzerland AG
The registered company address is: Gewerbestrasse 11, 6330 Cham, Switzerland

To our mentors,
Irene Sharp Rubin & A. Ann Sorensen

Preface

Like most, we were incredibly saddened by the events of January 6, 2021. On that day, a multitude of protestors stormed the U.S. Capitol in an effort to change the outcome of the United States presidential election from Joe Biden's victory to Donald Trump's. While they ultimately failed, it was a national tragedy in terms of the lives lost and the psychological and tangible damages inflicted on the American government's capacity to peacefully transfer democratic power from one administration to the next.

In many ways, the events of January 6th remain deeply scarring to us. However, we weren't really shocked by the turn of events.

In the years prior to that cataclysmic attack, we had been studying the concept of capacity in the federal bureaucracy through an analysis of administrative reforms and a series of interviews with high-level federal administrators, national advocacy groups, and public administration scholars. We had hoped to study innovations and discover current administrative strategies regarding capacity that could make federal programs successful into the future. What we heard and studied in 2018 and 2019 revealed two immediate findings that alerted us to the potential breakdowns of 2020 and 2021.

First, a significant majority of the interviewees expressed heightened concerns about the changes to federal administration occurring during the presidency of Donald Trump. They noted a number of administrative maneuvers implemented by the Trump administration that directly reduced federal administrative capacity. These included: refusing to fill agency leadership posts and vacancies in crucial human capital management boards, so that agencies floundered and the boards lacked the ability to function for years; threatening civil service employees with termination if they didn't follow mandates that contradicted the mission of the agency (and sometimes the law); moving agencies out of Washington DC ostensibly putting the agency "closer to the people" even though it would result in most civil service employees leaving the agency and the agency giving up its visibility to Congress; and preventing agencies from publishing or even using science-based data. Politicization accelerated in federal administration during the presidency of Donald Trump that made our earlier focus on "capacity strategies for the future" incomplete, absent a deep understanding of the drivers of the dysfunctions we saw unfolding. Administrative capacity wasn't being innovated for the future, it was being attacked and destroyed, day by day. As the COVID-19 pandemic spread across the nation in the early months of 2020, such damage to federal administrative capacity became even clearer.

Second, and surprising from an academic point of view, our discussions with the experts and our survey of the literature did not find a widespread agreement on a conceptual definition of administrative capacity. Experts knew it was important and realized that it appeared to be declining in some way, but no singular conceptualization of administrative capacity emerged. *What was administrative capacity?* Some scholars and practitioners thought it was about agency personnel numbers. Others thought that a focus on personnel was misguided as all programs depended on contractors to implement services. Still, others noted that federal administrative capacity could only be defined by comparative studies and determining if a baseline of capacity existed for effective governance. However, as we progressed through our inquiries, personal perspectives and published studies almost always came to the same conclusion: capacity was a very complex issue, included certain multiple dimensions, and seemed to be degrading at a very rapid pace in the Trump administration.

In this book, which is guided by the insights of our peers in academia and the good government community, we have explored the concept of administrative capacity with the hopes of defining it and showcasing how it has changed through history and especially in the years of the Trump presidency. As a result, our book is as much a reflective project as it is an effort to come up with a sensemaking framework on the components of capacity and their ebb and flow. We very much appreciate our interviewees as they lent us their ideas on capacity, informed us about administrative histories, and provided insight on how capacity had changed over the last two decades. To connect the present with the past, we grounded our understanding of administrative capacity by looking at the history of administrative reforms and the evolution of theories on administrative capacity. The result is a theoretical exploration, through time, of administrative capacity, to make sense of today's decline and tomorrow's challenge of rebuilding.

As this was our first time to work on a book, we realized as we worked that we were framing a larger theory, and that another volume might be needed to tease out some of our ideas. We still have many hours of interviews that can be coded for themes and used in a more conventional research project. We felt we had to first arrive at a good understanding of administrative capacity and explore how it evolved before the Trump administration and how it was transformed recently. Only then could we really understand what the future might hold for federal administrative capacity.

Since our grad school years at Northern Illinois University, we have nurtured a fascination with the abilities of governments to cope with change. Much as we have enjoyed our collaboration through the decades, we also would not have been able to complete this book without the ideas of the scholars ahead of us, the inspiration of our graduate students at San Francisco State and Central Michigan, and the support of a number of people. Robert Durant, Alasdair Roberts, Irene Rubin, Jason Briefel, John Kamensky, Terry Gerton, Dustin Brown, Bill Valdez, Brian Cook, and Robert Goldenkoff lent us nuggets of wisdom that led to our comprehensive approach, including connection to their network of reform-minded leaders. We also received insights into government reform from the perspectives of the agencies, legislature, academia, labor, contractor, and good government circles—some of which we have used for this book, and some that we hope to mine in a succeeding volume—from Mark Bussow, Dan Chenok, Jonathan Justice, Melvin Dubnick, Mordecai Lee, Shelley Metzenbaum, Richard Leob, Molly Jahn, Juniper Katz, Cynthia Vallina, Thomas Ross, Bill Brantley, Erik Bergrud, Katherine Smith Evans, David Mader, Susan Offutt, Steve Suppan, Richard Holden, Tony Corbo, Stan Soloway, Robert Tobias, Adam White, John York, and many others we could not list here.

Thomas would like to thank his family for their support as he worked on this project: Jerry and Joy Greitens, Lesley Hoenig, Walker Hoenig-Greitens, Silvio Hoenig, Chester Hoenig, and Phoebe (Phoebus) Hoenig.

Ernie is grateful for the support of her family and friends in this project: Patricia Joaquin, Felomina Tesoro, Pinky Ramos, Vicky and David Watters, Fely Magsalin Ramos, Thomas Hetherington, Katherine Mendoza, Yi Yen Chen, Erin Gotland, Vic San Vicente, and Cynthia Paralejas.

We want to thank Lorraine Klimowich, Faith Su, Maria David, and the rest of the team at Springer for their guidance and encouragement as we worked on this project. We humbly take responsibility for all that is said and all that is left unsaid in this book. Writing about the complexities of governing and conducting research amid pandemic and national tragedies have made this experience truly one of a kind. We are thankful to have gotten this far and we persevered thinking that this book could someday fall into your hands—as a public servant, a colleague, a student, or a citizen who will chart the future of the land we love.

San Francisco, CA, USA   M. Ernita Joaquin
Mount Pleasant, MI, USA   Thomas J. Greitens

Contents

About the Authors

Maria Ernita Joaquin is Associate Professor of Public Administration at San Francisco State University. She previously taught at The University of the Philippines and at University of Nevada-Las Vegas. Her earlier publications explored management development and Philippine government devolution. Recent works have examined budget and accountabilty reforms in American bureaucracy, e-democracy, and public administration pedagogy. She received her Political Science bachelor's degree and MPA degree from the University of the Philippines and her Advanced Certificate in Human Resource Studies from The University of Manchester (UK). She received her PhD in Political Science from Northern Illinois University.

Thomas J. Greitens is Professor of Public Administration and Director of the MPA program at Central Michigan University. His research explores the administrative challenges of implementing innovation in public sector organizations, from online service delivery to privatization to public engagement. He received his bachelor's degree and MPA degree from Arkansas State University, and his PhD from Northern Illinois University. His work has appeared in *Public Administration Review, Administration & Society, Public Performance & Management Review,* and several books on public management.

Abbreviations

ACIR	Advisory Commission on Intergovernmental Relations
AFGE	American Federation of Government Employees
APA	Administrative Procedure Act
BLS	Bureau of Labor Statistics
CBO	Congressional Budget Office
CBPP	Center on Budget and Policy Priorities
CDC	Centers for Disease Control and Prevention
CPSC	Consumer Protection and Safety Commission
CREW	Citizens for Responsibility and Ethics in Washington
CSC	Civil Service Commission
DHS	Department of Homeland Security
DOE	Department of Education
DOI	Department of the Interior
DOL	Department of Labor
EOP	Executive Office of the President
EPA	Environmental Protection Agency
ERS	Economic Research Service
FDA	Food and Drug Administration
FDR	Franklin D. Roosevelt
FEMA	Federal Emergency Management Agency
FEVS	Federal Employee Viewpoint Survey
FLRA	Federal Labor Relations Authority
GAO	Government Accountability Office
GPRA	Government Performance and Results Act
GSA	General Services Administration
HHS	Department of Health and Human Services
ICE	Immigration and Customs Enforcement
IHME	Institute for Health Metrics and Evaluation
MSPB	Merit Systems Protection Board
NAPA	National Academy of Public Administration
NPR	National Performance Review

NPR	National Public Radio
NSF	National Science Foundation
OMB	Office of Management and Budget
OPM	Office of Personnel Management
OSC	Office of Special Counsel
OSHA	Occupational Safety and Health Administration
OTA	Office of Technology Assessment
PACGO	President's Advisory Committee for Government Organization
PART	Program Assessment Rating Tool
PCAM	President's Committee on Administrative Management
PMA	President's Management Agenda
PMP	Personnel Management Project
PPS	Partnership for Public Service
SEA	Senior Executives Association
USAID	United States Agency for International Development
USCIS	US Customs and Immigration Services
USDA	US Department of Agriculture

Chapter 1
Introduction

> *(The) path toward a regeneration of American government*
> *requires the utmost caution, lest in disgust with bureaucracy we*
> *stumble upon a sense of the state far more threatening than we*
> *have yet known.*
>
> Stephen Skowronek (1982, p. 292)

1.1 A Crisis Finds a Nation as It Is

A federal agency that eradicated smallpox and polio, the US Centers for Disease Control and Prevention (CDC), fell hard in the face of a pandemic, its mistakes part of a chain of governance failures that contributed to untold suffering and the diminution of America's integrity in the eyes of the world (Bandler et al., 2020). From surveilling the threat to containing the outbreak, the CDC was joined by other public health agencies in demonstrating a stunning level of helplessness against what President Donald Trump called a flu-like disease. How could the most powerful nation on the planet allow itself to be brought to its knees so swiftly by a novel coronavirus? What happened to its administrative capacity?

Early in 2020, before the attempted overthrow of the November presidential election, no other puzzle of politics or administration was more disturbing. The alarm was not rising merely from the left of the political spectrum. David Frum (2020), a conservative critic of Trump, argued that the United States could have and should have suffered less than nations nearer to China, where COVID-19, the respiratory illness created by the coronavirus, broke out in January (Frum, 2020). Yet, within a span of months, the country marched itself toward the greatest number of deaths and the worst economic dislocation since the Great Depression. America's Cold War enemy, Russia, the oft-derided United Nations, and pandemic-stricken China had to send humanitarian aid to the richest country that seemed like a beggar nation in utter chaos (Packer, 2020, para. 3). Torn by the politicized science of the pandemic, the nation's health dwindled amid cultural wars and structural inequities, resulting in a failure to confront a threat that would shrink the economy by at least

© Springer Nature Switzerland AG 2021
M. E. Joaquin, T. J. Greitens, *American Administrative Capacity*,
https://doi.org/10.1007/978-3-030-80564-7_1

a trillion dollars, infect at least 25 million Americans, and kill almost half a million of them by the time the Trump administration passed the baton reluctantly to the Biden administration (Johns Hopkins University, n.d.). These cataclysmic failures compel an examination of administrative capacity. But what is administrative capacity? How is it lost? The perturbations of the Trump presidency made us want to dig up the past and find the right shovel with which to dig it. If capacity building is about "institutionalizing or embodying strengths" (Honadle, 1981, p. 578), what government reforms have influenced those strengths, and what dynamics could help explain the dissipation of capacity witnessed recently?

Warnings were not scarce about the potential collapse of administrative capacity to handle a national crisis (Walsh, 2017). However, in an environment bombarded with rallying cries to make one thing or another "Great Again," a well-functioning bureaucracy and a national regard for science that made America truly great were getting deconstructed out of sight. Countless experts, managers, and workers in public health, emergency management, occupational safety, and education at the federal, state, and local levels left the public service after absorbing immense duress. Political pressures shook the foundations of basic science and the tenets of a professional bureaucracy (Lane & Riordan, 2017). Those pressures only magnified as the Trump administration led attacks on the civil service, repelled the idea of neutral competence, and forced government workers to either endure troubling breakdowns in administration or leave the service completely (Rucker & Costa, 2019). Midway into Trump's term that began in 2017, the signs of a decaying administrative culture suggested that it was just a matter of *when*, not *if*, a catastrophe would illustrate the true severity of the federal government's diminished administrative capacity (Chait, 2019).

The threat to democracy witnessed in the aftermath of the 2020 election further indicated the severity of the decay in terms of collective values and administrative structures. Democracy, it is said, depends on the consent of the losers in an election to honor the legitimacy of the winners (Anderson et al., 2005). Yet, when voters decided to change the head of its administrative state in the 2020 election, Trump's reluctance to accept the verdict tested the country's constitutional, democratic, and moral resilience. What happened? On January 6, 2021, the country's sitting vice president, senators, and representatives were thrown in harm's way as Trump's supporters stormed the national Capitol to prevent a peaceful transfer of power. In the aftermath of the attack, investigations uncovered alarming breakdowns of capacity beyond the reportedly arcane and overly bureaucratic procedures that left no one single person responsible for securing the Capitol (Feuer & Hong, 2021). The capacity deficit – inside government as well as in the wider society – that gave the novel coronavirus so much lethality also allowed enemies of the state to intimidate the first branch of government and undermine democracy. To date, the new Congress struggles to rise above recriminations in exhuming the terrors of that day and the miscarriages of democracy that precipitated them.

To examine what blindsided the federal government at the onset of the pandemic and what helped cause the subsequent failures of federal administration, we explore the concept of administrative capacity and link its rise and fall with various administrative reforms passed over time. By anchoring our analysis of today's capacity decay to historical reforms, we can see how the problems of the modern administrative state are linked to problems present at its beginning, and how the challenges we confront in the aftermath of Trump's deconstruction of capacity are rooted, like so many issues of administration, in the reform solutions of the past (Skowronek, 1982, p. ix). In our analysis, a decayed capacity abetted the crises in the recent administration, and such decay was paved by reforms untethered to a comprehensive notion of administrative capacity. Looking at the vast history of bureaucratic reforms in the federal government, we thought it was reasonable to ask whether reforms enhanced administrative capacity, merely camouflaged its decline, or, worse, abetted its decay.

1.2 Avoiding Presentism

In this book that is part -conceptual reflection and part -theory building, we aim to show where the beginnings of capacity's decay can be traced and how capacity's reseeding toward resilience can occur. This goal requires avoiding presentism. In *Strategies for Governing: Reinventing Public Administration for a Dangerous Century,* Alasdair Roberts wrote that shorter timeframes for understanding governance strategies "create an illusion of robustness and stability" (2019, p. 25). Likewise, Robert Durant, in his incisive analysis of bureaucratic evolution, dissuaded researchers from focusing on proximate causes and effects or reducing the multidimensionality of important concepts in public administration. Durant instead suggested paying attention to the long-term, slow-moving secular forces as explanatory factors to what we now see (2010). Heeding both scholars, we inquired about capacity beyond the ambit of management and sketched it out within a developmental and political context. As Ezra Suleiman noted:

> the relevance of the questions that the field of public administration asks resides in the fact that what is raised and answered depends on where this field situates itself. Management specialists do not ask the same questions as those whose main concern happens to be the distribution of power and influence. (Suleiman, 2005, p. 5)

Recognizing those ideas, this book is an effort to reconceptualize capacity while tracing its evolution in the context of reform initiatives. This allows us to *formulate an understanding of what administrative capacity is, by figuring out how the reformers of various eras influenced it.* This approach is obviously challenging as it requires an understanding of the politics of reform movements and how those reforms then influenced administrative capacity. We hope that the product of our research, a capacity-centered framework and a multidimensional approach to capacity, can offer useful insights for future reformers. At the end, those insights converge around the idea of resilience and the tasks ahead for allies in good government to steer a new direction, even if the hour is already is late.

1.3   The Administrative Landscape

Some basic definitions and descriptions are in order. Prior to any analysis of administrative capacity, we have to discuss how it links back to the different conceptualizations of the administrative state. *Administrative state,* like *capacity,* evokes different things to different people. For example, Roberts observed that academics constantly discover and label new types of *states,* but the terms hardly capture the ultimate goals of political leaders:

> Sometimes their labels relate to features or circumstances (for example, fragile states or frontier states), and sometimes they relate to priorities and strategies for leaders (for example, developmental states or welfare states). The practice of labeling states is problematic, however, because no single adjective adequately describes all of the important conditions that influence strategy…(L)eaders respond in many ways to diverse circumstances and also that states change form constantly. (Roberts, 2019, p. 141)

Roberts suggested decoupling the terms and narrowing the definition of administrative state to avoid mistakenly triggering meanings that are loathed by conservatives. He pointed to an early, 1939 conceptualization that small government and anti-bureaucracy movements harbored. But Trump took that concept further with his *deep state* accusations that have less to do with abhorrence of central planning and more about loyalty as the litmus test for holding office. It might be useful, therefore, to avoid the confusion that could arise when bandying about a "timeless" notion of the administrative state. Instead, it must be clarified that "administrative state" originally referred to:

> a state that has acquired an extensive bureaucracy with responsibilities for regulating economic and social affairs. Introduced in the early 1940s, this term usually is used in discussions about the problems of accountability that arise as a consequence of delegating rulemaking and adjudicative power to administrative agencies. (Roberts, 2019, pp. 141–142)

Its provenance recognized, *administrative state* is the government that grew out of the New Deal, during which, Donald Kettl wrote, "more problems became governmental problems…and more governmental problems became federal ones" (2020, p. 62).

That view of the administrative state seems in congruence with much of the academic literature, until recent times, when authors started using it to refer to the administrative arm of government. For example, David Lewis, in his study of presidential appointment politics, equated "the modern administrative state" with the "governmental apparatus" (2008). Additionally, Joanna Grisinger, in her study of the New Deal era, used the term *administrative state* to mean "the whole of the agencies, departments, bureaus, and commissions sprawled awkwardly across the federal landscape" (2012, p. 3). *We take a similar view of the administrative state.* The term is used in this book interchangeably with the *federal bureaucracy* or the federal *agencies,* the administrative apparatus that is delegated authority by Congress to carry out the nation's laws and which it supervises under joint custody (Rosenbloom, 2015) with the executive branch. Our main unit of analysis is the administrative *apparatus* of the state, the *executive establishment*, and its capacity to undertake the charge it is given. It describes the following instruments:

> agencies wielding broad discretion through a combination of rulemaking, adjudication, enforcement, and managerial functions; the personnel who perform these activities, from the civil service and professional staff through to political appointees, agency heads, and White House overseers; and the institutional arrangements and issuances that help structure these activities. In short, it includes all the actors and activities involved in fashioning and implementing national regulation and administration. (Metzger, 2017, p. 8)

Our study's use of the term administrative state is different than other approaches famous in the public administration discipline. For example, in *The Administrative State* written by public administration icon Dwight Waldo (1984), a more value-laden approach to the administrative state was explored. Some of its themes overlap with our query into the influence of reforms on administration. But overall, Waldo's approach to the administrative state "carries a specific normative connotation: the triumph of the Progressive movement's ideal of the planned and administered society" (Rosenbloom & McCurdy, 2007, pp. 4–5). In contrast, our approach explores how various reforms, including those meant to enhance capacity, ended up contributing to its decline.

Understanding the development of administrative capacity within the context of reform required our own interpretation of the key events in history. To facilitate our analysis, we divided the major reform eras that shaped federal administration and influenced the evolution of capacity. They are:

- The *capacity mapping-out* period of Constitution framing and the "clerical pre-administrative state" (Durant, 2010), which was characterized by political party dynamics in controlling personnel appointment. In this era, the predominating value was that of having a strong national government to promote national unity, economy, and defense.
- The *capacity buildup* period, starting from the Progressive reform movement establishing the civil service system and budget system of the administrative state to the New Deal era. In this period, the value promoted was that of having a professional government that is effective in uplifting public welfare.
- The *capacity consolidation* period that saw reforms in administrative procedures and other management systems, from World War II through the Great Society, which strengthened the executive in federalism and agenda setting. In this era, value was placed on modernizing the economy and using government to promote civil rights and economic development.
- The *capacity dilution or decline* period beginning with the 1970s with the Civil Service Reorganization Act of 1978 (CSRA) through the 1980s with the Grace Commission. Here, fiscal conservatism dominated in a time of economic shocks worldwide, inducing public sector retrenchment and privatization of government functions.
- The *concealed capacity decline* period starting from the reinventing government movement and the National Performance Review (NPR) through the President's Management Agenda (PMA) of the 2000s. In this era, a gradual decline in

capacity was camouflaged by short-lived cost reductions, the use of performance scorecards, and digital engagement. The time of big government was officially over, it proclaimed, and a "results" mindset dominated considerations of agency performance.

- The *capacity decay* period, from 2017 onward, in which economic populism and cultural fissures coincided with the height of anti-government rhetoric and the "deconstruction of the administrative state." In this period, an assault on traditional institutions, the civil service system, and workers' rights eroded further the agencies' capacity and tested the resilience of the administrative apparatus amid natural and political crises.

In this overview of administrative history, *reformers* are those who advocate, design, legislate, and execute reforms. The key players consist of presidents and lawmakers, political parties and allies, as well as their "proxies" in the central agencies and those outside of government that push for reform: academics, think tanks, government worker and executive associations, and other entities in the policy and administration learning networks that liaise with Congress and key agencies. They include the National Academy of Public Administration (NAPA), the Partnership for Public Service (PPS), the Volcker Alliance, and the American Society for Public Administration (ASPA). A good term for them from Stephen Skowronek and Stephen Engel, editors of *The Progressive Century*, is the *parastate*, defined as the extensive web of "think tanks, universities, foundations, professional societies, and lobbying organizations that occupy a vastly expanded executive branch" (2016, p. 9).

By *reforms*, we mean what Paul Light (2006) called experiments in making government work or the adjustments and readjustments in the machinery of government, according to Herbert Kaufman (1956). Reforms encompass several *types*: reorganizations, restructuring, reductions in force, and other bureaucratic tweaks by Congress or the executive, as well as the manner by which agency actions or decisions are influenced, coordinated, or evaluated. One of the most consequential of reforms, reorganization, is a comprehensive reordering of authorities and structures, via abolition, consolidation, creation, transfer, or mergers of entire units, bureaus, or agencies. The *pace* of reform depends on the politics of the day, the partisan pressures, and the institutional capacity to reform or innovate, which has waned in recent decades, according to Light (2020). His metaphorical assessment of reforms as a series of tides or waves crashing on the shore over the last half of the twentieth century is integral to understanding administrative evolution. In *The Tides of Reform*, each reorganization or reform initiative was classified under four philosophies championed by different institutional players. Scientific management reforms accompanied the rise of professional bureaucracies toward the New Deal era; watchful eye reforms centered on getting the bureaucracies more accountable to its principals; war on waste reforms accompanied reforms to streamline bureaucracies; while liberation management reforms, like the war on waste, focused on loosening up authorities, such as hiring and firing, and outsourcing governmental functions.

Overall, reforms may address an agency's mission or purpose, its people, processes, or clientele (Gulick, 1937). Reforms are not always targeted across the board, and the values they espouse typically cycle between efficiency and its variants and accountability and its variants. In certain eras, reformers put more weight on controllability, requiring bureaucrats to submit their decisions to notice-and-commenting procedures. When capacity was being built, reformers adhered to *traditional approaches* or Constitution-based methods of bureaucratic controls. Through them, the executive and the legislative branches negotiated their supervision over the administrative state. After the New Deal, conservatives increasingly espoused *transactional approaches* that relied on short-term exchanges with organizations external to federal administration. More significantly, through transactionalism, the president gained more power in controlling the capacity within the federal bureaucracy. But no matter the approach to reform, the effect on administrative capacity had long-term value.

1.4   Force Multipliers, Proxies, and the Shadow Bureaucracy

Not all the agencies in government are equal. This involves bureaucratic politics, after all. In a *Harvard Law Review* article, Gillian Metzger argued that *administrative state* conveys the idea of a single monolithic entity, when, in fact, the system contains within it "tremendous variety, cooperation, and rivalry ---a pluralistic dynamics that obtains within individual agencies as well" (2017, p. 8). In fact, a few are *superagencies* or *capacity enhancers*, influential and often rivalrous in recalibrating capacity across the administrative state, what the Partnership for Public Service calls the "force multipliers" (Wagner, 2021). These are the Office of Management and Budget (OMB), the Office of Personnel Management (OPM), and the General Services Administration (GSA). The first two figure prominently in our developmental analysis, while the third emerges when we discuss presidential transitions and the Trump administration's attempt at OPM dismantling. As the agencies that sit atop federal budget, personnel, and general services and policies, they are often subjects and objects of capacity-changing reforms and serve as the proxies of the executive and Congress waging their war along bureaucratic lines.

Within the Executive Office, OMB puts together the president's annual budget to Congress, informs the appropriation process even if Congress deviates significantly from it, oversees spending, and sets policies on contracting, financial accounting, information technology, and other management functions. Because it reviews agency rulemaking, OMB's control can have consequential impacts on the public, the economy, and the environment (Schwellenbach, 2020). OMB also coordinates interagency councils populated by career and political executives involved in strategic planning and other initiatives as they navigate their mandates from, and relationships with, their executive and legislative principals. The development of OMB's management control side, in addition to its budget side control levers, makes OMB today's key operator of administrative capacity, allowing it to have a greater say in personnel policy that was historically the realm of OPM.

Unlike OMB, OPM is an independent agency created during the last civil service reorganization under President Jimmy Carter. Its provenance goes back to the Pendleton Act of 1883 when the country decided to divorce personnel management from the political machines of the day. Before the Trump administration released *Executive Order 13957 on Creating Schedule F Within the Excepted Service* (see Chap. 7), OPM, the chief human resource office of a bureaucracy of two million people (excluding the Postal Service and uniformed military), was the fulcrum of a multi-year effort to loosen up civil service rules. Congress had fought hard to block the plans to disassemble OPM but that hurdle might have prompted the more radical Executive Order 13957 to come forth, which would have remade the entire merit-based system on Trump's very last day in office.

Congressional bureaus or bodies follow in stature to the executive capacity enhancers. The most significant is the Government Accountability Office (GAO), which conducts investigations into agency programs and systems. GAO advises lawmakers in their policy and oversight tasks. Crucial to sound lawmaking also are research entities, like the Congressional Research Service (CRS) and science and analytic agencies critical to the problem-solving, management, and engagement dimensions of government work (e.g., USDA-Economic Research Service providing peer-reviewed information on agriculture, tariffs, or nutrition). In the past, these entities included the defunct Advisory Commission on Intergovernmental Relations (ACIR) and Office of Technology Assessment (OTA), whose revivals are brought up every now and then in Capitol Hill (Chappellet-Lanier, 2019).

It is impossible to talk about the administrative establishment without a discussion of the so-called third-party government or government by proxy (Salamon, 2002; Kettl 1988) – the network of contractors and service delivery vehicles that have acted on the state's behalf for decades. In 2020, contract spending showed the federal government was on pace to exceed the single-year record of $598 billion set in fiscal year 2019 (Konkel, 2020). Contracting promises immediate problem-solving capacity (e.g., for a surge order of a product or service that the government might not need again), but its consequences in administrative expertise, accountability, and management terms can be serious and inimical to administrative capacity, as GAO (n.d.) points out. Beth Honadle wrote decades ago that "if there is one thing that capacity building does not mean it is creating dependency on outsiders for expertise" (1981, pp. 577–579, p. 579). In-house capacity deficits, which are solved in some ways by outsourcing, are in other ways enlarged when reformers neglect the development of bureaucratic skills, rules, and structures necessary to manage those third parties. Privatization can harm sovereignty itself (Verkuil, 2017; Michaels, 2017), especially when a shrunken civil service is presided by an executive that increasingly sidelines Congress. Attending this dynamic is citizen perception that government does little relative to proliferating vendors and nonprofits, even though these act on behalf of the bureaucracy and use taxpayer dollars. A vicious cycle of bureaucratic skepticism and this skepticism forcing government to privatize even more, characterizes the "submerged state" (Mettler, 2011). Such dynamic only weakens the civic trust that is necessary to shore up flagging administrative capacity. With the key movements and actors unveiled, it is time to lay down our thesis.

1.5   The Structure of This Book

Juliette Kayyem, former Homeland Security official, wrote that "a crisis finds a nation as it is, not as its citizens wish it to be" (2020a, para. 7). *Chapter 2* opens with a story of a test, the dynamics of one of the coronavirus pandemic's key battle-fronts – the wearing of face masks in public – to illustrate what a decayed adminis-trative capacity looks like at a time of crisis. Pandemics weren't new; neither were recessions, a Great One of which the country climbed out under President Obama and whose administration wrote the "Pandemic Playbook," containing 15 years of preparatory insights. It was reportedly ignored (Harris, 2020). Instead, the Trump administration let a dangerous cocktail of anti-scientism, misinformation, and polit-icization infuse the work of government. As large-scale protests in the summer of 2020 packed individuals in dangerous proximity to one another and the capacity to make voting safe in the impending November elections vanished with the Republicans' underfunding of the US postal system, the public was forced to make a number of stark choices. The winter approached with Americans facing the dead-liest stage of the pandemic before any vaccine could reach a human arm (Balz, 2020).

In the good government community's diplomatic terms, America's ailment under Trump was due to "a legacy government that was unable to refresh its capacity" in both the executive and legislative branches (Balz, 2020, para. 3). In our analysis, the turmoil of 2020 was brought about by a combination of policies and forces seeded from the birth of the administrative state and ripe for a deconstructionist to carry to its fateful outcome, whether or not he personally understood the part he was playing in the anti-government reform movement.

Chapter 3 works through a haystack to grasp the concept of administrative capacity. Recalling those days when the pioneers of public administration tried to define "management" or explore the design of "management functions," the litera-ture on capacity is found to be still evolving. Based on the different typologies and "umbrellas" of capacities identified by various scholars, we conclude that the exist-ing perspectives, for our purposes, must be anchored in the politics of administrative reform. Embedding capacity in political development could help explain why reforms to improve things ended up destroying, or creating disparate impacts on, administrative capacity. Synthesizing various ideas, we arrive at our own *definition of capacity* in *five dimensions* that we believe capture the concept's commonly understood elements as well as their institutional and democratic context. These core dimensions are (1) problem-solving, (2) management, (3) administrative con-servatorship, or administrative leadership, (4) engagement, and (5) accountability.

After defining capacity and its dimension, in *Chapter 4*, a framework is devel-oped further to show how reform movements drawn by the electoral calculus and the battle for bureaucratic control contributed to the guardrails of capacity falling along the wayside. Indicators of *decline and decay* and the drivers behind them are elaborated, including the severance of the bonds between Congress and the bureau-cracy and between bureaucracy and citizens. We present two approaches to control-ling bureaucracy and capacity – one *traditional* and constitutionally/legislatively anchored and the other one *transactional* and coevolving with the unitary executive thesis – that influenced administrative capacity over time. Executive dominance over Congress was the tectonic shift that changed capacity in ways that enabled reformers to lean more toward short-term improvements, which yet concealed a gradual capacity decline. More modern presidential administrations, with support from the private sector, "sliced and diced" – as we colloquially dub the transactional approach – the authorities and resources of government to create capacities required by their political agendas.

Both the traditional and transactional approaches convey the role that capacity plays in the leaders' designs for the administrative state. Each approach espouses a political theory of public administration, the values it must uphold in the exercise, and the relationships between and among principals and agents. As these dynamics are played over a long period of time, rhetoric, ritualism, cyclicality, and nonlinearities suffuse the meanings of efforts in capacity building (March & Olsen, 1983). By tethering capacity to the politics of belief making over time, it becomes possible to see how capacity could decline despite persistent reformism.

In *Chapters 5 through 6* our framework is illuminated with historical evidence. We discuss how capacity began to be built and shaped by constitutional notions of control. Some reformers, then as in now, cast their lot with a strong presidency as the bulwark of capacity. Presidents tried to win the public over with "new deals" or "grand reorganizations" that favored executive centralization (Lee, 2012). During the traditional period, "scientific" administration advocates shepherded the establishment of a merit-based federal bureaucracy. Capacity rose to fit the state's intended goals – to address extreme poverty. During this long road to capacity building, the state expanded through the First World War and the Great Depression under President Franklin Roosevelt (FDR), "a masterful tactician and strategist on behalf of an expanded role of government" (Rockoff, 1998, p. 132). The inner workings of a progressive administration – from budgeting to the management of the economy, the burgeoning civil service, to the creation of centralized and independent bodies to cater to the concerns of various stakeholders – industries, workers, immigrants, consumers, were sorted and resorted. Programs expanded, and regulatory entities – "progressivism's most distinctive governmental achievement" (Grisinger, 2016, p. 361) – mushroomed.

But over time, approaches to capacity changed. Efforts to weaken federal administration commenced and led to a variety of reforms that eventually gave presidents even more power over administrative capacity relative to Congress while concurrently shifting capacity to entities external to the federal government. A tectonic shift ensued, as political calculus changed with national conditions. More outsourcing and more flashy reforms occurred. As a result, the campaign against government, by government, took hold. Economic theories of government failure replaced orthodox thinking from public administration. The heirs of FDR themselves embraced New Public Management (NPM). The retreat of the administrative state, in theory and practice, was in motion. Consequently, a "shadow" workforce (Light, 1999) encroached upon some functions that were inherently governmental.

The stage was set for a weakened administrative capacity to meet a deconstructive, *unitary executive*. In *Chapter 7*, we describe the result of the centralization of power in the executive and a diminished administrative capacity. The height of transactionalism and the unitary executive theory was demonstrated by the ease with which a populist president controlled bureaucracy and achieved the "deconstruction of the administrative state" despite the Constitution's vaunted checks and balance and the norms that had guided the Republic since the founding. While nobody in the Trump administration defined what it meant, policies revealed deconstruction to be a combination of administrative disinvestment, political delegitimization, and bifurcation of administrative capacity (Joaquin, 2018). It degraded institutional expertise in several agencies, sucked the vitality out of previous reform initiatives, and took greater advantage of congressional division and incapacity.

Previous decades' warnings about breakdowns, shutdowns, and tipping points accelerated under Trump's tenure, showing how capacity decline could easily turn to decay. Civil servants experienced some of the most intense accusations and political retaliation in modern history, while some agencies functioned as if they personally serviced the president and not the Office. The annals of deconstruction revealed the powerful legal and psychological tools that have accumulated in the executive, leading many to label the convergence of these streams as the democratic triumph of authoritarianism (Lieberman et al., 2017; Hetherington & Weiler, 2009). It was this political trajectory that made bureaucratic dismantling, unilateral reorganization, and *Schedule F* possible under a president whose two impeachments evidenced a sense of total control over the governing system.

In *Chapter 8*, we summarize our examination of capacity's rise, decline, and decay within the politics of reforming the administrative state. Overall, our work shows that Trump's presidency and the capacity failures of his time were catalyzing, not conditioning, events. They should alert us to the task of building resilient capacity in the years ahead. Politics ultimately dictate what capacities are created, maintained, or neglected (Roberts, 2019; Thompson, 2006; Knott & Miller, 1987). As explored in this book, a more nuanced understanding of capacity offers ways of capacity building in five dimensions and with a greater awareness of the macro forces in democratic systems. What is needed is not merely a repair of the federal government's human capital management issues; we advocate for a reconstitution of capacity with a greater role for Congress, administrator engagement, and citizen trust in professional bureaucracy. The path out of decay includes building a resilience movement, reconceptualizing capacity's theory and practice within a political process, and viewing the roles, relationships, and strategies of everyone with a stake in democratic government in this new light.

References

Anderson, C. J., Blais, A., Bowler, S., Donovan, T., & Listhaug, O. (2005). *Losers' consent: Elections and democratic legitimacy*. Oxford University Press.

Balz, D. (2020, May 16). Crisis exposes how America has hollowed out its government. *The Washington Post*. https://www.washingtonpost.com/graphics/2020/politics/government-hollowed-out-weaknesses/. Accessed 19 May 2020.

Bandler, J., Callahan, P., Rotella, S., & Berg, k. (2020, October 15). Inside the fall of CDC. *ProPublica*. https://www.propublica.org/article/inside-the-fall-of-the-cdc. Accessed 5 Nov 2020.

Chait, J. (2019, September 9). Trump has figured out how to corrupt the entire government. *Intelligencer.* http://nymag.com/intelligencer/2019/09/trump-corruption-sharpiegate-hotel-biden.html. Accessed 18 Jan 2020.

Chappellet-Lanier, T. (2019, December 26). 2019 in review: The year in building tech capacity on Capitol Hill. *FedScoop.* https://www.fedscoop.com/2019-review-congress-tech-capacity/. Accessed 13 Apr 2020.

Durant, R. F. (2010). Herbert Hoover's revenge: Politics, policy, and administrative reform movements. In R. F. Durant (Ed.), *The Oxford handbook of American bureaucracy* (pp. 153–178). Oxford University Press.

Feuer, A., & Hong, N. (2021, January 21). The first capitol riot arrests were easy. The next ones will be tougher. *The New York Times.* https://www.nytimes.com/2021/01/21/nyregion/capitol-riot-conspiracy-fbi.html?action=click&module=Top%20Stories&pgtype=Homepage. Accessed 24 Jan 2021.

Frum, D. (2020, April 7). This is Trump's fault. *The Atlantic.* https://www.theatlantic.com/ideas/archive/2020/04/americans-are-paying-the-price-for-trumps-failures/609532/. Accessed 9 Apr 2020.

Grisinger, J. L. (2012). *The unwieldy American state: Administrative politics since the New Deal.* Cambridge University Press.

Grisinger, J. L. (2016). The long administrative century. In I. S. Skowronek, S. M. Engel, & B. Ackerman (Eds.), *The progressives' century: Political reform, constitutional government, and the modern American state* (pp. 360–381). Yale University Press.

Gulick, L. H. (1937). Chapter 1: Notes on the theory of organization. In L. H. Gulick & L. F. Urwick (Eds.), *Papers on the science of administration.* Columbia University. Institute of Public Administration.

Harris, J. (2020, September 29). America wrote the pandemic playbook, then ignored it. *The New York Times.* https://www.nytimes.com/video/opinion/100000007358968/covid-pandemic-us-response.html. Accessed 30 Sept 2020.

Hetherington, M. J., & Weiler, J. D. (2009). *Authoritarianism and polarization in American politics.* Cambridge University Press.

Honadle, B. W. (1981). A capacity-building framework – A search for concept and purpose. *Public Administration Review, 61*(5), 575–580.

Joaquin, M. E. (2018, April 23). Questions in the aftermath of deconstruction: Public administration in a transforming world. *The PA Times.* https://patimes.org/questions-in-the-aftermath-of-deconstruction-public-administration-in-a-transforming-world/. Accessed 21 Oct 2019.

Johns Hopkins University. (n.d.). COVID-19 dashboard. Center for Systems Science and Engineering. https://coronavirus.jhu.edu/map.html. Accessed 17 Aug 2020.

Kaufman, H. (1956, December). Emerging conflicts in the doctrines of public administration. American Political Science Review, 50(4), 1057–1073.

Kayyem, J. (2020, March 8). The U.S. isn't ready for what's about to happen. *The Atlantic.* https://www.theatlantic.com/ideas/archive/2020/03/us-isnt-ready-whats-about-happen/607636/. Accessed 11 Mar 2020.

Kettl, D. F. (1988). Government by proxy and the public service. *International Review of Administrative Sciences, 54*(4), 501–515.

Kettl, D. F. (2020). *The divided states of America: Why federalism doesn't work.* Princeton University Press.

Knott, J. H., & Miller, G. C. (1987). *Reforming bureaucracy: The politics of institutional choice.* Prentice-Hall.

Konkel, F. (2020, September 30). Federal government to conclude fiscal 2020 with record spending. *Nextgov.* https://www.nextgov.com/cio-briefing/2020/09/federal-government-conclude-fiscal-2020-record-spending/168884/. Accessed 3 Oct 2020.

Lane, N., & Riordan, M. (2017, December 6). Science has made America great. *Scientific American.* Https://blogs.scientificamerican.com/observations/science-has-made-america-great/. Accessed 1 May 2019.

Lee, M. (2012). *Nixon's super-secretaries: The last grand reorganization effort.* Texas A&M University Press.

Lewis, D. E. (2008). *The politics of presidential appointments: Political control and bureaucratic performance*. Princeton University Press.

Lieberman, R. C., Mettler, S., Pepinsky, T. B., Roberts, K. M., & Valelly, R. (2017, August 29). Trumpism and American democracy: History, comparison, and the predicament of liberal democracy in the United States. *Social Science Research Network*. https://doi.org/10.2139/ssrn.3028990. Accessed 1 June 2019.

Light, P. C. (1999, January 1). The true size of government. *Government Executive*. https://www.govexec.com/magazine/1999/01/the-true-size-of-government/5921/. Accessed 7 June 2020.

Light, P. C. (2006). The tides of reform revisited: Patterns in making government work, 1945–2002. *Public Administration Review, 66*(1), 6–19.

Light, P. C. (2020, October 12). Washington has given up on big-ticket reform. *The Brookings Institution*. Washington, DC. https://www.brookings.edu/blog/fixgov/2020/10/12/washington-has-given-up-on-big-ticket-reform/. Accessed 29 Oct 2020.

March, J. G., & Olsen, J. P. (1983). Organizing political life: What administrative reorganization tells us about government. *The American Political Science Review, 77*(2), 281–296.

Mettler, S. (2011). *The submerged state: How invisible government policies undermine American democracy*. University of Chicago Press.

Metzger, G. E. (2017). The Supreme Court, 2016 Term — Foreword: 1930s redux: The administrative state under siege. *Harvard Law Review, 131*(1), 1–95.

Michaels, J. D. (2017). *Constitutional coup: Privatization's threat to the American republic*. Harvard University Press.

Packer, G. (2020, April). The president is winning his war on American institutions. *The Atlantic*. https://www.theatlantic.com/magazine/archive/2020/04/how-to-destroy-a-government/606793/. Accessed 10 May 2020.

Roberts, A. S. (2019). *Strategies for governing: Reinventing public administration for a dangerous century*. Cornell University Press.

Rockoff, H. (1998). By way of analogy: The expansion of the federal government in the 1930s. In M. D. Bordo, C. Goldin, & E. N. White (Eds.), *The defining moment: The Great Depression and the American economy in the twentieth century* (pp. 125–154). University of Chicago Press.

Rosenbloom, D. (2015). The public context. In M. E. Guy & M. M. Rubin (Eds.), Public administration evolving: From foundations to the future (pp. 3-17). New York: Routledge..

Rosenbloom, D., & McCurdy, H. (2007). Introduction. In D. Rosenbloom & H. E. McCurdy (Eds.), Revisiting Waldo's administrative state: Constancy and change in public administration (pp. 1-14). Washington DC: Georgetown University Press.

Rucker, P., & Costa, R. (2019, October 2). 'A presidency of one': Key federal agencies increasingly compelled to benefit Trump. *The Washington Post*. https://www.washingtonpost.com/politics/a-presidency-of-one-key-federal-agencies-increasingly-compelled-to-benefit-trump/2019/10/01/f80740ec-e453-11e9-a331-2df12d56a80b_story.html. Accessed 14 Oct 2019.

Salamon, L. M. (2002). *The tools of government: A guide to the new governance*. Oxford University Press.

Schwellenbach, N. (2020, December 2). Schedule Effed. *Project on Government Oversight*. https://www.pogo.org/analysis/2020/12/schedule-effed/. Accessed 15 Dec 2020.

Skowronek, S. (1982). *Building a new American state: The expansion of national administrative capacities, 1877–1920*. Cambridge University Press.

Skowronek, S., & Engel, S. M. (2016). Introduction. In S. Skowronek, S. M. Engel, & B. Ackerman (Eds.), *The progressives' century: Political reform, constitutional government, and the modern American state* (pp. 1–15). Yale University Press.

Suleiman, E. N. (2005). *Dismantling democratic states*. Princeton University Press.

Thompson, J. R. (2006). The federal civil service: The demise of an institution. *Public Administration Review, 66*(4), 496–504.

Verkuil, P. R. (2017). *Valuing bureaucracy: The case for professional government*. Cambridge University Press.

Wagner, E. (2021, January 19). Don't expect Trump's workforce policies to be reversed overnight. *Government Executive*. https://www.govexec.com/management/2021/01/dont-expect-trumps-workforce-policies-be-reversed-overnight/171488/. Accessed 10 Feb 2021.

Waldo, D. (1984). *The administrative state: A study of the political theory of public administration* (2nd ed.). Holmes & Meier.

Walsh, B. (2017, May 4). The world is not ready for the next pandemic. *Time*. https://time.com/magazine/us/4766607/may-15th-2017-vol-189-no-18-u-s/. Accessed 19 May 2020.

Chapter 2
The Mask Is Off

*Yeah, no, I don't take responsibility at all...And when you say
'me,' I didn't do it...It's the- it's the administration. Perhaps
they do that. You know, people let people go.*

Donald Trump quoted in Smith (2020, para. 17)

*The norm of bureaucratic professionalism and fairness is a
pillar of the political legitimacy and economic strength of the
American system, the thing that separates countries like the
U.S. from countries like Russia. The decay of that culture is
difficult to quantify, but the signs are everywhere.*

Jonathan Chait (2019, para. 13)

*I don't know how we go forward from here. Is America a failed
state and society? It looks truly possible.*

Paul Krugman (2016, para. 5)

2.1 A Global Test and an American Failure

When Colorado Governor Jared Polis told his constituents in the summer of 2020,
that "No state lives in a bubble. We live and die together" (*CNBC* Staff, 2020, para.
2), he was not talking about slinging 50 pounds of gear and heading toward a field
of combat to defend the American way of life; it was putting on something that
weighed less than 3.5 grams when picking up the groceries or visiting one's parents.
Polis and others like him were trying to engage citizens' cooperation amid an especially ruinous level of capacity on the part of the national government. Economically
ravaged, inequality-beset, politically polarized in the midst of a trade war, America
could not muster consensus among its citizens and even sub-national officials
around the wearing of *face masks in public* at the height of the coronavirus ("SARS-
CoV-2") pandemic. Polis' warning was already 4 months into the crisis. The respiratory disease had claimed around 140,000 lives at that point, a scale of tragedy
unsurpassed in public health history (Tompkins, 2021).

© Springer Nature Switzerland AG 2021
M. E. Joaquin, T. J. Greitens, *American Administrative Capacity*,
https://doi.org/10.1007/978-3-030-80564-7_2

What the Americans witnessed in horror months earlier, in the Hubei province of China, then in South Korea, Iran, and Italy, came with unnerving virulence to New York. It rapidly overwhelmed its hospitals and those of other cosmopolitan cities. The reckoning came for a healthcare system saddled by decades of private influence and shrunken public investment. Yet, despite the scientific consensus about the effectiveness of mask wearing to ameliorate the worst effects of the pandemic, not to mention the trillion dollars it could have saved the economy (Hansen, 2020), no more than half of the states had mask mandates by May. The other half, taking their cue from President Donald Trump, consumed by some political calculus of economic freedom and civil liberty, railed against the guidelines from the government's own Centers for Disease Control and Prevention (CDC) (IHME, 2020). His rhetoric, alarming in and of itself, found a fertile soil and generated personal and professional insecurities among the agencies that sorely needed leadership. The evolving mysteries of COVID-19, the near absence of an agile response infrastructure, and the CDC's own changing guidelines on who should wear masks, and where, and how, and the timidity with which the agency vouched for its effectiveness early in the pandemic, were met with confusion, distrust, and outright public hostility during a crisis where collective response mattered most of all.

The facial mask saga marked a breakdown of the government's consensus-inducing ability, traditionally anchored on science, expertise, and professionalism. It was part of a broader decay in administrative capacity whose various dimensions – problem-solving, management, engagement, administrative leadership, and accountability – manifested corrosion as a divided and institutionally weakened Congress lost its ability to ensure that the executive branch acknowledged that a national problem existed and that presidential power was geared toward capacity building, rather than its deconstruction.

From London to Taiwan, the pandemic was not merely a stress test for the supply chains tethered to China; it was a global test of governance (Diehl, 2020). The complexities and uncertainties surrounding it compelled regimes, small and big, autocratic and liberal, to show their mettle and national resilience. In the United States, the government's failures in *problem-solving, engagement,* and *communication* reverberated in all walks of life – inside frantic testing laboratories, unprotected government buildings, overrun intensive care units, overwhelmed unemployment aid centers, disrupted schools, indignant churches, reconfigured stores, parks, and other spaces where the public congregated with great unease and sometimes with outright hostility. The Federal Emergency Management Agency (FEMA) – the body historically in charge of logistical and relief support in times of disasters, but which suffered an identity crisis when it was consolidated into the new Department of Homeland Security (DHS) post-9-11 – became invisible as soon as it was designated the lead coordinating agency. The president instead directed the Office of the Vice President under Michael Pence to lead the White House Coronavirus Task Force. Calls for a unified disaster response led by the Department of Defense (DOD), another agency that would have had some capacity to lead the fight against the invisible adversary, went unheeded. The government's *management capacity* – in program administration, data collection and analysis, human capital and resource management, and coordination in a vast, federalized context – buckled under the heavy load of crisis mitigation. In many agencies, telework capacity was found to be limited, despite studies noting how alternative and flexible work schedules created a positive impact on the workforce (Park et al., 2018). The few agencies that teleworked in previous administrations had mostly lost it earlier in the Trump administration (Block & Longo, 2018). *Administrative leadership* cracked as decimated experts were muzzled from telling the nation the contours of the threat and the sacrifices it entailed. The capacity to *perform with accountability* also proved too much to expect. Asked to account for his government's inability to act swiftly to head off the crisis, the "unitary executive" declared "No, I don't take responsibility at all" (Smith, 2020, para. 15) and promptly passed the blame to the previous administration that had left behind a pandemic response playbook (EOP, n.d.). Though Trump later labeled the crisis a war and himself a wartime president, the pandemic exposed an incapacitated administrative state.

2.2 "Nobody Owns the Problem:" Failures of Problem-Solving and Management

Leading a nation is obviously difficult; political priorities and short- and long-term goals clash constantly. Contending with inherited and emerging national problems in rapidly changing environments also presents such brain-splitting complexity that leaders must rely upon administrative institutions capable of sound decision-making (Roberts, 2019). The Republic was founded upon many principles, and one of them was Hamilton's deep fear of governmental impotence (White, 1954, p. 463). Under COVID-19, a decayed capacity revealed just that – a decimated capacity for sound decision-making and politicization of whatever was left of it. The biggest issue that was confronted immediately centered around the government's anticipatory capabilities. For instance, who was given what intelligence about the brewing problem, and when, and what was done about it (Rascoe & Dwyer, 2020)? And while an investigative report uncovered the existence of a plan to meet the crisis early on, it fell by the wayside as a result of political opportunism that polarized the nation. The plan's dismissal was tragic in that its components appeared to recognize the most essential elements of an effective response, the apparent failures of the early response, and the urgent need for federal leadership. For example:

- It identified the challenges of uneven coronavirus testing capacity, significant delays in reporting results (4–11 days), and national supply chain constraints regarding protective personnel equipment, swabs, and certain testing reagents.
- It clarified the federal government's role in the distribution of test kits, so they could be surged to heavily affected areas.
- It proposed to lift contract restrictions on where doctors and hospitals sent tests, allowing any laboratory with capacity to test any sample.
- It proposed a massive scale-up of antibody testing to facilitate a return to work.

- It called for mandating that all COVID-19 test results from any kind of testing, taken anywhere, be reported to a national repository as well as to state and local health departments.
- It proposed establishing "a national Sentinel Surveillance System" with "real-time intelligence capabilities to understand leading indicators where hot spots are arising and where the risks are high vs. where people can get back to work" (Eban, 2020, para. 27–28).

This plan reportedly lost favor in the White House as the administration feared that more testing would lead to more cases being found and more bad publicity for the president heading toward the November elections. Since the virus at this time was ravaging New York and other Democrat-led states the hardest, the public would blame their own governors, the thinking went, instead of the president.

With heightened denialism, problem-solving naturally went in the opposite direction. This was especially evident to the US Postal Service (USPS) workers, no strangers to crises, like the anthrax scare of 2001, but who felt vulnerable as the pandemic intensified. A proposal in April 2020 to send face masks to every residential address failed to be implemented. Upon recommendation by the Department of Health and Human Services (HHS), the plan had called for USPS delivering masks to those who lived where the outbreak was worst. But like the plan discussed earlier, it was vetoed from the top, reportedly to prevent people from panicking (Budryk, 2020).

At the CDC, one of the earliest tests of its management capacity occurred when Americans started arriving back from China on the first weeks of the outbreak. For obvious reasons, these travelers needed to be monitored by government. But the CDC's decade-old notification system gave local officials who were tracking passenger information bad phone numbers and incomplete addresses. At one point, when the CDC was asked about the possibility that infected travelers might slip away, local officials listened in disbelief as the CDC responded to "Just let them go" (Lipton et al., 2020).

Most seriously, chaos and delay marked the rollout of coronavirus testing, in one of the most shocking governmental failures in history. Testing guidelines were published on the CDC website against the objection of scientists and the consideration of a standard review process (Mandavilli, 2020). State laboratories around the country received testing kits that were too complicated to use. In manufacturing these kits, the CDC also contaminated many of them through sloppy laboratory practices. The agency also was unable to ramp up commercial and academic labs. An agency that had been waiting its entire existence for this moment failed what it was set up to do (Lipton et al., 2020).

It was during the gnawing weeks of March 2020 that states and communities lost faith in federal leadership and resolved to take the bold steps on their own. These included (1) restrictions on mass gathering, (2) business closures, (3) educational facility closures, (4) nonessential services closures, (5) travel restrictions, and (6) stay-at-home orders. The first-in-the-nation order to shelter in place came from the City and County of San Francisco, California. Governors of the states that bore the brunt of the first wave of infections, like Washington and New York, ordered nonessential businesses to close. However, in the absence of a strong and coherent national strategy, the disjointed attempts of contiguous localities could not meet the challenge posed by the pathogen.

Securing lifesaving equipment, in addition to failures in the areas of testing, contact tracing, and social distancing, was another flashpoint where surge capacity simply was not there. At this point the federalist system showed both its strengths and weaknesses. As the pandemic spread, American states had to compete with other nations for a limited supply of face masks, protective gear, and hospital equipment. But rather than lead in strategic decision-making, the president scolded the governors and informed them they had to get what they needed, themselves. The White House resisted immediately invoking the 1950 Defense Production Act, a vestige of the Korean War era, to engage companies in the national effort to produce more protective gear and hospital equipment (Rascoe, 2020). The Act could have federalized the medical supply chain and sped up the manufacturing of lifesaving masks and respirators; instead, the federal government even outbid some states on those critical supplies, many of which were sourced from virus-ravaged China (Relman, 2020). At one point, HHS rewrote its website to accommodate the administration's view that the national stockpile of equipment belonged to them and not the states (Porter, 2020).

The incoherence of national government actions made the situation in the states much more challenging. In an alert circulated through *The New England Journal of Medicine*, a medical executive described the nightmare of the first wave:

> Hours before our planned departure, we were told to expect only a quarter of our original order. We went anyway, since we desperately needed any supplies we could get. Upon arrival, we were jubilant to see pallets of KN95 respirators and face masks being unloaded…Before we could send the funds by wire transfer, two Federal Bureau of Investigation agents arrived, showed their badges, and started questioning me. No, this shipment was not headed for resale or the black market. The agents checked my credentials, and I tried to convince them that the shipment of PPE was bound for hospitals…Only some quick calls leading to intervention by our congressional representative prevented its seizure. I remained nervous and worried on the long drive back, feelings that did not abate until midnight, when I received the call that the PPE shipment was secured at our warehouse. (Artenstein, 2020, para. 4)

Jared Kushner, advisor to the President as well as the President's son-in-law, was later revealed to have been running a coronavirus "shadow" task force to the Vice President's own, adding to the White House' disjointed response. His role caused confusion and required a delicate balancing act among those involved with regular agency response efforts. "Project Airbridge," said to be his brainchild, had the federal government striking a deal with six medical supply companies for subsidized flights to pandemic hotspots identified by the administration. It was mired, however, in controversy after severe discrepancies were reported in the amount, types, and destination of the supplies brought into the country. Some state officials were reportedly told by the FEMA that they could not share information of what medical supplies had arrived through Project Airbridge (Brittain et al., 2020).

A report to the House Committee on Oversight and Reform described how Kushner precipitated "bureaucratic cycles of chaos" in chasing critical supplies by layering over experts in emergency planning with volunteers that he recruited from private equity and consulting firms. Volunteers were said to have no significant experience in healthcare, procurement, or supply chain operations or a clear understanding of customs requirements or FDA rules (Abutaleb & Parker, 2020). "An old saying in emergency management," according to a former deputy administrator at the FEMA, is that "disaster is the wrong time to exchange business cards...And it's absolutely the wrong time to make up new procedures" (Confessore et al., 2020, para. 5). Hospitals and clinicians were also not sure why some medical centers were chosen to receive coveted doses of an important drug, remdesivir, while others were not, and where those decisions were coming from in the first place (Boodman & Ross, 2020). A former senior official regarding this emergency management landscape with utter frustration concluded that "There's no point of responsibility. It keeps shifting. Nobody owns the problem" (Pilkington & McCarthy, 2020, para. 15).

The HHS, parent agency of the CDC and the FDA, immediately lost the ability to control the condition and the message amid ethics investigations, the ousting of one of its career scientists, and uncertainties over the future of its own Secretary: "I don't think people appreciate how tired the department is," a former HHS appointee told journalists. "Your effectiveness wears down after you've been in a fight— and...HHS has been kicked in the teeth" (Diamond, 2020, para. 4). The White House further undercut the agency when it wrested control of the coronavirus reporting system. The administration privatized the system's management, throwing off efforts to understand the disease and the pressures on healthcare capacities nationwide. Data – crucial to the allocation of resources from the federal government – immediately became suspect as HHS and the private contractor refused to share procurement information with Congress (*The New York Times*, 2020).

The vertical and horizontal failures were so severe that 2 months into the pandemic, the Project on Government Oversight (POGO) had already uncovered 31 whistleblower disclosures and federal employee complaints describing retaliation for reporting pandemic response concerns (Schwellenbach, 2020). Several inspectors general who would have helped keep the pandemic response effective and honest, and seasoned workers who could have bridged state and nongovernmental efforts resigned, were forced out of office or were undermined by political appointees when they revealed information that the White House deemed embarrassing (*45chaos*, n.d.).

2.3   From Disorientation to Collapse: Failures of Engagement

Early in the crisis, doctors had noticed that COVID-19 exhibited strange symptoms among the elderly: they might seem "off" – unusually apathetic or confused. Losing balance, sometimes they simply collapsed (Graham, 2020). The year revealed how federal administration was as stricken as the patients described above. With a fast-spreading menace, the country needed rapid and coherent engagement from federal authorities in a hyper-turbulent environment, for which Ali Farazmand (2009) warned administrative capacity ought to be geared. But capacity was compromised in a system that crowded out expert collection, digestion, and communication of the facts by inflammatory rhetoric, high-speed Internet conspiracies, and a disorienting lack of coordination among the government's crisis management units.

No single national-level body or elected figure truly led the American people with enough integrity or epistemic authority to draw the connections for them between the pathology of the COVID-19 virus and the policy measures imposed on individuals and businesses to mitigate it. An administrative body has legitimate epistemic authority, according to public administration scholar Larry Terry (2003, p. 95), if it possesses and is perceived by others to have superior knowledge and competence in a particular field or realm. This was demonstrated in Germany's response during the first wave of the crisis. Unlike Trump, whose background was in real estate and entertainment business, Chancellor Angela Merkel happened to have a doctorate in quantum physics. She and other prominent scientists engaged the German public about the virus and the necessary policy measures to control it. Her video explaining concepts like the basic reproductive number ("R0") of the virus immediately went, so to speak, viral. Germans credited the educational access they were freely afforded as a factor in letting rationality prevail; others saw it as a matter of civic trust and the art of engagement: people didn't feel like they were on their own when information and rules were communicated well (Farr, 2020).

Engagement could have shored up the flagging management capacity of the state, but that would have meant creating and maintaining people's belief in the integrity of public institutions, something that made America at this point in history especially vulnerable to this virus. Governors and mayors often tried to convey such concepts, but their approach was overwhelmed by the Trump administration's own communication efforts. The substance and rhetoric of their engagement was starkly different from the president's, as an article in the *Los Angeles Times* captured the prevailing atmosphere in April:

> We have become a nation of castaways, combing the bandwidth from a hundred million islands fearfully, hopefully for news… for the look of distress that says Someone Cares… Woodrow Wilson held the first presidential press conference in 1913…Dwight D. Eisenhower was the first to put one on television, in 1955, though it was shot on film and edited; JFK was the first to go live and unedited on TV, days after his inauguration in 1961. The present occupant of 1600 Pennsylvania Ave. has been all over the television, for hours, in recent weeks.
>
> But to get a clearer picture of what's up in America—a picture of things getting done—I recommend a visit to the country's governors and mayors, who are closer to the front line…The officials appear flanked by flags, with doctors and administrators on hand, sometimes joined by a general… listening to (New York's governor) Cuomo can reduce stress, not because he sugarcoats but because he shoots straight…(and governor) Newsom…likes to call California a "nation state," which, for a native, reinforces the comforting sense of a bulwark against whatever madness might reign elsewhere. (Lloyd, 2020, para. 2–6)

Leaders naturally wanted to look decisive in the face of the COVID-19, but with this virus, discovery was slow. Scientific knowledge was not enough to shield officials from criticisms as they attempted to save the sick while preventing the "worried well" from panicking and unnecessarily burdening hospitals everywhere. In instances where scientific uncertainty is high and values consensus is low, according to Roger Pielke (2007, p. 18) in *The Honest Broker*, information plays a different role in decision-making. Some policymakers use scientific knowledge to rationalize a values-based choice, while others are more comfortable when information leaves room for a wider, instead of a narrower, set of policy choices. Similarly, some would like to see scientists advocate within the policy arena, while some would rather that scientists "stick to the science" and leave the policy to the politicians. This complexity was on full display. For a long time since it had broken out of Wuhan, the coronavirus remained mysterious, leaving the medical community one step behind as the virus surged. Compared to previous pandemics, scientists worldwide were collaborating at a much quicker pace, with thousands of pages published on COVID-19 and made available to the scientific community. Yet the evolving knowledge could not back up policy measures with 100% certainty. According to Natalie Dean, scientific understanding "oscillates at first, but converges on an answer. That's the normal scientific process but it looks jarring to people who aren't used to it" (Yong, 2020a, para. 22).

That ambiguity left room for certain elements to muddle the message for political purposes. During one breathtaking moment that was broadcast globally, Trump turned to the government's infectious disease specialists and asked if they could study injecting people with disinfectants, "like a cleaning" (Clark, 2020). Pressured, the scientists could not speak truth to power on TV: administrative leadership had been eroding behind the scenes. It fell to the makers of Lysol™ and Clorox™ to caution the public against ingesting their cleaning products. In that crystallizing moment, many lost the sense that Trump's government could lead the nation out of the crisis. The newsrooms of the world were quick to ridicule the American president, but a deep perturbation about decay had spread. The televised event was"

> not so much a turning point as *an acceleration point, the moment when a transformation that began much earlier suddenly started to seem unstoppable*...the outline of a very different, post-American, post-coronavirus world is already taking shape. It's a world in which American opinions will count less, while the opinions of America's rivals will count more. (Italics ours) (Applebaum, 2020, para. 12)

Worldwide sentiment against Trump was already negative, to be sure, with his trade wars and abrupt retreat from multilateral bodies and hard-fought treaties. His foreign policy before the pandemic was seen as purely transactional, with no larger purpose of building a better world (Wright, 2020). The global liberal order unsettled by his economic nationalism also contributed to the difficulties of securing protective equipment for Americans. Government had not seemed more relevant in people's lives than at this point, and the world itself needed a leader of leaders. Yet, on both counts, America under Trump was fading. It shrunk to the metaphor beloved by the anti-tax movement: a government so small one could "drag it into the bathroom and drown it in the bathtub" (*NPR,* 2020, para. 1).

2.4 "Ask China": Failures of Accountability

A pandemic may be thought of as a wicked problem in that policymakers should have no right to be wrong (Rittel & Weber, 1973). But making government account for its performance outside of the ballot mechanism is easier said than done when many layers exist between the government and the citizen, information is costly, and the variables to be considered in assessing accountability are many and fast moving, such as what prevails in a pandemic. During the crisis, accountability or impression management (Romzek & Dubnick, 1987) – where facts are reframed in ways that compromise accountability – often dominated communications emerging from the Trump administration. Much of this reframing concentrated on personal image making rather than communicating how the government could protect and serve the public during the pandemic. For example, the administration's impulse was to calm the stock market and excoriate the Democrats for the 2019 impeachment and creating a COVID "hoax." The coronavirus was just like the flu; it would magically disappear, the president insisted. At various points during the pandemic Trump blamed the "co-opted" World Health Organization (WHO), Obama's FDA, former Vice President Joe Biden, "lamestream media," Trump's own appointees, hospital staff, Democratic governors, and the watchdog community. Beyond domestic political rivals, the president and his allies laid the blame on China, promoting racial epithets like the "China virus" or "Kung Flu" that served nothing more than politics and division. During another broadcast:

> (A) correspondent…asked the president why he so frequently claims that the United States is doing "far better than any other country" at testing for coronavirus…Trump started by deflecting—"they're losing their lives everywhere in the world"—before pivoting suddenly: "And maybe that's a question you should ask China. Don't ask me, ask China that question, okay?" (Wilkie, 2020, para. 8–10)

The strategic twin of dodging blame was credit grabbing. More focused on his brand than leadership, the president bragged that his coronavirus briefings had such high viewership (Milbank, 2020). At one point, he asked, "Did you know I was No. 1 on Facebook? I just found out I'm No. 1 on Facebook" (Lloyd, 2020, para. 17). Many lamented the wasted time that could have been better used to enhance the capacity for reopening the country.

Trump's discordant notes made the American tragedy "surreal" in the eyes of the world. He could have tapped the wattage of the living former presidents in the pandemic response, but he disliked sharing the limelight. During the terrified atmosphere of September 2001, the horror of the 2010 Haiti earthquake, and the tragic aftermath of Hurricane Katrina in 2015, US presidents called on their predecessors for national emotional succor; but not this one (Bower, 2020). Peter Wehner, author of *The Death of Politics: How To Heal Our Frayed Republic After Trump*, remarked that:

> This constellation of characteristics would be worrisome in a banker or a high-school teacher, in an aircraft machinist or a warehouse manager, in a gas-station attendant or a

truck driver. To have them define the personality of an American president is downright alarming. (Wehner, 2019, para. 12)

American political development scholar Stephen Skowronek observed that the personalization of executive power renders the whole of American government more volatile (Skowronek, 2009, p. 2100). The administrative state appeared to dissolve in the mind of a president who often spoke of the bureaucracy as his (Stirling, 2020). He could not accept how government scientists could contravene his opinion, as when he castigated the FDA for refusing to give authorization to unproven treatments as quickly as he would like (Silverman, E., 2020).

The challenge of taking someone like Trump – who had mastered the art of priming his audience, honing his arguments, and channeling attention in the age of social media – into account may be explained using political ethicist Melvin Dubnick's (2005) social mechanism approach to understanding accountability and performance in government. Based on the works of social scientists such as Richard Mulgan, Marvin Scott, and Stanford Lyman, Dubnick argued that account-giving is not simply reporting what a public official has done. Reporting, mitigating, and reframing are three forms of account-giving behaviors that depend on the balance of power between the one giving account and the principal. *Reporting* is a subordinate's kind of action, providing information to the principal that the latter uses as a control mechanism. *Mitigating* occurs when the two parties are on a more equal footing, and an account-giver who may be in the wrong can employ excuses – emphasizing his or her lack of control over the deed and the appropriateness in their mind of what they have done. *Reframing* is what many American leaders employed to account for their decisions or performance during the pandemic. Reframing occurs when the agent is engaged in impression management to control or transform how a problematic situation is defined or perceived by their principal. Instead of being subject to control, the account-giver becomes an account-"maker" through diversion, avoidance strategies, manipulation of account, changing of the subject, and other strategies to preempt negative reactions or provide grounds for later mitigation (Dubnick, 2005; Joaquin & Greitens, 2011). The coronavirus pandemic displayed Trump's reframing style of accountability. Were it not for the November election and the second impeachment he received on his way out, his failures of accountability might have forever damaged America's sense of good government.

2.5   Resilience and the Breakdown of a Sense of Shared Fate

The cascading failures in administration along with explicit political messaging from the Trump administration depleted civic energy as the months passed. However, resilience also manifested itself. When the White House refused to help the states immediately secure protective equipment, civilians, much like in wartime, mobilized and made masks for frontline workers (Enrich et al., 2020). The crisis had forced many people to resort to "crowdfunding" (like *GoFundMe*) and other means of securing civic generosity to tutor kids, help the sick, feed the hungry, entertain lonely seniors, and support exhausted essential workers. But digital organizing and private generosity could never replace the work of a national government operating with sufficient capacity (Lowrey, 2020).

During the pandemic, experts around the world noted that a form of power was emerging and proving to be much more effective in this crisis, having nothing to do with military might but an ability to absorb shock and adapt to the changing conditions by understanding the necessary trade-offs to be made and having the capacity to respond to insight or expert knowledge (Friedman, 2020b). At the core of this resilient power was trust: the level of trust people had in other people and their own governments, workplaces, communities, and neighbors. In several nations, trust led to resilience and proved vital in mitigating the pandemic. Trust was essential as the virus required not merely that governments coordinated their actions. As the infections surged, public authorities needed the public to *come together psychologically while distancing physically*. This required trust in the scientific endeavor, trust that the government informed its policy with expert knowledge (that evolved over time), trust that the public would heed government guidelines, and public trust among themselves. The pandemic showed how much one's fate was linked to the fate of one's neighbors (Friedman, 2020a).

Countries marked by a high level of trust carried out less stringent lockdowns during the first wave of the pandemic, as governments relied on their citizens to voluntarily observe guidelines (*The Economist,* 2020a, b). In the United States, where extreme polarization, high inequality, and low levels of trust had existed for decades, confrontations increased. The president's insurgent message about the pandemic found its way among militant protesters who defied the lockdowns. His message also resonated at county meetings and town halls – celebrated in textbooks as the fulcrum of direct democracy – where parents argued with other parents over the mask requirement for their school children. As for hospital capacity, the Pew Research Center found that Americans were divided by religion on who should get critical care if there was a shortage of ventilators (Kramer, 2020). Political affiliation was the immediate "centrifugal force" that acted on society as social distancing measures visited one American community after another:

> According to the data, 42% of Republicans believe that stay-at-home orders infringe on their rights (only 6% of Democrats agree) and 34% want social-distancing measures to end by June 1st (against 7% of Democrats). Half of Republican-affiliated adults also approve of protests against restrictions, whereas only 14% of Democrats feel the same way. Republicans are also more than twice as likely as Democrats to believe that owners who reopen their businesses in compliance with their state's plans should not be held responsible if their workers contract the virus, and nearly four times as likely to believe that employers should fire workers who refuse shifts for fear of contracting SARS-CoV-2. (*The Economist,* 2020a, p. 1)

In this setting, the face mask easily became a token of tribal affiliation (Lizza & Lippman, 2020). Within months, increased harassment was reported by several groups, such as Asian-American immigrants, reporters covering the unrest, and travelers from pandemic-hit states.

The coronavirus also victimized those holding jobs in the service industry, which the Trump administration's reopening calls would have impacted more severely, while their white-collar counterparts were afforded the safety of remote work modalities. The National Academy of Sciences found that suppressing the virus was extremely challenging for the poor who had to keep moving, while the rich was able to lock down as the disease spread (Weilla et al., 2020). People of color – Black, Indigenous Americans, Latino, and Asian immigrants – were felled disproportionately, something that was foreseen by the Federal Reserve. The bank's analysis of the 1918 pandemic led to a conclusion that a modern-day equivalent of the Spanish flu could result in greater nonwhite mortality rates in the United States, as a greater percentage of the nonwhite population live in urban areas (Garrett, 2007).

2.6   Reopening Problems: Second-Order Failures

If the failure to prepare for the pandemic was a first-order failure, second-order failures flummoxed the reopening push as the fall of 2020 came closer. Economic, housing, and financial insecurities were driving a wider unrest as the weather warmed in April. Since February, industry after industry had been asphyxiating, beginning with the travel industry. Because the virus first devastated the provinces of China – supermarket for the world, manufacturer of much of the world's cheap indulgences, and source of vital ingredients critical for medicine, protective gear, and emergency equipment – the pandemic upended the global supply chains, first, and then in terms of demand, as the pathogen spread, and cities halted movement and commerce. The world economy was estimated to shrink by 1.3% and the US Gross Domestic Product by 12%, year-on-year, in the first quarter of 2020. Experts warned that "if Americans chose to avoid person-to-person proximity of the length of an arm or less, occupations worth approximately 10% of national output would become unviable" (*The Economist,* 2020b). Despite some states refusing to shut down in order to prop up their economies, by July, the Department of Labor (DOL) reported that a staggering 33 million Americans had filed for unemployment, the highest in history. Many needed the economy restarted in order to feed their families; the social safety net built up from the Great Depression was proving tremendously weak.

But the weaknesses at the top and the patchwork and conflicting responses only made the conditions riskier for schools, students, and businesses. The federal government could not even model the safe way to reopen. Having undermined the dwindling number of experts left in government from the outset, the White House appeared to force a CDC guideline revision in July to mimic "a political statement" that downplayed the threat of reopening (CDC, 2020). Pressured to return, federal employee and contractor unions decried the lack of protective gear, hazard pay, and a voice at the table amid worker illnesses, from veteran workers to prison employees (AFGE, 2020). The Occupational Safety and Health Administration (OSHA), which would have been another agency central to an effective federal response, failed to assure Congress that public and private employers nationwide had sufficient return-to-work guidelines. According to the National Employment Law Project, OSHA feebly received thousands of complaints but did little and relied on a voluntary approach to worker safety. The federal failure especially victimized workers of color (Berkowitz, 2020).

For their part, school districts felt it extremely challenging to reopen despite fiscal stimulus or threats of withholding funds (and tax-exempt status) from the Department of Education (DOE). In some states like Florida, teacher unions went to court to battle the return- to- work order. The complexity of the variables to manage in reopening K–12, colleges, and universities was enormous compared to reopening restaurants or malls. Until this pandemic, education simply was not seen as an essential infrastructure: "Four months of stay-at-home orders have proved that, if schools are unavailable, a city cannot work, a community cannot function, a nation cannot safeguard itself" (Kayyem, 2020, para. 10).

There was no good answer to school reopening questions from those who feared that their children were being left behind by remote learning, due to governmental weaknesses and a spiral of bad choices that trapped the nation. *The Atlantic*'s Ed Yong, observing the breakdown of problem-solving capacity, noted that decision-makers were reactive, relying on lagging pandemic data like the light of distant stars, emitting records of the past instead of the present. False binaries (e.g., save the country or the economy? shut down or reopen?) prevented consideration of a mix of remedies that could have offered some relief to communities that were mentally paralyzed by the word, *lockdown*. Some solutions were erroneously regarded as pandemic-ending strategies, when the crisis was in fact one of a long haul. Theatrical comforts – scrubbing and bleaching surfaces when the virus was clearly airborne, temperature checks that could not detect asymptomatic infections, and porous travel bans – only worsened the crisis when they took the place of stronger measures, such as expanding testing and enacting policies to protect workers infected at their jobs. The nation's leaders led the country in magical thinking, individual-level fixes, and the habituation of horror, normalizing the tragedy in the same way they did police brutality during the Trump administration (Yong, 2020b).

2.7 "And the Governors Know That:" Pandemic Federalism

The politicization of disaster response is common in the literature, but the problem is compounded when pathogens are involved. Nathan Myers' *Pandemics and Polarization* (2019) describes the partisan standoff over the government budget in 2016 that adversely affected the response across all levels of government to the outbreak in certain states of the Zika virus, whose health impacts included birth defects. With COVID-19, the advantages as well as the constraints to capacity arising from federalism were seen in regard to the pandemic restrictions, gear procurement, aid to states and local government, and the deployment of federal agents in cities torn by unrest. The pandemic seemed to break the trend toward federal expansion when Trump made it known that the coronavirus was a local problem if it made his government look bad (Greenblatt, 2020). His political tactics were obvious to everyone. During the first phase of the crisis, the president shoved responsibility down to the states while denying the lethality of the pandemic. The abdication forced some governors to form a multistate pact to coordinate their reopening plans. On the East Coast, New York, New Jersey, and Rhode Island led the effort; California, Oregon, and Washington worked together on the West Coast to create a plan based on science. The governors were reacting to the president who thought he could escape responsibility at the same time arrogate unto himself the power to reopen economies based on a belief that the pandemic was easing. One of his exchanges with a reporter during the White House press briefings captured his dim view of federalism:

Q Mr. President, just to clarify your understanding of your authority vis-à-vis governors—just to be very specific: For instance, if a governor issued a stay-at-home order—
THE PRESIDENT: When you say "my authority"—the President's authority. Not mine, because it's not me.
Q If I could just ask the question—
THE PRESIDENT: This is—when somebody is the President of the United States, the authority is total, and that's the way it's got to be.
Q It's total? Your authority is total?
THE PRESIDENT: It's total. It's total.
Q Your authority is total?
THE PRESIDENT: And the governors know that. (Brady 2020, p. 1)

When he could not overpower the states, the president turned to intimidation with a series of "LIBERATE!" tweets inciting the public to defend their Second Amendment rights that was supposedly "under siege" with the mitigation measures from the CDC and state governments (Trump, 2020). Soon, protests erupted in Virginia and in Minnesota; and in Michigan, a mask-defying, gun-toting rally against the Democratic governor ended up in a plot to kidnap her. Trump would later on contract COVID-19 himself, receive extraordinary care at Walter Reed Hospital, and urge the country to wear face masks when Republican governors started abandoning his stance amid spiraling deaths. It left experts wondering if the president was instigating a civil war as the election approached – something that historians later on mulled in light of the post-election Capitol attack by his supporters.

Shades of punitive federalism (Goelzhauser & Konisky, 2020) against Democrat-led states marred federal aid to states and local governments, including schools and hospitals that reeled from the economic collapse. Republican lawmakers like Mitch McConnell pushed the idea of letting the blue states go bankrupt, as if the Constitution would allow it. The hyper-partisan policy posture merely weakened local governments' capacities to enforce their own guidelines and augment the holes in national capacity. Across the land, the divisions pushed governors to take mayors to court and legislatures to overrule their governors. Behind the scenes, the toll mounted on expert bureaucrats at the state capitols and municipal halls.

The accountability chain was admittedly complex in a federated system where externalities, veto powers, and clashing rationalities marked the landscape. It was not always clear which level the public blamed at different times, and bureaucrats were in the mix often. It was too easy for the president to blame the "deep state" for any lagging response; for the states, in turn, to blame the president and the federal agencies; and for the public to blame all sorts of public figures. Experts watching America were not at all sure that the Constitution was fulfilling its goal of furthering accountability through federalism. The pandemic was, for sure, at both local and national levels, expanding the power of the executive relative to legislatures (Selin, 2020).

2.8   The Broken Branch

Transfer of power to the president often occurs during crises. Due to their deliberative nature, the courts and Congress require more time to act, compared to the president (Selin, 2020). Deliberativeness was not the only reason for their diminished stature. COVID-19 revealed an attendant decline of congressional capacity, defined as its "relative ability to influence the country's legal landscape" (Feinstein, 2013, p. 140). Like millions of workers that suddenly had to telework, the 535-member national legislature found the reality forced by the pandemic quite awkward and, in some ways, diminishing. A frustrated speaker said: "People think we can do Congress by Zoom. Zoom is a Chinese entity that we've been told not to even trust the security of. So, there are challenges. It's not as easy as you would think." Another representative added, "I do worry about the optics… People expect Congress to be working, and we absolutely are right now, but we also have to be voting and conducting hearings and oversight" (Cheney & Ferris, 2020, para. 15–17).

Optics, however, were the least of their problems. Looming large was Congress' diluted ability to restrain an increasingly powerful executive that could do more damage than help. Ordinarily, a crisis crying out for energetic fiscal policy would have put Congress front and center. But Congress, like the public, was divided as the catastrophe hit. The coronavirus came on the heels of the Senate acquittal of Trump on his first (2019) impeachment. With impeachment failing, the budget system long ago broken, and Trump agency officials either snubbing or barred from attending congressional hearings, Congress kept running out of tools to assert itself. Institutional checks were dismal with the president's party controlling the Senate. Despite Congress enacting the biggest fiscal stimulus packages in history, and at least four oversight bodies established to track coronavirus spending, the White House effectively thwarted legislative wishes in distributing and managing the trillions of stimulus dollars, unemployment benefits, and bridge loans to mitigate the pandemic's effects on millions of employers and their workers. Although Congress had its own budget office, the White House OMB did not provide Congress and the public a mid-session budget update in July as required by the Congressional Budget and Impoundment Control Act of 1974. Lawmakers worried the president would use outdated projections to disguise the current crisis (Nicholson, 2020). The Democratic House leadership repeatedly found it frustrating to design with the Republican Senate and the White House a broad-based relief package for the states and the millions of unemployed. Neither could they find out the extent to which the Treasury and the Small Business Administration (SBA), which suffered from Trump budget cuts like many agencies, reached the intended recipients of COVID-19 relief, speedily or effectively.

The stonewalling of legislators by the agencies – a stance that conservatives typically rail against when the presidency is held by a Democrat – was in flagrant display under the unified Republican control of the presidency and the Senate. Congress' institutional independence and identity, the separation of powers, was no match to partisanship, the separation of parties (Levinson & Pildes, 2006). Heads of the CDC, the White House Coronavirus Task Force, and other experts failed to appear at some hearings meant to obtain adequate information on the supply chains for treatment drugs and protective equipment. Nor was insight offered into the significant decisions to award billions to drug companies for accelerated vaccine development through *Operation Warp Speed*, the contracting out of the coronavirus hospital reporting system and data management that the CDC had long controlled, or the CDC's changing guidance for reopening schools. Before and especially during the pandemic, the White House evaded oversight by firing inspectors general and running several agencies with acting heads that paid no heed to congressional demands for information.

Caught in the middle of this institutional hostility were the bureaucrats, even veterans in the health field, whose expertise in another era might have calmed the waters. But now they lacked autonomy and their legitimacy was strained. For that they took heat from lawmakers, as well. Thundered speaker Nancy Pelosi, "I don't have confidence in anyone who stands there while the president says swallow Lysol and it's going to cure your virus" (Breuninger, 2020, para. 16).

2.9 Designed Incapacity

To the World Health Organization (WHO), too many countries were headed in the wrong direction as COVID-19 spread. America stood out among those lost. While many were drawing on preexisting strengths in data systems, surveillance systems, and well-resourced local infrastructures to combat the pandemic, America seemed to have intentionally rendered itself incapable of meeting the challenge (Garrett, 2020). In the eyes of the world, America did not just do badly – it did "exceptionally badly…in the first global crisis in more than a century where no one was even looking for Washington to lead" (Bennhold, 2020, para. 1). The coronavirus landed in a country whose resilience was immuno-compromised from years of externalizing capacity and of polarization. Many assumed wrongly that the country was still endowed with the agencies and personnel devoted to responding to pandemics when the virus broke out (Frum, 2020). Trump promised to "drain the swamp" of special lobbies, but he appeared to have drained capacity, instead. Janet Napolitano, former DHS secretary, argued that:

you have to maintain a certain base level so that, when an event like a pandemic manifests itself, you can quickly activate what you have and you have already in place a system and plan for what the federal government is going to do and what the states are going to do. (Balz, 2020, para. 3)

The central organizations that should have been bolstering the capacity of the rest of the instruments of the state and leading the activation of intergovernmental problem-solving, management, leadership, accountability, and engagement were weakened by the previous years of deconstruction. By the first half of 2020, more than 1000 scientists had left various agencies (Packer, 2020), a staggering blow to administrative conservatorship and bureaucratic resilience. They had become casualties of a "war" against the administrative state, whose severe impact was laid bare by the coronavirus. Such war was signaled by presidential adviser Stephen Bannon's three-pronged agenda for the then newly installed Trump government, years before the coronavirus pandemic. Speaking to a conservative caucus, Bannon said:

The first is kind of national security and sovereignty, and that's your intelligence, the Defense Department, Homeland Security. The second line of work is what I refer to as economic nationalism, and that is Wilbur Ross at Commerce, Steven Mnuchin at Treasury, Lighthizer at—at Trade, Peter Navarro, Stephen Miller, these people that are rethinking how we're gonna reconstruct the—our trade arrangements around the world The third, broadly, line of work is what is deconstruction of the administrative state. (Blake, 2017, para. 13)

Disinvestment and delegitimization would mark the landscape afterward. In fact, *on the same week* that COVID-19 would claim its first casualty in the United States, White House spokesman Hogan Gidley was on *Fox* TV confirming the impending purge of the so-called NeverTrumpers from "the bowels of the federal government:"

It's not a secret that we want people in positions that work with this president, not against him, and too often we have people in this government—I mean the federal government is massive, with millions of people—and there are a lot of people out there taking action against this president and when we find them, we will take appropriate action. (Katz, 2020, para. 3)

Since Bannon's announcement, the pandemic response capacity from previous administrations appeared to have been dismembered. Looking back, according to Elaine Kamarck, the Obama administration had insisted on conducting a pandemic exercise with Trump's incoming officials during the transition period in 2017. Three hours of tabletop exercise appeared to have had little impact on readiness because only 8 of the 30 Trump attendees were still working for the administration at the onset of the coronavirus pandemic (Tenpas, 2020). The timing could not have been worse. More than two-thirds of staff including epidemiologists at a key US public health agency operating inside China were cut, making the CDC office in Beijing a shell. The administration shut the Beijing offices of the National Science Foundation (NSF) and the United States Agency for International Development (USAID), whose roles included helping China monitor and respond to outbreaks. The US Department of Agriculture (USDA) also transferred out of China in 2018 the manager of an animal disease monitoring program (Taylor, 2020). In 2018, the disease-fighting cadres of the US Public Health Service Commissioned Corps went down by 40%, steadily eroding as retiring officers went unreplaced. An independent, bipartisan panel had warned that the lack of preparedness was so acute that the "United States must either pay now and gain protection and security or wait for the next epidemic and pay a much greater price in human and economic costs" (Garrett, 2020, para. 12).

Capacity was the road not taken. The pandemic was already brewing when the public health cuts were proposed. The president boasted that he was a businessperson who didn't like "having thousands of people around when you don't need them." He explained that those experts "hadn't been used for many years," and if necessary, "we can get them all back very quickly," because "we know all the good people" (Roig, 2020, para. 1–5). As the next chapters will show, the private sector has occupied an outsized role in the discourse, design, and practice of modern governmental capacity, with long-term implications.

Among the experienced personnel who left the administration within months of the crisis were the White House Domestic Policy Council head and coronavirus task force member, a deputy assistant administrator for the FEMA's response group and a 13-year FEMA veteran, and the head of the National Security Council's unit on pandemic preparedness before it was disbanded in 2018 (Bublé, 2020). FEMA remained obscure throughout the first year of the pandemic, unable to perform what its framers imagined it to do. Likewise, OSHA, an agency like the CDC whose reason for existence came at this moment, suffered from having the lowest number of occupational safety and health inspectors since 1975 (Berkowitz, 2020).

Certain long-serving executives, dubbed in this book as "administrative conservators" (Terry, 2003) for their protective stance regarding agency mission, dared speak truth in an administration marked by denialism. Of them, Dr. Anthony Fauci, head of the National Institute of Allergy and Infectious Diseases and frequent target of White House denigration, stood out and called the testing response a failure. Such conservators manifest neutral competence as they advanced their views to those who must make the final call. Reflecting on the scale of tragedy and the process of decision making, Fauci noted that:

> if you had a process that was ongoing and you started mitigation earlier, you could have saved lives...But there was a lot of pushback about shutting things down back then. We look at it from a pure health standpoint. We make a recommendation. Often, the recommendation is taken. Sometimes it's not. (Cole, 2020, para. 4)

Administrative conservators were getting to the end of a harrowing year caught between an insurgent executive, a divided and weak Congress, and a fractious and suffering public. Deconstruction would later move on to the arena of vaccine. During the vaccine development, agency decisions seemed to be framed in the light of the president's reelection campaign. At the FDA, the agency's embattled head sought to reassure the public that the FDA would remain data-driven, despite the pressure. However, hollowing out and politicization of capacity would eventually harm the government's efforts long after Trump: vaccine rollout and vaccine documentation would confront the same problems discussed in this chapter.

2.10   A Failure of Capacity in Five Dimensions

When the future looks back to this time, they would wonder how a country that used to rank first, according to the WHO, in pandemic preparedness, which comprised 40% of the total global spending in pharmaceuticals and represented 24% of global economic output, ended up having little capacity when it mattered (Cohen, 2020). The inability to induce a consensus on the wearing of face masks in public unmasked a decaying capacity that met the coronavirus. Civic resilience was able to tide some people over, but the magnitude of the crisis required a capacitated government. The buried fault lines of American society also weakened the pockets of unity across the land. By summertime, businesses took it upon themselves to impose their own policies, creating signs that read like this:

> In addition to posting *clear signage* at the front of our stores, Walmart has *created the role* of Health Ambassador and will station them near the entrance to remind those without a mask of our new requirements. Our ambassadors will receive *special training* to help make the process as smooth as possible for customers. The ambassadors, *identifiable* by their black polo shirts, *will work with customers* who show up at a store without a face covering *to try and find a solution.* (Italics ours) (Shrikantm, 2020, para. 4)

That contained, in a single paragraph, a capacity mindset that was sorely lacking from the state's initial response. It revealed important *dimensions of capacity*, problem-solving, management, engagement, and accountability that were necessary for action, strategic visibility and clarity, management and workforce training to minimize conflict with a public that might or might not adhere automatically to a new behavioral rule. Ultimately, the goal was to work together and solve the problem.

In sum, the coronavirus pandemic response exhibited the decline and decay of American administrative capacity in several dimensions:

- It showed a decayed capacity for *problem surveillance and problem-solving*. To foreign policy experts, the coronavirus pandemic was the biggest intelligence failure in US history, more glaring than Pearl Harbor or the September 2001 attacks. Unlike those, this one was precipitated by unprecedented indifference, even willful negligence (Zenko, 2020). Calls to mobilize the agencies with a reputation for crisis management capacities went unheeded. Federalist principles were attacked even though the states stepped up where national capacity failed. The White House admission that it was not really trying to control the pandemic was effectively a form of surrender in this dimension (Pramuk, 2020). As the crisis dragged on, government kept reprising the tactical and conceptual errors of the deadly first wave, trapping the nation in a spiral of failures (Yong, 2020b). As for the COVID vaccine rollout – as politicized as the coronavirus epidemiology – Congress under Trump would not come to the aid quickly enough of states, local governments, hospitals, and schools. The FDA, meanwhile, encountered the same capacity issues and pressures that plagued the CDC.

- It manifested a decayed capacity for *organization and management*. Having lost or muffled the experts, neophytes fumbled the effort and blurred the lines of authority, leading to nobody owning the problem. Relative to Asian and European countries, whose bureaucratic infrastructure displayed nimbleness in adapting to the contours of the pandemic (Penn, 2020; Abe, 2020), the American government's crude coordination and even harassment of the states in getting lifesaving equipment manifested signs of a "failed state" that some had feared happening when Trump captured power (Krugman, 2016). Government revealed inadequate telework capability or plans to safeguard their own employees. According to several workers' unions, the pandemic exposed every fracture in workplace safety. "Even an enthusiastic OSHA would be fighting with one arm behind its back;" instead, the OSHA's weaknesses were magnified under Trump (Feuer, 2020, para. 10).
- It demonstrated a decay in *administrative conservatorship*. Instead of seeking, retaining, and harnessing expertise in anticipation of novel emergencies, it was deconstructed, along with much of the administrative state. Scientists and crisis management veterans were undermined, fired, or exiled. The exodus signaled the breakdown of a professional culture. As the pandemic deepened, the Office of Special Counsel reported having received 20,505 complaints from federal employees alleging government wrongdoing, retaliation for whistleblowing, or other improper treatment – a 36% jump from Obama's first term (Rein et al., 2020).
- It showed a decayed capacity for *engagement and communication*. A pandemic of misinformation muzzled vertical and horizontal coordination, scientific collaboration, and the civic body's ability to deliberate carefully, if not rationally. A hollowed-out government struggled to marshal expertise and educate the fiercely divided, cognitively strained populace on the linkages among social distancing, business reopening, school safety, and capacity of hospitals and medical communities. Databases used for pandemic management information disappeared, lacked coherence, or were contracted out without transparency, leading to dubious updates and furthering conspiracy theories and citizen mistrust.
- Finally, the saga manifested a decayed capacity for *accountability*. Congress failed to ensure executive honesty to the public and responsibility in crisis response. Civic trust in the government's ability to address a national problem, a crucial element in getting the work done in a vast, diverse, and complex system, was eroded from within and by the top. No sense of sacrifice was evoked by the president; no cultivation of resilience and unity in the face of flagging administrative capacity. Instead, accountability fell victim to an alternative reality that put the blame on almost anyone else but the leader of the land.

References

45 Chaos. (n.d.). *Trump administration departures.* https://www.45chaos.com/. Accessed 3 Aug 2020.

Abe, K. (2020, December 29). The lessons from East Asia's coronavirus successes. *The Japan Times.* https://www.japantimes.co.jp/opinion/2020/12/29/commentary/world-commentary/api-east-asia-response/. Accessed 4 Jan 2021.

Abutaleb, Y., & Parker, A. (2020, May 5). Kushner coronavirus effort said to be hampered by inexperienced volunteers. *The Washington Post.* https://www.washingtonpost.com/politics/kushner-coronavirus-effort-said-to-be-hampered-by-inexperienced-volunteers/2020/05/05/6166ef0c-8e1c-11ea-9e23-6914ee410a5f_story.html. Accessed 4 June 2020.

American Federation of Government Employees (AFGE). (2020, August 19). Federal workers feel unsafe, lack resources to protect themselves during coronavirus pandemic, AFGE survey shows. Washington, DC. [Press Release]. https://www.afge.org/publication/federal-workers-feel-unsafe-lack-resources-to-protect-themselves-during-coronavirus-pandemic-afge-survey-shows/. Accessed 21 Sept 2020.

Applebaum, A. (2020, July 23). Trump is putting on a show in Portland. *The Atlantic.* https://www.theatlantic.com/ideas/archive/2020/07/trump-putting-show-portland/614521/. Accessed 1 Aug 2020.

Artenstein, A. (2020, April 30). Correspondence, COVID notes: In pursuit of PPE. *The New England Journal of Medicine.* https://doi.org/10.1056/NEJMc2010025. Accessed 1 May 2020.

Balz, D. (2020, May 16). Crisis exposes how America has hollowed out its government. *The Washington Post.* https://www.washingtonpost.com/graphics/2020/politics/government-hollowed-out-weaknesses/. Accessed 19 May 2020.

Bennhold, K. (2020, April 23). 'Sadness' and disbelief from a world missing American leadership. *The New York Times.* https://www.nytimes.com/2020/04/23/world/europe/coronavirus-american-exceptionalism.html. Accessed 19 June 2020.

Berkowitz, D. (2020, April 28). Worker safety in crisis: The cost of a weakened OSHA. *National Employment Law Project.* https://www.nelp.org/publication/worker-safety-crisis-cost-weakened-osha/. Accessed 3 June 2020.

Blake, A. (2017, February 23). Stephen Bannon's nationalist call to arms, annotated. *The Washington Post.* https://www.washingtonpost.com/news/the-fix/wp/2017/02/23/stephen-bannons-nationalist-call-to-arms-annotated/. Accessed 13 Aug 2020.

Block, E., & Longo, A. (2018, March 7). More D.C. commuters as USDA slashes telework for all employees. *WUSA9.* https://www.wusa9.com/article/news/local/dc/more-dc-commuters-as-usda-slashes-telework-for-all-employees/65-526612469. Accessed 5 June 2019.

Boodman, E., & Ross, C. (2020, May 6). Doctors lambaste federal process for distributing COVID-19 drug remdisivir. Stat. https://www.statnews.com/2020/05/06/doctors-lambaste-federal-process-for-distributing-covid-19-drug-remdesivir/. Accessed 13 August 2020.

Bower, K. A. (2020, April 27). Trump's contempt for the ex-presidents is costing us right now. *The New York Times.* https://www.nytimes.com/2020/04/27/opinion/coronavirus-trump-presidents.html. Accessed 30 Apr 2020.

Brady, J. S. (2020, April 14). Remarks by President Trump, Vice President Pence, and members of the coronavirus task force in press briefing. *The White House.* https://www.whitehouse.gov/briefings-statements/remarks-president-trump-vice-president-pence-members-coronavirus-task-force-press-briefing-19/. Accessed 11 Apr 2020.

Breuninger, K. (2020, August 3). Trump attacks Dr. Birx after she said U.S. reached 'new phase' in coronavirus fight. *CNBC.* https://www.cnbc.com/2020/08/03/trump-attacks-dr-birx-after-she-said-us-reached-new-phase-in-coronavirus-fight.html. Accessed 5 Aug 2020.

Brittain, A., Stanley-Becker, I., & Miroff, N. (2020, May 8). White House's pandemic relief effort Project Airbridge is swathed in secrecy and exaggerations. *The Washington Post.* https://www.washingtonpost.com/investigations/white-house-pandemic-supply-project-swathed-in-secrecy-and-exaggerations/2020/05/08/9c77efb2-8d52-11ea-a9c0-73b93422d691_story.html. Accessed 11 May 2020.

Bublé, C. (2020, May 6). Trump administration faces departures of key health and emergency response officials during pandemic. *Government Executive*. https://www.govexec.com/management/2020/05/trump-administration-faces-departures-key-health-and-emergency-response-officials-during-pandemic/165185/. Accessed 14 May 2020.

Budryk, Z. (2020, September 17). White House nixed Postal Service plan to send face masks to every household in US: Report. *The Hill*. https://thehill.com/policy/healthcare/516893-white-house-nixed-plan-to-send-facemasks-to-every-household-in-us-report. Accessed 19 September 2020.

Chait, J. (2019, September 9). Trump has figured out how to corrupt the entire government. *Intelligencer*. Http://nymag.com/intelligencer/2019/09/trump-corruption-sharpiegate-hotel-biden.html. Accessed 18 Jan 2020.

Cheney, K., & Ferris, S. (2020, April 17). 'I do worry about the optics': Congress struggles to get off the sidelines. *Politico*. https://www.politico.com/news/2020/04/17/congress-sidelines-coronavirus-192351. Accessed 21 Apr 2020.

Clark, D. (2020, April 23). Trump suggests 'injection' of disinfectant to beat coronavirus and 'clean' the lungs. *NBC News*. https://www.nbcnews.com/politics/donald-trump/trump-suggests-injection-disinfectant-beat-coronavirus-clean-lungs-n1191216. Accessed 25 Apr 2020.

CNBC Staff. (2020, July 17). Coronavirus live updates. *CNBC*. https://www.cnbc.com/2020/07/17/coronavirus-live-updates.html. Accessed 18 July 2020.

Cohen, D. (2020, August 22). Why a PPE shortage still plagues America and what we need to do about it. *CNBC*. https://www.cnbc.com/2020/08/22/coronavirus-why-a-ppe-shortage-still-plagues-the-us.html. Accessed 26 Aug 2020.

Cole, D. (2020, April 12). Fauci admits earlier covid-19 mitigation efforts would have saved more American lives. *CNN*. https://www.cnn.com/2020/04/12/politics/anthony-fauci-pushback-coronavirus-measures-cnntv/index.html. Accessed 13 Apr 2020.

Confessore N., Jacobs, A., Kantor, J., Kanno-Youngs, Z., & Ferré-Sadurní, L. (2020, May 5). How Kushner's volunteer force led a fumbling hunt for medical supplies. *The New York Times*. https://www.nytimes.com/2020/05/05/us/jared-kushner-fema-coronavirus.html. Accessed 9 May 2020.

Diamond, D. (2020, April 28). 'HHS has been kicked in the teeth.' *Politico*. https://www.politico.com/news/2020/04/28/hhs-coronavirus-218923. Accessed 28 Apr 2020.

Diehl, J. (2020, March 21). The winners and losers of the coronavirus's global test of governance. *The Washington Post*. https://www.washingtonpost.com/opinions/global-opinions/the-winners-and-losers-of-the-coronaviruss-global-test-of-governance/2020/03/30/f53fe19e-6f71-11ea-b148-e4ce3fbd85b5_story.html. Accessed 25 Mar 2020.

Dubnick, M. (2005). Accountability and the promise of performance: In search of the mechanisms. *Public Performance and Management Review, 28*(3), 376–417.

Eban, K. (2020, July 30). How Jared Kushner's secret testing plan "went poof into thin air". *Vanity Fair*. https://www.vanityfair.com/news/2020/07/how-jared-kushners-secret-testing-plan-went-poof-into-thin-air. Accessed 2 Aug 2020.

Enrich, D., Abrams, R., & Kurutz, S. (2020, March 25). A sewing army, making masks for America. *The New York Times*. https://www.nytimes.com/2020/03/25/business/coronavirus-masks-sewers.html. Accessed 28 Mar 2020.

Farazmand, A. (2009). Building administrative capacity for the age of rapid globalization: A modest prescription for survival in the 21st century. *Public Administration Review, 69*(6), 1007–1020.

Farr, C. (2020, July 21). Germany's coronavirus response is a master class in science communication. *CNBC*. https://www.cnbc.com/2020/07/21/germanys-coronavirus-response-masterful-science-communication.html. Accessed 24 July 2020.

Feinstein, B. D. (2013). Congressional government rebooted: Randomized committee assignments & legislative capacity. *Harvard Law and Policy Review, 7*, 601–634.

Feuer, W. (2020, April 28). Coronavirus has 'exposed every fracture' in US workplace safety, top labor union leaders say. *CNBC*. https://www.cnbc.com/2020/04/28/coronavirus-has-magnified-us-workplace-safety-weaknesses-unions-say.html. Accessed 16 May 2020.

Friedman, U. (2020a, March 25). Why America is uniquely unsuited to dealing with the coronavirus. *The Atlantic*. https://www.theatlantic.com/politics/archive/2020/03/coronavirus-united-states-vulnerable-pandemic/608686/. Accessed 21 Apr 2020.

Friedman, U. (2020b, November 15). The pandemic is revealing a new form of national power. *The Atlantic*. https://www.theatlantic.com/ideas/archive/2020/11/pandemic-revealing-new-form-national-power/616944/. Accessed 21 Nov 2020.

Frum, D. (2020, April 7). This is Trump's fault. *The Atlantic*. https://www.theatlantic.com/ideas/archive/2020/04/americans-are-paying-the-price-for-trumps-failures/609532/. Accessed 9 Apr 2020.

Garrett, T. A. (2007, November). Economic effects of the 1918 influenza pandemic implications for a modern-day pandemic. *Federal Reserve Bank of St. Louis*. https://www.stlouisfed.org/~/media/files/pdfs/community-development/research-reports/pandemic_flu_report.pdf. Accessed 23 June 2021.

Garrett, L. (2020, January 31). Trump has sabotaged America's coronavirus response. *Foreign Policy*. https://foreignpolicy.com/2020/01/31/coronavirus-china-trump-united-states-public-health-emergency-response/. Accessed 16 July 2020.

Goelzhauser, G., & Konisky, D. M. (2020). The state of American federalism 2019–2020: Polarized and punitive intergovernmental relations. *Publius: The Journal of Federalism, 50*(3), 311–343.

Graham, J. (2020, April 23). Seniors with COVID-19 show unusual symptoms, doctors say. *CNN*. https://www.cnn.com/2020/04/23/health/seniors-elderly-coronavirus-symptoms-wellness-partner/index.html. Accessed 28 Apr 2020.

Greenblatt, A. (2020, December 8). How the pandemic broke the trend toward federal expansion. *Governing*. https://www.governing.com/now/how-the-pandemic-broke-the-trend-toward-federal-expansion.html. Accessed on 14 February 2021.

Hansen, S. (2020, June 30). A national mask mandate could save the U.S. economy $1 trillion, Goldman Sachs says. *Forbes*. https://www.forbes.com/sites/sarahhansen/2020/06/30/a--national-mask-mandate-could-save-the-us-economy-1-trillion-goldman-sachs-says/#2e9a7d6256f1. Accessed 30 June 2020.

IHME COVID-19 Forecasting Team. (2020, October 23). Modeling COVID-19 scenarios for the United States. *Nature Medicine, 27*, 94–105. https://www.nature.com/articles/s41591-020-1132-9?utm_source=newsletter&utm_medium=email&utm_campaign=newsletter_axiosvitals&stream=top#Abs1. Accessed 30 Oct 2020.

Joaquin, M. E., & Greitens, T. J. (2011). The accountability-performance link. *Public Performance & Management Review, 34*(3), 323–349.

Katz, E. (2020, February 25). White House confirms it's purging disloyal employees 'from the bowels of the federal government'. *Government Executive*. https://www.govexec.com/workforce/2020/02/white-house-confirms-its-purging-disloyal-employees-bowels-federal-government/163316/. Accessed 11 Feb 2020.

Kayyem, J. (2020, July 6). Reopening schools was just an afterthought. *The Atlantic*. https://www.theatlantic.com/ideas/archive/2020/07/reopening-bars-easy-schools-are-difficult/613861/. Accessed 21 July 2020.

Kramer, S. (2020, April 24). Americans are divided by religion on who should get critical care if there is a shortage of ventilators. *Pew Research Center*. https://www.pewresearch.org/fact-tank/2020/04/24/americans-are-divided-by-religion-on-who-should-get-critical-care-if-there-is-a-shortage-of-ventilators/. Accessed 21 Oct 2020.

Krugman, P. (2016, November 8). Our unknown country. *The New York Times*. https://www.nytimes.com/interactive/projects/cp/opinion/election-night-2016. Accessed 14 Apr 2020.

Levinson, D. J., & Pildes, R. H. (2006). Separation of parties, not powers. *Harvard Law Review, 119*(8), 2314–2315.

Lipton, E., Goodnough, A., Shear, M., Twohey, M., Mandavilli, A., Fink, S., & Walker, M. (2020, June 3). The C.D.C. waited 'its entire existence for this moment.' What went wrong? *The New York Times*. https://www.nytimes.com/2020/06/03/us/cdc-coronavirus.html. Accessed 11 June 2020.

Lizza, R., & Lippman, D. (2020, May 1). Wearing a mask is for smug liberals. Refusing to is for reckless Republicans. *Politico*. https://www.politico.com/news/2020/05/01/masks-politics-coronavirus-227765. Accessed 2 June 2020.

Lloyd, R. (2020, April 2). Forget Trump's daily briefings. Watch these coronavirus messengers instead. *Los Angeles Times*. https://www.latimes.com/entertainment-arts/tv/story/2020-04-02/press-conferences-trump-cuomo-newsom-garcetti. Accessed 1 May 2020.

Lowrey, A. (2020, August 21). The lesson Americans never learn. *The Atlantic*. https://www.theatlantic.com/ideas/archive/2020/08/gofundme-economy-was-never-going-work/615457/. Accessed 19 Sept 2020.

Mandavilli, A. (2020, September 17). C.D.C. testing guidance was published against scientists' objections. *The New York Times*. https://www.nytimes.com/2020/09/17/health/coronavirus-testing-cdc.html. Accessed 1 Oct 2020.

Milbank, D. (2020, March 30). What kind of person calls 100,000-plus dead a 'very good job'? *The Washington Post*. https://www.washingtonpost.com/opinions/2020/03/30/what-kind-person-calls-100000-plus-dead-very-good-job/. Accessed 1 Apr 2020.

Myers, N. (2019). *Pandemics and polarization: Implications of partisan budgeting for responding to public health emergencies*. Lexington Books.

Nicholson, J. (2020, May 28). Trump violating law by not updating budget, outside experts say. *MarketWatch*. https://www.marketwatch.com/story/trump-violating-law-by-not-updating-budget-outside-experts-say-2020-05-28. Accessed 20 May 2020.

NPR. Morning Edition. (2001, May 25). Conservative Advocate. https://www.npr.org/templates/story/story.php?storyId=1123439. Accessed 27 Oct 2019.

Park, S. M., Joaquin, M. E., Min, K. R., & Ugaddan, R. G. (2018). Do reform values matter? Federal worker satisfaction and turnover intention at the dawn of the Trump presidency. The American Review of Public Administration, 48(6), 506–521.

Packer, G. (2020, April). The president is winning his war on American institutions. *The Atlantic*. https://www.theatlantic.com/magazine/archive/2020/04/how-to-destroy-a-government/606793/. Accessed 10 May 2020.

Penn, M. (2020, August 12). How some Asian countries beat back COVID-19. *Global Health Institute*. https://globalhealth.duke.edu/news/how-some-asian-countries-beat-back-covid-19. Accessed 24 Aug 2020.

Pielke, R. A., Jr. (2007). *The honest broker: Making sense of science in policy and politics*. Cambridge University Press.

Pilkington, E., & McCarthy, T. (2020, March 28). The missing six weeks: How trump failed the biggest test of his life. *The Guardian*. https://www.theguardian.com/us-news/2020/mar/28/trump-coronavirus-politics-us-health-disaster. Accessed 4 Apr 2020.

Porter, T. (2020, April 3). The Department of Health and Human Services rewrote its definition of the federal health-equipment stockpile so it didn't contradict Jared Kushner. *Business Insider*. https://www.businessinsider.com/dhhs-rewrites-national-stockpile-definition-to-not-contradict-kushner-2020-4. Accessed 19 June 2020.

Pramuk, J. (2020, October 26). Stimulus deal before election day looks less likely as Pelosi pushes Mnuchin over virus testing. *CNBC*. https://www.cnbc.com/2020/10/26/coronavirus-stimulus-update-pelosi-slams-trump-over-virus-testing.html. Accessed 30 Oct 2020.

Rascoe, A. (2020, March 25). Trump resists using wartime law to get, distribute coronavirus supplies. *NPR*. https://www.npr.org/2020/03/25/821285204/trump-sends-mixed-messages-about-invoking-defense-production-act. Accessed 2 Apr 2020.

Rascoe, A., & Dwyer, C. (2020, May 2). Trump received intelligence briefings on coronavirus twice in January. *NPR*. https://www.npr.org/sections/coronavirus-live-updates/2020/05/02/

849619486/trump-received-intelligence-briefings-on-coronavirus-twice-in-january. Accessed 19 June 2020.

Rein, L., Hamburger, T., Eilperin, J., & Freedman, A. (2020, October 29). How Trump waged war on his own government. *The Washington Post.* https://www.washingtonpost.com/politics/trump-federal-civil-servants/2020/10/28/86f9598e-122a-11eb-ba42-ec6a580836ed_story.html. Accessed 1 Nov 2020.

Relman, E. (2020, March 20). The federal government outbid states on critical coronavirus supplies after Trump told governors to get their own medical equipment. *Business Insider.* https://www.businessinsider.com/coronavirus-trump-outbid-states-on-medical-supplies-2020-3. Accessed 25 Mar 2020.

Rittel, H. W. J., & Webber, M. M. (1973). Dilemmas in a general theory of planning. *Policy Sciences, 4*(2), 155–169.

Roberts, A. S. (2019). *Strategies for governing: Reinventing public administration for a dangerous century.* Cornell University Press.

Roig, J. Z. (2020, February 27). Trump defends huge cuts to the CDC's budget by saying the government can hire more doctors when we need them' during crises. *Markets Insider.* https://markets.businessinsider.com/news/stocks/trump-defends-cuts-cdc-budget-federal-government-hire-doctors-coronavirus-2020-2-1028946602. Accessed 1 Mar 2020.

Romzek, B. S., & Dubnick, M. J. (1987). Accountability in the public sector: Lessons from the challenger tragedy. *Public Administration Review, 47,* 227.

Schwellenbach, N. (2020, May 4). Watchdog examining dozens of federal coronavirus whistle-blower cases. *Project on Government Oversight.* https://www.pogo.org/investigation/2020/05/watchdog-examining-dozens-of-federal-coronavirus-whistleblower-cases/. Accessed 14 May 2020.

Selin, J. (2020, June 8). How the Constitution's federalist framework is being tested by COVID-19. *The Brookings Institution.* https://www.brookings.edu/blog/fixgov/2020/06/08/how-the-constitutions-federalist-framework-is-being-tested-by-covid-19/. Accessed 16 June 2020.

Shrikantm, A. (2020, July 5). Walmart and Sam's Club will join Costco, other chains in requiring shoppers to wear masks. *Grow.* https://grow.acorns.com/walmart-requires-face-masks-at-all-us-locations/#:~:text=Starting%20Monday%2C%20Walmart%20and%20Sams,locations%20to%20wear%20face%20masks. Accessed 7 July 2020.

Silverman, E. (2020, August 22). FDA commissioner needs to push back and tell Trump the agency is not part of the 'deep state.' Stat. https://www.statnews.com/pharmalot/2020/08/22/fda-hahn-trump-vaccine-covid19-deep-state-coronavirus/. Accessed 24 Aug 2020.

Skowronek, S. (2009, October 29). The conservative insurgency and presidential power: A developmental perspective on the unitary executive. *Harvard Law Review, 122*(8), 2070. https://harvardlawreview.org/2009/10/the-conservative-insurgency-and-presidential-power-a-developmental-perspective-on-the-unitary-executive/. Accessed 23 Oct 2020.

Smith, D. (2020, March 13). 'I don't take responsibility': Trump shakes hands and spreads blame over coronavirus. *The Guardian.* https://www.theguardian.com/us-news/2020/mar/13/donald-trump-coronavirus-national-emergency-sketch. Accessed 17 Mar 2020.

Stirling, D. (2020, March 7). Trump treats the military as his own—and the troops could suffer. *The Conversation.* https://theconversation.com/trump-treats-the-military-as-his-own-and-the-troops-could-suffer-130019. Accessed 21 Oct 2020.

Taylor, M. (2020, March 25). Exclusive: U.S. slashed CDC staff inside China prior to coronavirus outbreak. *Reuters.* https://www.reuters.com/article/us-health-coronavirus-china-cdc-exclusiv/exclusive-u-s-slashed-cdc-staff-inside-china-prior-to-coronavirus-outbreak-idUSKBN21C3N5. Accessed 28 Mar 2020.

Tenpas, K. D. (2020, May 7). *How instability and high turnover on the Trump staff hindered the response to COVID-19.* The Brookings Institution. https://www.brookings.edu/blog/fixgov/2020/05/07/how-instability-and-high-turnover-on-the-trump-staff-hindered-the-response-to-covid-19/. Accessed 12 May 2020.

Terry, L. D. (2003). *Leadership of public bureaucracies: The administrator as conservator.* M.E. Sharpe.

The Economist. (2020a). Checks and balance. [Audio podcast]. Accessed 1 Oct 2020. https://www.economist.com/briefing/2020/04/30/the-90-economy-that-lockdowns-will-leave-behind. Accessed 2 May 2020.

The Economist. (2020b, May 2). *Do low-trust societies do better in a pandemic?* https://www.economist.com/europe/2020/05/02/do-low-trust-societies-do-better-in-a-pandemic. Accessed 15 May 2020.

The New York Times. (2020, August 14). *Firm helping run U.S. coronavirus database refuses senators' questions.* https://www.nytimes.com/2020/08/14/world/covid-19-coronavirus.html?action=click&module=Top%20Stories&pgtype=Homepage. Accessed 20 Aug 2020.

Tompkins, L. (2021, January 23). 'An incredible scale of tragedy': The U.S. records 25 million virus cases. *The New York Times.* https://www.nytimes.com/2021/01/22/us/covid-coronavirus-25-million-cases.html. Accessed 2 Feb 2021.

U.S. Centers for Disease Control and Prevention (CDC). (2020, July 23). *The importance of reopening schools this fall.* Accessed 28 July 2020.

U.S. Executive Office of the President (EOP). (n.d.). *Playbook for early response to high-consequence and emerging infectious disease threats and biological incidents.*

Wehner, P. (2019, March 18). A damaged soul and a disordered personality. *The Atlantic.* https://www.theatlantic.com/ideas/archive/2019/03/trump-tweets-attack-john-mccain/585193/. Accessed 5 Dec 2019.

Weilla, J. A., Stiglerb, M., Deschenesc, O., Springborn, M. R. (2020). Social distancing responses to COVID-19 emergency declarations strongly differentiated by income. *PNAS.* https://www.pnas.org/content/early/2020/07/28/2009412117. Accessed 6 Feb 2021.

White, L. D. (1954). *Introduction to the study of public administration* (4th ed.). The Macmillan Company.

Wilkie, C. (2020, May 11). Trump abruptly ends press conference after reporters challenge him on coronavirus testing. *CNBC.* https://www.cnbc.com/2020/05/11/coronavirus-trump-ends-press-conference-after-reporters-challenge-him-on-testing.html. Accessed 18 June 2020.

Wright, T. (2020, August 28). Will Trumpism change republican foreign policy permanently? *The Atlantic.* https://www.theatlantic.com/ideas/archive/2020/08/will-trumpism-change-republican-foreign-policy-permanently/615745/. Accessed 6 Sept 2020.

Yong, E. (2020a, April 29). Why the coronavirus is so confusing. *The Atlantic.* https://www.theatlantic.com/health/archive/2020/04/pandemic-confusing-uncertainty/610819/. Accessed 29 Apr 2020.

Yong, E. (2020b, September 9). America is trapped in a pandemic spiral. *The Atlantic.* https://www.theatlantic.com/health/archive/2020/09/pandemic-intuition-nightmare-spiral-winter/616204/. Accessed 10 Sept 2020.

Zenko, M. (2020, March 25). The coronavirus is worst intelligence failure in US history. *Foreign Policy.* https://foreignpolicy.com/2020/03/25/coronavirus-worst-intelligence-failure-us-history-covid-19/. Accessed 8 Apr 2020.

Chapter 3
The Concept of Capacity

Capacity – noun: competency or fitness, the potential or suitability for holding, storing, or accommodating; mental or physical ability; duty, position, or role; the facility or power to produce, perform, or deploy.

Merriam-Webster Dictionary (n.d.)

3.1 Capacity in the Spotlight

On his first day, President Joseph Biden vowed to devote a full-scale, wartime effort to defeat the coronavirus pandemic: "We will manage the hell out of this operation. Our administration will lead with science and scientists," he declared (Mervosh et al., 2021, para. 7). Clearly, capacity would be involved in "letting the science speak," as Dr. Anthony Fauci, the popular White House adviser on infectious diseases, saw it (Mason & Holland, 2021, para. 1). But what administrative capacity was needed to address the crisis? Was it something that could be maintained or made resilient over time? Could it even be recognized once it eroded? What were ways of thinking about administrative capacity within a political context? Was it an executive branch construct alone? Could a president have no need for certain administrative capacities?

To answer these questions, we had to first explore how capacity was defined previously. The Merriam-Webster (n.d.-a) Dictionary offers these meanings for the noun, capacity: *competency or fitness, the potential or suitability for holding, storing, or accommodating; mental or physical ability; duty, position, or role; the facility or power to produce, perform, or deploy.* That would mean that administrative capacity is the bureaucracy's fitness, ability, power, or suitability to be that which we would expect bureaucracy to be, and to do those things we would expect it to carry out, in a manner consistent with the standards we set. Some social scientists define *capacity* – without the qualifier "administrative" – as that which allows the government to respond intelligently to changing circumstances (Roberts, 2019b,

© Springer Nature Switzerland AG 2021
M. E. Joaquin, T. J. Greitens, *American Administrative Capacity*,
https://doi.org/10.1007/978-3-030-80564-7_3

p. 9), its ability to accomplish intended actions (Huber & McCarty, 2004, p. 481), or simply that of having an adequate number of people with the right training and skills to carry out the tasks they are assigned (Fukuyama, 2020). As a research construct, there seem to be many interpretations of what capacity consists of or what it is supposed to do. Across the disciplines, the levels of analyses or the metrics for capacity vary. In the organization, business, and nonprofit literatures, its usages call to mind the early 1900s when pioneers tried to define what "management" or "administration" consisted of, with some studies adopting more prescriptive and others more descriptive approaches to the term.

Recent applications of capacity appear to be influenced by the New Public Management (NPM) movement, which put great emphasis on performance analysis and capacity's role in engendering successful performance. Surveying the literature, Robert Christensen and Beth Gazley, in "Capacity for Public Administration: Analysis of Meaning and Measurement" (2008), navigated the conceptual disarray that Beth Honadle observed in 1981. They discovered that capacity was a favorite topic among management researchers, with 16 top journals devoting an average of more than 2% of their published articles to capacity. Though the authors intended to focus on *administrative* capacity, they discovered works on *organizational* capacity, *managerial* capacity, and *governance* capacity, all of whose operationalizations depended on an understanding of the contexts in which capacity's meaning was used. The authors also intended to examine capacity at the firm level but came across other applications as well, from the individual (person) to the nation (state). Thus, capacity as a concept was used not just in discussions at the organizational level but also in broader discussions of governance and policy implementation.

Capacity could describe both inputs and outputs, the ends/goals of organizational effort (e.g., "collaborative capacity," "absorptive capacity"), and the means to an end (the resources needed to achieve effectiveness or some measure of success). Capacity could also be framed in terms of the policy process, as when "delivery capacity" is understood synonymously with the capacity for "administration" in the politics/administration distinction, with the "implementation" phase of the policy process, or with "performance" in the study of public management (Hupe & Hill, 2014).

Capacity's features could be internal (e.g., human and capital resources) and external (networks of relationships), tangible and intangible, and quantitative and qualitative. Capacity could be reduced to a matter of resource acquisition or funding but also be expanded to include multidimensional, financial, human, physical, and technological attributes. As both a process and a structure, capacity could be a function of, among others, institutionalization, leadership, alignment across systems, and feedback loops. For example, when the concept of capacity is explored in the crisis management literature, a multi-dimensional approach to capacity emerges:

> *Coordination capacity* is about bringing together disparate organizations to engage in joint action; *analytical capacity* is about analyzing information and providing advice as well as risk and vulnerability assessments; *regulation capacity* is about control, surveillance, oversight, and auditing; and *delivery capacity* is about handling the crisis, exercising power, and providing public services in practice. (Christensen et al., 2016, p. 888; Lodge & Wegrich, 2014)

While no single discipline consistently used such definitions, most often employed "relatively simple conceptual frameworks of capacity focusing on internal and external dimensions that comfortably captured different definitions of capacity" (Christensen & Gazley, 2008, p. 273).

In addition to defining the concept of capacity, many studies focused on how to build it via research on *capacity building*. However, the term *capacity building* also lacks consistency in the literature. Some studies used it to specify the activities that should be performed, while others used the term to specify the results that should be sought. Some studies had a "survival view" of capacity building to describe the capacity of an organization to take action that enables it to survive. Additionally, some studies had a "service" view, in that capacity building was the ability of an organization to become more competent in using its powers and resources to accomplish purposes. Then there were uses of the term that stressed the rationality or the "perfection" of administrative systems, those that involved the political dynamics constraining capacity-building efforts, definitions that focused on inputs versus the total systems, and definitions that signified the means of accomplishing goals versus results improvement (Honadle, 1981).

At the *institutional* level, capacity was described as a clutch of abilities that included anticipating and influencing change; making informed, intelligent decisions about policy; developing programs to implement policy; attracting and absorbing resources; managing resources; and evaluating current activities to guide future action. At the *organizational* level, capacity involved the ability to forge links with other organizations, processes for solving problems, coordination among disparate functions, and mechanisms for institutional learning. Capacity building was framed as "how well" things are being done. Benchmarking across agencies was often suggested to measure capacity building, though "admittedly" Honadle (1981) wrote, "the goals of administrative development are hard to quantify" (p. 579), making measurement context-dependent.

3.2   Administrative Capacity as the Core of Government

One could scarcely find a more comprehensive listing of capacity concepts than in Ali Farazmand's paper "Building Administrative Capacity for the Age of Rapid Globalization." To calibrate capacities for a rapidly changing world, three types of capacity would be necessary: governance, instrumental, and administrative. With *governance* capacities or the capacity to govern, Farazmand called for redirecting capacity for chaos management, building collaborative management, balancing the strong hand of the state with checks and balance and legislative oversight, and developing strategic human capital for anticipatory capacity or "knowing what we do not and cannot know" (2009; Dror, 2001). *Instrumental* capacities referred to the capacity to manage and the application of innovative tools, techniques, and other know-how areas. They involved new thinking beyond traditional public management as we know it. Under this, the author spoke of designing *macro-strategic capacities to manage* in rapidly changing environments involving three key strategies: adaptive strategy, service delivery performance strategy, and development and advancement strategy. As for *administrative capacities*:

> Administrative capacity is a broad concept that entails running the machinery of a political or economic system, a government, and its international or global affairs, executing policy decisions, and translating political and collective will into actions through implementation and management. Administrative capacity also entails the capability to develop and deliver services that include system maintenance and provision of security and social order; it is the "core of government."

> Administrative capacity embodies many dimensions, functions, values, processes, and issues that require close attention…upgraded and geared for anticipatory, future-weaving, and history - making purposes in governance and administration. (Farazmand, 2009, pp. 1016–1017)

The main attribute of such capacities was "facilitative…dynamic, professionally trained" administrators "armed with the brains and bodies of a 'surprise management' system" (Farazmand, 2009, p. 1017). In his framework, supporting this attribute were multiple dimensions of different capacities including structural capacity; process capacity; cultural or normative capacity; institutional and organizational capacities that were noted earlier; learning leadership and managerial capacities; strategic human resource capacity; financial resource capacity; cognitive capacity; technological capacity; ethical, accountability, and other capacities of democratic representation, responsiveness, and fairness; and developmental capacity (Farazmand, 2009, p. 1017). The exhaustive list leaves no doubt about the complexity of governing in this age.

3.3   Formative and Reflective Operationalizations

Capacity was therefore an important and a popular concept, discussed far and wide in business, public administration, nonprofit, and civil society journals. But capacity could also be seen as a self-referential concept where clear meanings were sometimes lost. For example, if too many types and definitions of capacity exist, can the idea of capacity still be useful to practitioners? If capacity stands for a multitude of concepts, can those concepts overlap one another? Are different capacities complementary or substitutive of each other? Could one concept of capacity be emphasized at the expense of another, or is one capacity concept a prerequisite for another? The variety of capacity definitions and concepts peppering the broader literature suggests to us that capacity is a dynamic concept and capacity building a dynamic process that tracks the fluidity of the challenges confronting an individual, organization, or larger policy system. Capacity is essentially a label for the ingredients of an adaptive response, for calibrated action, to manage an ever-present uncertainty, but which also presents significant operationalization issues.

Helen Addison noted some of these problems in her review of the concept within political science. While she echoed some of the confusion surrounding the capacity concept, she also advised utmost care in dealing with it, else capacity gets trapped in tautological analyses that blur useful findings. She warned against falling for the fallacy of "best practice thinking" by simply declaring that certain structures, systems, mechanisms, or resources were needed to constitute capacity. She noted the risk of such an ideal -type conceptualization of capacity and suggested the need to ground capacity analysis within particular contexts (Addison, 2009). For example, she noted the utility of *formative* and *reflective* modeling in capacity: the former identifies antecedent factors when constructing indices that determine a level of capacity necessary to achieve a goal. The latter measures bureaucratic performance outcomes to infer the existence of a particular level of capacity (Addison, 2009, pp. 11–12).

Based on such classification, previous studies of contract management capacity (Joaquin & Greitens, 2012a) in American municipal governments viewed the concept in both formative and reflective senses with applications to specific managerial decisions. These studies identified contracting decisions as being influenced by a variety of factors ranging from competition, vendors' management capacity, municipal government's form, asset specificity, budget, performance measurement, planning, training, evaluation, financial management capacity, decision-making capacity, and political control of the contract management process (Hefetz & Warner, 2012; Johnston et al., 2004; Romzek & Johnston, 2002; Kelleher & Yackee, 2008; Shick & Weikart, 2009; Brown & Potoski, 2006). Other studies teased out in more detail the components of contract management in terms of four capacities – agenda-setting capacity, formulation capacity, implementation capacity, and evaluation. Adding nuance to this research stream, Yang, Hsieh, and Li adopted a long-term perspective of capacity with a recognition of the institutional and political constraints involved (Brown & Potoski, 2003; Yang et al., 2009).

For this book, based on the two models that Addison presented, we tap both the *reflective* and *formative* senses of qualitatively assessing capacity. We employ the *reflective* sense in Chap. 2 when reflecting on the performance and actions involved in the federal pandemic response and inferring the factors that gave rise to such performance. The idea of eroded capacity baselines is inferred from the vantage points of government careerists and agency watchdogs like the GAO – entities that have a sense of the erosions or shifts in the baseline, from institutional memory. We employ the *formative* sense moving forward. In Chap. 8, we develop the capacity-centered framework for future rebuilding efforts. In essence, we reflect on the bases of decline, and we also reformulate elements of capacity for future reconstitution efforts. This comports, we believe, with Addison's (2009, p. 16) admonition to treat capacity as a unified concept or "a distinctive phenomenon… a collective outcome of the dynamic operation of an administrative system that exerts a common influence on the performance of all parts of the system."

3.4   Agency Capacity from a Watchdog's Perspective

Given the history of research on administrative capacity, we can begin to sketch our capacity-centered framework. We view administrative capacity as consisting of five core dimensions: *problem-solving, management, engagement, administrative conservatorship* (Terry 2003, p. 43), and *accountability*. The first three dimensions embody the work of administration, while the latter three (engagement is included again, if one could imagine overlapping discs) are capacities that pertain to administration *in a democracy*. Capacity consists of the ability not only to perform or adapt but also to uphold administrative leadership and accountability in the process (Durant 2007). It describes an administrative apparatus that is receptive, responsive, and responsible in a political system, in those inward and outward dimensions.

In public administration, capacity is typically viewed from a human capital perspective, with many experts regarding the workforce as the fundamental element of administrative capacity, along with resource management. Such views can be found in GAO's mission to uncover critical or "high-risk" areas plaguing American government programs. Landing on the high-risk list invites greater scrutiny from congressional committees and interest groups, which by itself makes the job harder and makes the program a bone of contention between Congress and the executive branch. Human capital management has been on GAO's radar since 2001. Nonetheless, in some cases, being labeled a high- risk does not always mean reduced appropriations or political infamy for a program; some agencies like the DOD are so powerful and can take advantage of Congress' institutional weakness to get away with chronically poor audit results (Gould, 2019).

Agencies and their programs come and go on the list, gradually. According to the GAO, for an agency to make progress in an identified high-risk program, it must demonstrate response along five criteria, only one of which is called capacity:

(1) Leadership commitment
(2) *Capacity (i.e., people and resources) to resolve the risk(s) (italics ours)*
(3) Action plan
(4) Monitoring
(5) Ability to demonstrate progress in implementing corrective measures and in resolving the high-risk area (GAO, 2019, p. 3)

We view administrative capacity as involving all of those points – they represent the dimensions of capacity. Note that in the GAO criteria, leadership commitment is made separate from the human and other resources. GAO's leadership commitment is the equivalent of the dimension we call *administrative conservatorship*; its capacity is similar to our *management* and *engagement* dimensions; its action planning and monitoring invoke our *problem-solving* dimension; and its criteria on monitoring and demonstrating progress are embedded into our *accountability* dimension.

The GAO's criteria were adopted in 2015, more than a decade since the congressional body launched this special category of agency audit. When the GAO started publishing its High-Risk Series in 1992, capacity did not appear on the text of its first report on farm loan programs. In 1995, capacity showed up for the first time, and only once, when the report spoke of agencies' "capacity to manage for results" in connection with the Government Performance and Results Act of 1993 or GPRA. The preconditions for those were said to be complete and reliable information and an aggressive use of information technology (GAO, 1995, p. 78). By 2021, capacity showed up at least 78 times in GAO's report. Mapping out where the word showed up in the report, they appeared to support our idea of capacity's dimensions, including notions of baselines and capacity declines (GAO, 2021). Capacity in GAO's view includes allocating or reallocating funds or staff; establishing and maintaining procedures or systems; establishing workgroups with specific responsibilities; improving collaboration with other agencies, stakeholders, and the private sector; and providing guidance and training to staff and addressing skills gaps (GAO, 2021, p. 37). All allude to leadership, management, and problem solving actions that are also community engaged and democratically accountable.

3.5 Surge Capacities, Tipping Points, and Breakdowns

The GAO's framework shows that what we call administrative capacity operates along those five core dimensions and interacts with the governmental and instrumental capacities identified by Farazmand in getting people to work with resources, structures, systems, and authorities to fix areas of high risk in a fast-changing context. It is evident that a federal agency's capacity must match the changes in the agency's critical environment, which could overwhelm existing capacities if they are not planned around them. To speak of fluidity and changeable contexts, one may employ additional concepts – surge capacity, tipping points, baselines – that are commonly associated with capacity. They are overlapping but distinct, difficult to establish before the fact in an environment of complexity and uncertainty. Collectively, they test resilience, and convey the importance of having a resilient capacity in government.

From the medical world, *surge capacity* refers to "the ability to care for a large and unexpected volume of patients, as might occur after a mass-casualty event" (Kamarck, 2021, para. 13). Possessing that capacity allows an entity or a system to absorb a rapid escalation in pressure without a lot of disruption to existing functions. COVID-19 has forced organizations everywhere to understand the limits of their capacities, and the rules, interrelationships, and resources necessary to prepare for surges in demand. The most fervent appeals for the public to mask up during COVID-19 (and, later on, to get vaccinated) came from the medical community that knew this concept so well in a line of work where skills and equipment are maximized and lives are risked daily to save the ill, maskers or not, anti-vaxxers or not. To engage the public meaningfully about the waves or surges of infection and hospitalization, scientists worldwide, such as the Institute for Health Metrics and Evaluation (IHME) strived to develop the public's vocabulary about "peak resource use" in hospital ventilators, beds, and ICU beds, among others. Decision-makers as well as citizens were encouraged to grasp the importance of preparing hospitals' resources for the upper range of values in their forecasts (IHME, n.d.). Surges are unexpected demands upon capacity, which means they may taper down as unexpectedly. If surges are not met or absorbed, however, they may lead to a breakdown.

Capacity is also associated with *tipping points* and *breaking points*, and both connote a breaching some sort of a threshold. The capacity baseline is the floor, from which any more reduction or disinvestment in agency capacity produces a breakdown or a failure to provide a current level of service; conversely, any additional demand without addressing existing capacities invites a breakdown. Breakdowns not merely result in a failure to meet regular needs; they can have cascading effects and ruin even the accomplishments made prior to the breach, creating a greater rip in the service fabric.

A breakdown of administrative capacity (of the problem-solving sort) was evident in the foreign interference with the 2016 American presidential election, when all the 50 states' systems were hacked (Parks, 2019). After that, many complained that government attention was not being paid enough to the threat amid political polarization under Trump, and the risks of that breach reoccurring were escalating as the 2020 election approached. If a system is resilient enough, however, a breakdown in capacity may be repaired. For example, capacity proved to be resilient in that the 2020 election was sufficiently secure, despite claims otherwise by the losing candidate (Pelley, 2020).

Tipping points, unlike breakdowns, suggest a more fatal shock, a point of no return, a failure of resilience while waiting for capacity to be rebuilt. A "failed state" conveys that idea of a nation reaching its tipping point. Breakdowns can be mended if there is resilient human capital within the nation, system, or organization. Flirting with either tipping point or breaking point or driving agencies to constantly have to work within enormous resource constraints or political pressure reduces their ability to bounce back even if new infusions of resources are obtained.

As the November 2020 election approached, many historians felt that the nation would not have survived a second Trump term (Frum, 2020). A stalwart of the good government coalition who gave Trump's reorganization plans the benefit of the doubt in 2017 minced no words about the grave situation the president was about to leave behind. Max Stier thought Trump was:

> crashing the car before turning back the keys…Can you simply fix the car? Perhaps, but (1) people will get hurt in the crash, including the public and public servants; (2) you can't use the car while it is getting fixed; and (3) not clear the car will ever drive the same. (Rampell, 2020, para. 17)

With the January 2021 Capitol attack, the country almost hit a breaking point or a tipping point. Americans told a Gallup poll that governmental leaders and national discord had become *their top concern, surpassing the coronavirus*, which at this point had infected 100 million globally and killed almost half a million people in the United States (Budryk, 2021). Regard for national leadership was extremely shaky. Many equated Biden's charge with nothing less than the burden of Abraham Lincoln with the Civil War and Franklin D. Roosevelt's with the Great Depression. Within hours of the Capitol attack, thinned-out, disillusioned careerists thought of leaving their posts, but they were prevailed upon to stay to prevent any more capacity hemorrhage during the transition (Carney, 2021). Administrative conservators at the middle levels held the fort until the Biden administration could come in and fill the depleted agencies with seasoned managers (Katz, 2021). The coronavirus pandemic was still raging, whatever disputes the parties might have about the election. We could say that the capacity of workers in the federal government in 2020 likely reached its breaking point, its baseline capacity deconstructed over the years, but resilient capacity residing among the career employees prevented any more damage from occurring. Some of these notions are evident in the words of Jason Briefel, president of the Senior Executives Association, who noted colorfully that "we can't just keep throwing career folks under the bus for not being able to squeeze this totally screwed up and broken system to produce more results" (J. Briefel, personal communication, July 8, 2020). Congress and presidents sometimes fail to see instances when capacity breakdowns could result from their politics or policies. Those include:

> adopting meek solutions to major problems, rescinding or diluting policies that could have prevented a future breakdown, creating so much ambiguity that implementation cannot proceed, or even delegating action to a high-risk, vulnerable agency. Policies do not have to be perfect to be implemented, and Congress often gives agencies significant authority to smooth the edges of ambiguous statutes. Nevertheless, some policies are simply "unimplementable" under even the best of circumstances. (Light, 2015a, p. 13)

Reforms, depending on their goals and design, can be a type of turbulence that cause breakdowns. The deconstruction of the administrative state is one from recent times that expended capacity and tested agency endurance and limits. When reforms are mandated across the board, the inability of reformers to create meaningful distinctions among the agencies can lead to degradation of capacity in some units. An example from the past is when the Bush administration carried out the 2001 President's Management Agenda (PMA) in competitive sourcing (A-76). With quotas of full-time equivalent positions coming down to them from OMB, many agencies complied with a directive that could potentially privatize a significant number of jobs as a result of bidding competitions with contractors, but some, notably small, non-Cabinet agencies resisted competitive sourcing to avoid ruining their capacity.

   In organization theory, the notion of a starting point is important when considering the abilities of organizations to recover or adapt to a changing or hostile environment. The variance in the A-76 starting points among the federal agencies was exemplified by the compliant posture from the DOD relative to the resistance to the competitive sourcing directive coming from the National Science Foundation (NSF). The former was a huge, contracting savvy Cabinet agency that could absorb the presidential mandate without hampering its baseline capacity, while the latter was a small bureau without a lot of competitive sourcing experience and/or "low-hanging fruits" of functions that could be outsourced without hurting its mission. The two agencies' baselines before the reform were at extreme opposites, as they carried out A-76 competitions with differing resource slack. The smaller agencies found other ways of meeting the spirit of the PMA without damaging their capacity baseline (Joaquin, 2009). Those strategies buffered the agencies during a cutback era – a form of resilience. Such actions would also determine the extent of potential rebuilding that could happen afterward.

3.6   The Imperative of Resilience

To what extent could we anticipate these milestones or gauge these thresholds? Tipping points are hard to formally model for a government agency, which has an aura of immortality, though its fortunes could swing wildly with the politics of reform. The problem with tipping points and resilience is that they often are known only in hindsight, once the crisis has arrived or has passed (GAO, 2012, p. 19). Crises also can reveal how organizations could perform at a higher level than is normally expected. Perhaps due to a hidden slack or an unknown synergy that may be created from existing resources, it is tantamount to exacting greater and greater bang for the buck. This may be rooted in organizational practice during normal times, in terms of technical efficiency in using administrative resources or prioritizing resources across a host of demands – when capacity is recognized as finite but the needs to be met seem to just keep increasing (J. Justice, personal communication, August 23, 2019). From constant adaptation, memories of organizational limits, possibilities, and resilience are built.

The concepts of tipping points and resilience are therefore intimate to one set of stakeholders: the agency's long-serving administrators. In *Leadership of Public Bureaucracies: The Administrator as Conservator*, Larry Terry described the Constitutional underpinning of the administrative leader's role as not merely *serving*, but more importantly *preserving*. Conservators lead in "protecting institutional processes, values, and unifying principles that determine an institution's distinctive competence" (Terry, 2003, p. 43). Echoing John Rohr's writings on justice, Terry wrote that administrators have a moral obligation to preserve and sustain Constitutional principles because they took the oath when they joined the service (Rohr, 1986, p. 181). Exercising with morality the authority delegated them through administrative law, conservators support the legitimacy of the administrative state (Sunstein & Vermeule, 2020). Implicit also in this theory is that career leaders would have an internal gauge of the radical shifts in capacity's demand and supply, with their institutional memory. These actors, in essence, possess "depth" (Skowronek et al., 2021). They guard against the dissipation of power to accomplish their mission (Long, 1949). Given these attributes, conservators are the key element of resilience. With these propositions, we can arrive at some definitions, beginning, almost counter-intuitively, with resilience as the ultimate goal of capacity building.

Resilience may be defined as *the ability of the administrative state or of an individual agency to absorb and navigate extreme disruptions to mission and organization and evolve the agency's political and technical responses to a changed resource and political environment.* Resilience may be demonstrated by particular agencies or the administrative state as a whole, i.e., the population of agencies. Resilience allows an agency to endure despite disruptions, undertake rebuilding actions, and calibrate the agency to new demands or emerging issues. Resilience means preserving some baseline capacity or some "stock" to rehabilitate capacity or rebuild capacity. Resilience makes rebuilding less onerous. Capacity (re)building simply means securing of the necessary supports vital to enhancing the problem-solving, management, conservatorship, engagement, and accountability of the administrative state.

The aim of resilience is to design systems so that they can "fail gracefully and recover nicely" (Friedman, 2020, para. 1). According to Uri Friedman, the pandemic revealed a new form of national power, one that had nothing to do with a military arsenal, population size, or Gross Domestic Product: as resilient power or the "capacity to absorb systemic shocks, adapt to these disruptions, and quickly bounce back from them." A form of soft power, a term coined by political scientist Joseph Nye, resilient power was evident when the United States recovered from the Great Depression to fight World War II. What makes this current era demand "a new dimension of resilience" on the part of governments worldwide is that today's challenges have less historical precedent, yet have greater complexity. In addition, the twentieth century's drive for increased efficiency created an industry and society whose interconnected systems have spawned new vulnerabilities. Scholars at the Paris-based Organisation for Economic Co-operation and Development (OECD) warn that the successful states of tomorrow are those that invest in resilient infrastructure, knowledge, and relationships, including the development of widespread public confidence in government. They also recognize when adaptive skills have become more important than market-inspired priorities. This "imperative of resilience," according to Friedman, is being seen in the approaches to governing of countries like New Zealand, Australia, and Singapore, where decision-makers demonstrated resilience in adversity, developed supportive systems, and recognized the trade-offs that are necessary between systems (e.g., resilience versus efficiency) to promote adaptability (2020).

The deadly coronavirus gauged the resilience of administrative conservators in American government agencies. A workforce survey by the ACT-IAC, MeriTalk, and Partnership for Public Service found some intriguing evidence that explored this resilience in government. One in two respondents associated agency resilience with an agile workforce, one that is adaptable to changing circumstances and public demands. The report noted that such resilience could be rooted in federal employees' commitment to service and mission, with scientific studies showing evidence that a strong sense of purpose improves an individual's resilience in facing adverse situations. Eighty-five percent of the respondents thought their agencies had capacity gaps before the pandemic and that had affected resilience during the crisis. After adapting to the pandemic, 67 percent reported improvement in agency resilience, but only 27 percent graded that capacity as an "A" (Partnership for Public Service, 2021, p. 3).

To get to resilient capacity, we need to nurture conservators and their collaborative networks in the innovation community, establish the connection between democratic and bureaucratic resilience, and redefine bureaucratic engagement. Capacity may be revived if agencies retain enough administrative conservators to "reseed" their agencies during times of organizational stress. Their collective intelligence and network strength could support them as their agencies address their capacity gaps.

In addition, the notion of resilient power and the breakdown of democratic norms seen recently mean that we need more than just administrative capacity building – we need to reconstitute democratic administrative capacity – a *Reconstitution*. With antidemocratic, extremist elements capturing the base of the Republican Party during Trump's presidency (Boot, 2017) and voting rights in great peril in many states that the party controls, the social contract is fraying. No capacity rebuilding effort would last long without everyone's explicit assent to democracy, the rule of law, or the legitimacy of its instruments. Repairs in bureaucratic matters would not amount to much if the underlying democratic compact was tenuous. Stakeholders in good government need to renew the democratic bargain, and voters must develop a greater awareness of how much the battle for political control of bureaucracy injures accountable capacity (Knott & Miller, 1987). Finally, because politicians would listen only to the voters for the most part, administrative conservators need to engage politically and reach the public effectively. They need to compete smartly in the highly technologized market of influence for citizens' attention and educate them about the importance of a shared sense of fate, of realizing the need for an accountable, capacitated government. With these key assumptions from research and practice, grounding them in the efforts to reform the bureaucracy is next in developing our theoretical framework.

3.7 The Political Development Context

In a system as complex as the American government, an analysis like ours that attempts to make sense of recent governmental failures by looking for their seeds in history, and which tries to develop a forward-looking framework for reformers as well, involves more than one plane of understanding. We wish to explore not only what capacity is but also how capacity has evolved in such a way that it has become possible for a president to dismantle it more easily than to build it. We do not wish to risk oversimplifying capacity as a concept and the factors giving rise to capacity deconstruction hampering the pandemic response efforts, as the previous chapter showed. We therefore in this book try to locate its discussion within two conceptual planes: one has to do with what this chapter tackles, the concept of capacity, and how its dimensions could illuminate and be illuminated by the history of capacity development within Alexander Hamilton's ideals of the *energetic executive* (Chap. 5 and Chap. 6). As we have seen, the literature often serves up views of capacity that are organizational, resource-driven, and management-level focused, when it is much more multidimensional than that. In looking at the capacity-inducing measures applied to the administrative state over the past hundred years, we attempt to take the concept's internal and resource-based moorings and plant them within various approaches to build and influence federal administration, from the pre-civil service era to the years before Trump's deconstruction.

The second plane of understanding built within this book's framework is the juxtaposition of capacity being developed within the energetic executive, with the emergence of the *unitary executive* wresting control of capacity from Congress and removing bureaucracy away from clients that are not the president. We elaborate that further in the succeeding chapter. This approach not only takes the long view; it puts the dimensions of capacity within the macro-political context to make sense of the shifts in how bureaucracy was designed and its performance viewed by its sovereigns.

Capacity is conceptually wobbly without anchoring it to a consistent feature of the American political system – the need to submit bureaucracy under control, through direct and immediate political action and through the inculcation of beliefs about what the government can properly do, and the means to do it. Public administration demands the difficult reconciliation of politics and administration (Lane, 1992, p. 116), and any framework of capacity building must reflect this reconciliation. As Gerald Garvey (1995) observed:

> Administrative action in any political system, but especially in a democracy, must somehow realize two objectives simultaneously. It is necessary to construct and maintain administrative capacity, and it is equally necessary to control it in order to ensure the responsiveness of the public bureaucracy to higher authority, most particularly to elected representatives in the legislative branch. (p. 87)

Such control has become much more unbalanced and *presidentialized*, which means examining in this book how the macro strategies of leaders influence the capacity that gets built at the lower or meso-level and micro-level administrative apparatus (Roberts, 2019a; Rosenbloom, 2015). For example, the management innovations underway before the Trump deconstruction era floundered with the politicization and "deep state" distractions of a powerful executive. Presidents could easily build capacity, if desired, but their power could so much more effectively demolish it or, in Trump's case, bifurcate it (see Chap. 7), with consequences that could last longer than it took to build what was destroyed. Thus, our approach is to sketch out capacity in political and historical terms, cognizant that the questions we raise reside not in management theory, but in power and democracy's intersection with administration (see Suleiman, 2005). The political developmental context instead places bureaucracy within the historical battles among the branches of government, political parties, and their allies in society. As a guide, in *Building a New American State*, Stephen Skowronek framed the development of the American state from 1877 to 1920 as administrative capacity building, involving processes of organizing state power, with administrative institutions at the center of partisan dynamics and the relationship of government with citizens. Those power battles shifted with politicians' electoral fortunes and political crises – Congress sometimes prevailed over the president, and presidents since FDR were often victorious in imposing their philosophies. But present always were institutional dynamics and a recognition that the Constitutional system was fashioned to work through and around bureaucracy. Politicians saw reforms that controlled the expanding bureaucracy and its capacity as the door to power. The seeds of obdurate incapacity seen today may be found in the institutional politics of early state building when politicians ably imposed control over the bureaucracy but without defining political responsibility, creating, instead, "an ill-geared system" containing a vast, rational-looking machinery (Skowronek, 1982, p. 211). Over time, this system that looked rational but was actually ill-geared for capacity would promote not only the decline of capacity but also the rise of the unitary executive.

Such nuanced views of the historical cleavages and complex forces of reconstitutions in political development give us a richer canvass on which to paint capacity and are embedded in our framework. Capturing these ideas entails a definition of capacity that has an adaptive character for the purposes of future reform efforts, yet still be malleable within the politics of reforms and institutional animosities, and dynamic enough to accommodate the trade-offs that frequently occur in politics. We present that definition in the following section.

3.8   Definition and Framework of Administrative Capacity

To the interdisciplinary literature on capacity, we add the following definitions and framework that integrate the instrumental and institutional aspects and political as well as organizational influences on the changing capacity of the administrative state:

> Administrative capacity refers to the capacity of the administrative state to marshal the authority, expertise, resources, and relationships needed to respond and adapt in an accountable way to the changing problems of the nation.

> Depending on leaders' political strategies of governing, it is the capacity of the bureaucracy to engage with citizens and organized sectors in defining national needs and priorities and in crafting and managing solutions that uphold democratic and public service values.

> To reform or control administrative capacity is to address it in its five core dimensions: problem solving, management, administrative conservatorship, engagement, and accountability. Imbalance in reforming and controlling administrative capacity results in declining capacity. Creating resilient capacity must be the ultimate goal of capacity building.

We prefer *capacity* over *ability* or *capability* due to the former's broader, formal, and informal multidimensional attributes found by previous reviewers of the literature. We may mention ability in a secondary way in parts of the book, that is, administrative capacity may consist of a collection of abilities or capacities. The definition integrates the common elements of people, processes, institutions, and resources that the literature say are basic to capacity, as well as *realpolitik*. The definition puts context and political awareness by paying attention to who gets to frame the uncertainties or issues to which a capacitated bureaucracy must respond and who controls the tools of response.

The definition conveys the need for nimbleness in an environment of risk, mega-changes, and uncertainty. Because the pendulum of reform may swing from one ideological spectrum to another or from the executive to Congress, different aspects or dimensions of capacity could be changing over time. Balancing is necessary within the politics of reform. Reformers may seek to address only some dimensions of capacity, depending on their span of attention, lessons learned from previous reforms, the political tools at their disposal, and the type of problems that they choose to frame and address. Trying to achieve too many goals in government, such as efficiency and equity, sometimes backfires when policymakers are unable to design their programs or actions well (Salamon, 2002; Wilson, 1989). Initiatives promoting engagement and accountability overlap in many respects, as do problem-solving and management. Administrative conservatorship relies on bureaucracy's engagement, while it supports the capacities for problem-solving, management, and accountability. A reform of one dimension may impact another dimension, whether or not intended by the reformers. For example, cutting administrative capacity in the vast, blended context of the federal government is difficult to do without having multiplier effects. Contract management is one of those areas where, if you squeeze one part of the balloon in the hopes of shrinking the cost through outsourcing, it only moves the costs to another part of the balloon or increases the burden elsewhere. That such considerations were normally ignored was shown during one House Budget Committee deliberation in 2014, when Rep. Chris Van Hollen, a friend to workers' unions, expressed concern about a 10 % cut to the federal work-force as part of reforms to reduce the national deficit. He noted that proposals often did not consider trade-offs between all aspects of government operations, such as cutting federal employee vis-à-vis the contracting workforce. When he asked the CBO to prepare a report describing such trade-offs, CBO could not produce one due to the difficulty of obtaining the information (AFGE, 2014; Light, 2020c).

It is also possible that one dimension's rise engenders a decline in other capacities or that one dimension's decline is compensated for by slack in another dimension. For instance, when we marvel at agencies "doing more with less," it is possible that we assume low capacity in staffing, but there might be strength in some other dimensions that could temporarily compensate for the eroded dimension. Agencies such as FEMA had, in different eras, demonstrated such up-and-down dynamics, when it was able to perform well despite known impairments in some of its capacities. Uncertainty, of course, accompanies any reform. (In)efficiencies can be also generated in unanticipated ways, and initial moves can set off chain reactions (both positive and negative) well beyond the terms and sights of reformers; hence, the ideas of bounded rationality and first-mover advantages (Pierson, 2004) are recurrent themes in the political development literature.

The continuum under the core dimensions signifies how capacity as a whole could "move" –decline or be rebuilt – depending on political development (see Fig. 3.1). Decline may be imagined of the discs shifting in one direction, while resilience and the work of capacity rebuilding are the shift in the opposite direction. The next chapter continues the elaboration of this framework and situates the concept of capacity within those reform movements and its decline and decay arising

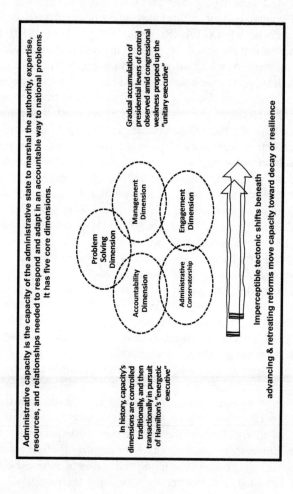

Administrative capacity is the capacity of the administrative state to marshal the authority, expertise, resources, and relationships needed to respond and adapt in an accountable way to national problems. It has five core dimensions.

Gradual accumulation of presidential levers of control observed amid congressional weakness propped up the "unitary executive"

Problem Solving Dimension

Management Dimension

Engagement Dimension

Accountability Dimension

Administrative Conservatorship

In history, capacity's dimensions are controlled traditionally, and then transactionally in pursuit of Hamilton's "energetic executive"

Imperceptible tectonic shifts beneath advancing & retreating reforms move capacity toward decay or resilience

Fig. 3.1 Core dimensions and coevolution of capacity with presidential control

out of a tectonic shift after the New Deal: *the ground had shifted* in favor of executive control over a balanced capacity, so that it is now even harder to arrest declines or to reconstitute capacity.

3.9   The Core Dimensions of Capacity

Based on the foregoing review, the five core dimensions of administrative capacity are built off the literature's notions of anticipatory, resource-absorbing, and link-forging capacities necessary in addressing public concerns and the idea that capacity must be held up against the promises made within the political system. A connective thread runs through all dimensions: capacity in promoting the public welfare in a democracy is first and foremost a problem-solving matter, abetted by managerial, engagement, and mission-protecting capacities, and, ultimately, is an ability marked by accountability.

3.9.1   Problem-Solving

This dimension of capacity refers to the ability of the agencies to connect the dots, make competent inferences and assessments, and induce consensus within the political system in framing national problems and crafting agile solutions. It includes sense-making and the intelligence activity and analytical capacity involved in risk assessments and vulnerability assessments (Lodge & Wegrich, 2014). It is akin to what Marc Eisner identified as the capacity to engage in search processes when established policies fail. With problem-solving, we need to realize that learning (from mistakes or not) is not guaranteed and therefore building the capacity to learn (e.g., using data analytics) is intricately bound to this dimension. This capacity necessitates evidence-based decision-making; preserving institutional data; surveilling loopholes in systems, rules, and procedures; scanning the present environment; and imagining the future to prepare an adaptive solution. What are ways of thinking about problem-solving capacity? It is said that with the coronavirus pandemic, America readied itself for the wrong kind of war: "It prepared for a new 9/11, but instead a virus came" (Bennhold, 2020, para. 4). When it came, both the dimensions of problem-solving and management suffered from a lack of surge capacity. Elaine Kamarck explains how the practice from the armed forces could have alleviated some of the problems of the hospital systems during the pandemic:

> What the reserves, the National Guard, and the Individual Ready Reserve provide the military is surge capacity. Night after night during the pandemic, Americans watched exhausted nurses and doctors try to cope with the influx of patients. What our health-care system lacked was something like an organized reserve corps. (Kamarck, 2021, para. 19)

Problem-solving capacity may be impacted by new rules that curtail enforcement of agency missions or contradict or swamp the old ones, as when the Trump administration reformulated agency mission statements, in a symbolic first action of executive power (Clark, 2018; Emba, 2018). Problem-solving capacity is harmed by appointing agency leaders that fundamentally oppose the missions of their agencies or undermine evidence-based decision-making processes. Loss occurs especially with the rapid turnover of people with institutional memory and excessive contracting that leaves mission accomplishment outside of agency control (I. Rubin, personal communication, April 5, 2019).

Capacity, according to John Kamensky, a veteran of government reform, may revolve around the question of how to reduce the failure rate in government (J. Kamensky, personal communication, March 10, 2019). As the previous chapter showed, there were failures of infectious disease surveillance abroad and missed opportunities to flatten the curve at home. Before 2020, instances of government "breakdowns" identified by Paul Light and the Volcker Institute, like the failure to anticipate the rise of the Islamic State in Iraq and Syria (Light, 2015b), may have occurred due to a decline in this dimension. Under Trump, even more instances were tallied by Light (2020d):

> the number of breakdowns, as determined by surveys of public interest in major stories and investigations of federal government performance, is well above average compared to his predecessors. Ronald Reagan, George H. W. Bush, and Bill Clinton together averaged just 1.5 breakdowns per year, and George W. Bush and Barack Obama averaged 3.3. Trump has averaged 5.25 annually to date. He also just set a single-year record with nine breakdowns in 2020—with three months left to go. (para. 4)

Increasingly, technological intelligence is central to the problem-solving capacity of the virtual state (Fountain, 2001). It is also at the center of national vulnerability. The US government has been failing to arrest its cyber-weaknesses, unable to prevent the hacking of OPM twice in 2015, state election infrastructure in 2016, and the Internal Revenue Service (IRS) in 2016. Even more gravely, the government fell victim in 2020 to sophisticated attacks conducted against the Office of the President and key agencies likes the DOD, DHS, Treasury, Commerce, National Security Agency (NSA), and the country's nuclear labs during the SolarWinds hack that also penetrated the company's 33,000 business customers. The State Department identified Russia as behind the massive theft of information, yet Trump – sowing confusion without actually providing evidence to back his claim – deflected the blame toward the media and China once more (Bing, 2020; Bing & Lunday, 2020). Right in the middle of such crisis, he fired the head of the government's Cybersecurity and Infrastructure Security Agency (CISA) not for the breach, but for rejecting Trump's claim of massive voter fraud in the election he lost to Joe Biden (Pelley, 2020).

But nothing speaks of a decaying problem-solving capacity more than a failure to acknowledge that a crisis exists. Deflection, confusion, and insinuating politics over "dull, technocratic honesty" (Friedman, 2020) in the nation's battle with the coronavirus could only lead to tragic consequences.

3.9.2 Management

This dimension embodies *administrative* capacity in public administration, business, and organization literatures, with human capital management at the center. This dimension encompasses the human, financial, technical, and material systems – or what may be called mission support capabilities (Chenok & Kamensky, 2021, p. 6) involved in organizing a government unit and its performance of core tasks. It is the quest for the "philosopher's stone" of coordination (Seidman, 1970) across the executive branch, the separate branches of government, the different levels of government, and their partners in the private sector. Management depends upon congressional direction, delegation, and appropriation, submits to the direction of the executive through OMB, and yields to public and judicial opinions. Agencies manage with an eye to what James Wilson called contextual goals to ensure procedural fairness and transparency (Wilson, 1989, pp. 130–131; Rosenbloom, 2015).

Because of privatization, this dimension intersects *delivery* capacity in the policy literature (Hupe & Hill, 2014). Management becomes network management – needing the skills that Salamon (2002) called enablement, activation, and orchestration of the different relationships in policy and program management. To these skills, Kettl (2015) adds network bargaining, financial oversight, smart contracting, technological operation, and adeptness at administrative law.

The obstacles to adequate management capacity are plenty. Human capital is said to be the most important resource of government, yet the aging federal workforce is ill-equipped to adapt to the changing nature of work, the deficit in workforce skills and agility becoming more pronounced each year. Management capacity is harmed by a mindset dominated by compliance, bean-counting, and an output mentality in the agencies. Workers' unions aren't spared their share of the blame for the lack of management innovation. The absence of widespread agreement as to what constitutes performance (measuring it, interpreting it, utilizing it), a running saga since the Clinton years, also slows down efforts to make agencies rely more on data and evidence in program analysis and decision-making (Clark, 2017; House of Representatives, 2019; Congress, 2019).

In the National Academy of Public Administration's (NAPA, n.d., p. 2) view, fragmentation is one of the grand management challenges in public administration today, as seen in the "conflicting rules, competing objectives, organizational stovepipes, and overlapping programs" that arise from the complex structures and relationships in governance. A lot of these weaknesses have to do with the agencies' political environment and principals having an imbalanced view of capacity. Like the problem-solving dimension, management capacity is affected by the politicization of agency mission. A mismatch between the mission and resources likewise damages capacity. Management capacity is vulnerable to staff cutbacks, such as a reduction in legal offices or other enforcement offices. Budget threats that result in breaking up grants into small, earmarked programs in an agency's efforts to court congressional support do not accomplish much by way of mission (I. Rubin, personal communication, April 5, 2019). Congress' weak support for program evaluation in agencies due to politics and budget scorekeeping rules also reduces agency capacity. Finally, decisions that lead to excessive reliance on contractors for expertise can dry out management capacity (Joaquin & Greitens 2012a).

3.9.3   Administrative Conservatorship or Leadership

One of the commonest ingredients found in studies of capacity are people. In our framework, they are more than "staff" or human resources. Resilient capacity requires character that connects the agency to its members. Administrative conservatorship is the dimension of capacity that has to do with the leaders, the agencies' executives, careerists, or what Larry Terry (2003) called the "administrative conservators." Terry's concept involves the capacity of these leaders to maintain the agency's distinctive competence and autonomy, fend off organizational rivals, proactively attract and absorb resources, exercise leadership in administration, and imbue agencies with resilience (Terry, 2003; Honadle, 1981; Peters, 2015; Fukuyama, 2013; Wilson, 1989). Along these lines, Charles Goodsell (2010) described administrators' effort to buttress against defunding and institutional weakening as a product of public agencies' "mission mystique."

Implicit in conservatorship is the idea that long-serving agency leaders would have an internal gauge of the changes to the capacity baseline of their agencies; they keep a sufficient level of capacity, or slack, which cushions the impact of radical reforms on organizational capacity. Descendants of the New Deal, their brethren were known for "building reputations for their agencies, erecting coalitions…and securing policies that they favor despite the opposition of the most powerful politicians" (Carpenter, 2001, pp. 3–4). The conservators' resilience is tested when they bear the brunt of the pathologies of the three political branches (Grisinger, 2016, pp. 362–363).

Because of the built-in tensions in the governmental system, conservatorship is fraught in bureaucratic politics each time a reform is launched by a new administration intent on pushing new priorities (Golden, 1992). During transitions, politics shows in the trust (or mistrust) that develops between careerists and political appointees within the agencies. Some agencies are more conducive than others in developing that bond. Some departments are used to being the political football between the parties, never pleasing either, and perennially neglected in capacity, while some are good at promoting their mission during the good times, hunkering down in bad times, and crafting game-like strategies to cope with any perceived threat to agency mission. They evoke admiration or contempt from citizens, depending on their bureaucratic sympathies. Close watchers of administrative reform are familiar with the "exit, voice, and loyalty" of the 1980s, the "guerrilla administrators" of the Edward Snowden era, the "autonomy-forging" agencies of the 1920s, and the wiggle room creating A-76 organizations of the George W. Bush presidency (Wood, 2010, pp. 153–178, 198; Joaquin, 2009; Joaquin & Greitens, 2009; O'Leary, 2006;

Hirschman, 1970). When confronted with reforms that would compromise their agency's capacity, some manage to comply with minimal threat to integrity, or play off one principal against another to create some breathing room, while delaying compliance and expanding alliances.

A good example of administrative conservatorship was seen recently when the DOD and other government security experts resisted political pressures to be drawn into the politics of the November 2020 elections. The Pentagon leadership as well as the Joint Chiefs stood their ground by refusing to behave like the DOJ or DHS. The latter were widely viewed as catering to the president's reelection agenda by turning the streets into battle zones with civilian protesters or by hounding the states to find support for discredited election claims (Applebaum, 2020; Pelley, 2020). The military chiefs did not like their sense of integrity besieged.

In theory, all of those strategies are available to bureaucrats; administrative conservatorship is the capacity for controlled or *selective adaptation* as a means of responsiveness to political principals – it does not yield to every political whim and chooses strategy carefully:

> All environmental pressures are not created equal when measured against their effect on institutional integrity. The determination of which pressure to seriously consider and when to do so is a complex process that should be guided by a fidelity to the institution's distinctive competence, values, and roles. (Terry, 2003, p. 55)

Career executives and managers also look at the long-term health and evolution of the agency or its programs (J. Kamensky, personal communication, March 10, 2019). Hence, they are crucial in identifying and fixing systemic vulnerabilities. GAO's report on high-risk practices and programs noted that leadership commitment is the most important ingredient in getting agencies to address the riskiest elements of policy and program administration (2021). Because these career executives possess an innate sense of the mission and capacity baseline, it is necessary to find ways of preserving such institutional capacity in the middle of the retirement wave (NAPA n.d.). Recent efforts to delegitimize bureaucrats and de-professionalize agencies harm conservatorship. Delayering and thinning may create short-term savings, but it weakens long-term capacity (Rosenbloom & McCurdy, 2007, p. 11) and the resilience needed to rebuild capacity.

Although Terry's idea of conservators connotes careerists instead of political appointees who might harbor short-term identification with their agencies, political appointees from the career ranks are also conservators. And while Terry identified conservators as the executive cadre, such leaders may be found at middle level, too. Middle management retains a special quality that Leonard White described half a century ago in his public administration compendium:

> Here it is that the substantive action of governments on behalf of citizens comes to fruition; here it is that citizens deal with government when they pass beyond their first contacts; here it is that the spirit and temper of the public service and its reputation are largely made. Middle management is in itself a career. It is also a training ground from which a considerable part of top management emerges. It deserves more attention that it has yet had. (White, 1954, p. 90)

Hollowing out may have thinned the middle ranks of civil servants in some agencies as an unintentional consequence of the Clinton/Gore reinvention (J. Kamensky, personal communication, March 10, 2019). Today, administrative leaders can build their alliances and resilience by tapping in-house innovation ideas and by collaborating with good government communities or public service networks. Laboratories of leadership resilience may include the Volcker Alliance *Government-To-University Initiative* and the Trump administration's attempt at creating government's own think tank, the Government Effectiveness Advanced Research (GEAR) Center. G2U, the brainchild of OMB's Deputy Assistant Director for Management Dustin Brown, aimed to bring government and university leaders together in strengthening government's capacity, while the GEAR Center, an OMB-GSA initiative, aimed to tackle government's complex management challenges by seeking and rewarding interdisciplinary ideas from the public and private sectors for modernizing government.

3.9.4   Engagement and Communication

In this dimension lies the vertical and horizontal relationships necessary for the agencies to advocate, get their message across, and build effective and lasting relationships with citizens and other actors (O'Leary, 2015, p. 93). This dimension refers to the bureaucracy's communicative, educative, and boundary-spanning relationships.

Engagement gets to the consensus-inducing capacity found in the institutional literature. It involves advocacy work by bureaucrats: the "power to persuade," if not to control (Cole & Brannon, 2017, p. 4) the opinion of stakeholders in carrying out the mission. One challenge of communication and advocacy, according to former USDA-ERS Administrator Katherine Smith Evans, is that it is hard for the agencies to make the general public aware of real bureaucratic-political dynamics. In the past, when employees were not doing advocacy directly, they used to have veteran administrators that did that work for them, but that did not always amount to much, and citizens could not always join the dialogue. "A lot of it is arcane, the significance is difficult to explain, unless you're a stakeholder to begin with," Smith noted (K. Evans Smith, personal communication, April 23, 2019). She also argued that is not enough that agencies perceive their own work to be good or produce outputs in metrics intelligible only to themselves. They must be perceived in quality and quantity that make sense *to the public*, if they must be engaged.

This dimension also recognizes the crucial task of communicating "what is and what may be," in generating or producing information, and in eliciting desired policy outcomes (Weiss, 2002, pp. 218–252). There are significant barriers in this dimension. How agencies share information influences the kind of stakeholder engagement that takes place (Piotrowski & Liao, 2012). Reforms to improve the bureaucracy-citizen nexus also are not a strong suit of reformers. In the past, the low enthusiasm among administrators to engage citizens was blamed on the citizens, themselves: their lack of deliberation expertise, overemotionality about the issues, unfamiliarity with bureaucratic routines, and, like bureaucracy itself, difficulty in controlling. Their decision-making input was also perceived to be tough to incorporate. "In an ideal bureaucracy," wrote Kweit and Kweit, "there is no place for citizen participation" (1984, p. 235; Callahan, 2000). But at this point in the evolution of the administrative state, agencies must effectively and equitably engage their customers, partners, and citizens, as the NPM parlance goes (Thomas, 2012).

Engagement capacity is integral to effective problem-solving and management. With governments frequently limited by resource constraints, agencies must engage various types of co-producers, including citizens, to secure capacity for joint action. As budgeting scholar Jonathan Justice expressed to us, budget and staff are just one piece of capacity:

> You've got the transformation process that takes financial inputs and converts them into activities and then outputs and outcomes. And there are so many linkages there that also are going to determine what your capacity is... (including) synergistic or coordinated resources in a network of stakeholders. In terms of co-production, especially if it's a social service, you need the focal populations to be active participants, and that's going to multiply your capacity, both potential and realized...The budget is an important determinant of capacity, but it's also only one of a really large number, and so in terms of determining capacity, it's not necessarily the most important. (Personal communication, August 23, 2019)

The need for effective capacity to engage and communicate is driven to the fore by the pandemic of misinformation that has stress-tested the system. In 2016, on Trump's way to the White House, false stories generated more engagement than factually reliable news (Silverman, 2020). When "alternative facts" became a famous line of thinking (Gajanan, 2017), the public's mechanisms for obtaining authoritative, timely, and useful information from government were impaired. By 2020, the disinformation was amplified by the politicization of the top layers of the federal bureaucracy. Trump added more layers at the top of government than any president in recent history, from 71 in 2017 to 83 in 2020, while boosting the number of people over people by 50%, from 3,200 to 4,900. As a result, the bloat escalated the "distortion of information, as it moves up and down a muddled chain of command" (Light, 2020d, para. 6). While the agencies lost their voice and even became foil for presidential aggrandizement, the tools of social media amplified the president's capacity, not the agencies', to grab the stage, control the debate, and alter political deliberation in a profound way. The 45th president exercised unsurpassed communication control. In "Presidential Administration," Justice Elena Kagan noted how the modern press' insatiable demands exert a lot of pressure on the presidency, reflecting and reinforcing the public's focus on him or her (Kagan, 2001, p. 2310). During the Trump presidency, administrative conservators found it hard to explain or defend their programs to policymakers and citizens. Offices that used to facilitate agency advocacy were whittled down or filled with political appointees who were not cozy with the agencies' mission (Lartey, 2017).

Engagement capacity is of utmost importance in an Internet democracy that pushes everything to the extreme (*The Economist,* 2021). In this hyper-technologized and transactional era, administrators must recognize that citizens may want more from their governments than efficient management: "They may want a sense of attachment to it" (Stivers, 2008, p. 111) – to foster ownership of their own bureaucracy and by renewing the pact between administrators and citizens through a process of "mutual promising" (Stivers, 2008). Technology-amplified falsehoods, however, test the limits of thinking and judging in political life. In *Governance in Dark Times: Practical Philosophy for Public Service*, Camilla Stivers described the complexity of the challenge in the post-truth era:

> Separating truth from lying is not a simple technical operation. Facts in political life are based on eyewitness testimony, data, or other evidence. They are not true by necessity, in the way of an equation; rather, they are contingent. They depend on how strong the evidence is, and what it means. (2008, p. 57)

Administrators need to hone their political engagement skills to battle misinformation among citizens that are inundated with data and have a short attention span (B. Valdez, personal communication, March 11, 2019). Especially in a crisis, ways must be found to ensure the public is clearly aware of the government's goals, including the constraints the agencies face (Wilson, 1989). As of this writing, engaging the public to participate in the national vaccine effort and surmount the mistrust and misinformation around COVID-19 is hounding the Biden administration. Efforts to loop in all the living former presidents (Samuels, 2021) in the vaccine campaign may be useful, but it also demonstrates the presidentialization of capacity that neglects the foundational work that must be done within the agencies or with bureaucracy's own administrative capacity.

3.9.5   Accountability

Francis Fukuyama observed that all governments need to have a strong executive branch to serve and protect their people, but what distinguishes authoritarian states from liberal democracies is the rule of law and democratic accountability (2020). Particularly in times of crisis, the executive is delegated a lot of power to act swiftly, as seen not just at the federal level but also in the state capitols across America during the pandemic (Selin, 2020). The energetic executive must be made to demonstrate accountability and return its emergency powers once the need has passed (Fukuyama, 2020).

A dynamic picture of administrative accountability may be borrowed from Appleby's essay, "Toward Better Public Administration," in which he spoke of "the process of adjusting administration to popular criticism, attitudes, and needs, a process that goes on, and should go on, every minute of every day at every level, within the limits of law and fair dealing" (1947, p. 94). Rounding out the dimensions, this capacity speaks to the ability of the administrative state to yield to democratic oversight. Harking back to the early days of the Republic, accountability reflects government's due dependence on the people (Hamilton et al., 2008) to prevent governmental excesses, as when leaders yielded to the municipal reform movement's demands for transparency in financial affairs (Rubin, 2006).

Accountability connects politics and administration when it elicits spirited public participation. Accountability is not simply that of a government to its public; in the most fundamental sense, it is the people that have to make a government accountable (Berner & Smith, 2004; Ebdon & Franklin, 2004; Simonsen & Robbins, 2000; Joaquin & Greitens, 2012b). Yet to trust the government, people must first *believe* that their government has expert and impartial capacity (Fukuyama, 2020). Absent that, they retreat. That is a sticky dilemma because trust and accountability require repeat interactions. A trust-based governance is contingent on the ability of partners to "read" each other and learn about counterpart behavior (Carson et al., 2003, p. 45). Repetitive engagement facilitates this reading process, a positive reflexivity often seen in political development literature. When the dimensions of engagement and accountability are effectively linked, we get public spiritedness, *a process of infusing governmental processes and programs with a sense of a shared fate between the citizens and the administrative state.* It rebels against definitions of government from a transactional perspective and argues that we are all in one boat, or in the same storm, and mutually accountable.

The capacity for accountability is harmed when there is an imbalance in control over the bureaucracy, as well as leaky accountabilities with third-party government. This dimension also is where we require agency capacity to oversee the shadow bureaucracy. As Durant (2007, p. 186) asked, "Who is responsible…when government programs fail if government agencies lack the capacity to oversee their agents?"

Citizen disaffection also goes up when politicians try to look accountable by refusing to govern, instead externalizing capacity and passing the onus to the "unaccountable, unelected" bureaucrats for the system's failures in problem-solving. Technology amplifies this "permanent campaign" at the expense of capacity. The mix of image making and strategic calculation that "remakes government into an instrument designed to sustain an elected official's popularity" (Heclo, 2000, p. 2) crowds out the more deliberative mechanisms that connect administrators and citizens, squeezing the space for a grounded puzzling over societal demands and the means to meet them.

In sum, administrative capacity is the capacity of the agencies to perform services effectively and professionally, maintain the integrity of their mission and organization, and engage the different sectors in defining the issues and crafting strategic solutions in the public interest. Beyond internal and resource concerns, capacity connects mission to expertise and integrity with an eye to the linkages among the civic, political, and bureaucratic dimensions. In the next chapter, we continue our framework development by explaining how capacity's decline and decay coevolved with executive dominance.

References

Addison, H. J. (2009). Is administrative capacity a useful concept? Review of the application, meaning and observation of administrative capacity in political science literature. London School of Economics Department of Government. *Research Papers* https://personal.lse.ac.uk/addisonh/papers/ac_concept.pdf. Accessed 16 Sept 2020.

American Federation for Government Employees (AFGE). (2014, December 11). House budget committee ranking member shines spotlight on expensive contracted workforce. Washington, DC. [Press Release] https://www.afge.org/article/house-budget-committee-ranking-member-shines-spotlight-on-expensive-contracted-workforce. Accessed 20 Oct 2020.

Applebaum, A. (2020, July 23). Trump is putting on a show in Portland. *The Atlantic.* https://www.theatlantic.com/ideas/archive/2020/07/trump-putting-show-portland/614521/. Accessed 1 Aug 2020.

Appleby, P. (1947). Toward better public administration. *Public Administration Review, 7*(2), 93–99.

Bennhold, K. (2020, April 23). 'Sadness' and disbelief from a world missing American leadership. *The New York Times.* https://www.nytimes.com/2020/04/23/world/europe/coronavirus-american-exceptionalism.html. Accessed 19 June 2020.

Berner, M., & Smith, S. (2004). The state of the states: A review of state requirements for citizen participation in the local government budget process. State and Local Government Review, 36(2), 140–150.

Bing, C. (2020, December 13). Suspected Russian hackers spied on U.S. Treasury emails – sources. *Reuters.* https://www.reuters.com/article/us-usa-cyber-treasury-exclsuive/suspected-russian-hackers-spied-on-u-s-treasury-emails-sources-idUKKBN28N0PG?edition-redirect=uk. Accessed 14 Dec 2020.

Bing, C., & Lunday, J. (2020, December 19). Trump downplays impact of massive hacking, questions Russia involvement. *Reuters* https://www.reuters.com/article/cyber-breach/trump-downplays-impact-of-massive-hacking-questions-russia-involvement-idUSKBN28T0R1. Accessed 12 Jan 2021.

Boot, M. (2017, March 14). The GOP is America's party of white nationalism. *Foreign Policy* https://foreignpolicy.com/2017/03/14/the-gop-is-americas-party-of-white-nationalism/. Accessed 11 July 2019.

Brown, T. L., & Potoski, M. (2003). Contract management capacity in municipal and county governments. *Public Administration Review, 63*(2), 153–156.

Brown, T. L., & Potoski, M. (2006). Contracting for management: Assessing management capacity under alternative service delivery arrangements. *Journal of Policy Analysis and Management, 25*(2), 323–346.

Budryk, Z. (2021, January 25). Concern about government tops coronavirus for first time since July: Gallup. *The Hill.* https://thehill.com/homenews/administration/535631-concern-about-government-tops-coronavirus-for-first-time-since. Accessed 25 Jan 2021.

Callahan, K. (2000). Citizen participation run amok. *Public Productivity and Management Review, 23*(3), 394–398.

Carney, J. (2021, January 7). GOP senators urging Trump officials to not resign after Capitol chaos. *The Hill.* https://thehill.com/homenews/senate/533187-gop-senators-urging-trump-officials-to-not-resign-after-capitol-chaos. Accessed 11 Jan 2021.

Carpenter, D. P. (2001). *The forging of bureaucratic autonomy: Reputations, networks, and policy innovation in executive agencies, 1862–1928.* Princeton University Press.

Carson, S. J., Madhok, A., Varman, R., & George, J. (2003, January-February). Information processing moderators of the effectiveness of trust-based governance in interfirm R&D collaboration.

Chenok, D. & Kamensky, J. (2021). Government reform: Lessons from the past for actions in the future. *Special Report.* IBM Center for the Business of Government. http://www.businessofgovernment.org/sites/default/files/Government%20Reform-Lessons%20from%20the%20Past%20for%20Actions%20in%20the%20Future.pdf. Accessed 17 Mar 2021.

Christensen, R. K., & Gazley, B. (2008). Capacity for public administration: Analysis of meaning and measurement. *Public Administration and Development, 28*, 265–279.

Christensen, T., Laegreid, P., & Rykkja, L. H. (2016). Organizing for crisis management: Building governance capacity and legitimacy. *Public Administration Review, 76*(6), 887–897.

Clark, C. S. (2017, November 16). House Passes bipartisan evidence-based policymaking bill. *Government Executive.* https://www.govexec.com/oversight/2017/11/house-passes-bipartisan-evidence-based-policymaking-bill/142590/. Accessed 4 Nov 2019.

Clark, C. S. (2018, April 27). Groups monitoring agency website changes see deeper Trump agenda. *Government Executive.* https://www.govexec.com/technology/2018/04/groups-monitoring-agency-website-changes-see-deeper-trump-agenda/147806/. Accessed 14 Apr 2020.

Cole, J. P., & Brannon, V. C. (2017). Chevron deference: A primer. US Congressional Research Service.

Dror, Y. (2001). *The capacity to govern: A report to the club of Rome.* Frank Cass.

Durant, R. F. (2007). Institutional values and the future administrative state. In D. Rosenbloom & H. E. McCurdy (Eds.), *Revisiting Waldo's administrative state: Constancy and change in public administration.*

Ebdon, C., & Franklin, A. (2004). Searching for a role for citizens in the budget process. *Public Budgeting and Finance, 24*(1), 32–49.

Emba, C. (2018, March 15). Opinion: The rewritten mission statements of Trump's federal agencies, annotated. *The Washington Post.* https://www.washingtonpost.com/blogs/post-partisan/wp/2018/03/16/trumps-edits-to-democracy-annotated/. Accessed 21 Mar 2020.

Farazmand, A. (2009). Building administrative capacity for the age of rapid globalization: A modest prescription for survival in the 21st century. *Public Administration Review, 69*(6), 1007–1020.

Fountain, J. E. (2001, August 1). Building the virtual state: Information technology and institutional change. *The Brookings Institution.* https://www.brookings.edu/book/building-the-virtual-state/. Accessed 12 Sept 2020.

Friedman, U. (2020, November 15). The pandemic is revealing a new form of national power. *The Atlantic.* https://www.theatlantic.com/ideas/archive/2020/11/pandemic-revealing-new-form-national-power/616944/. Accessed 21 Nov 2020.

Frum, D. (2020, November). Last exit from autocracy. *The Atlantic.* https://www.theatlantic.com/magazine/archive/2020/11/last-exit-trump-autocracy/616466/. Accessed 1 Dec 2020.

Fukuyama, F. (2013). What is governance? *Governance, 26*(3), 347–368. https://doi.org/10.1111/gove.12035

Fukuyama, F. (2020, March 30). The thing that determines a country's resistance to the Coronavirus. *The Atlantic.* https://www.theatlantic.com/ideas/archive/2020/03/thing-determines-how-well-countries-respond-coronavirus/609025/. Accessed 14 Apr 2020.

Gajanan, M. (2017, January 17). Kellyanne Conway defends White House's falsehoods as 'alternative facts'. *Time.*

Garvey, G. (1995). False promises: The NPR in historical perspective. In D. F. Kettl & J. J. Dilulio (Eds.), *Inside the reinvention machine: Appraising governmental reform* (pp. 87–106). Brookings.

Golden, M. M. (1992, January). Exit, voice, loyalty, and neglect: Bureaucratic responses to presidential control during the Reagan administration. *Journal of Public Administration Research and Theory, 2*(1), 29–62.

Goodsell, C. T. (2010). Mission mystique: Belief systems in public agencies. Washington, DC: CQ Press.

Gould, J. (2019, November 20). Pentagon audit's secret to success is failure. *Defense News.* https://www.defensenews.com/congress/2019/11/20/pentagon-audits-secret-to-success-is-failure/. Accessed 11 Dec 2020.

Grisinger, J. L. (2016). The long administrative century. In I. S. Skowronek, S. M. Engel, & B. Ackerman (Eds.), *The progressives' century: Political reform, constitutional government, and the modern American state* (pp. 360–381). Yale University Press.

Hamilton, A., Jay, J., & Madison, J. [1788] (2008). The Federalist papers. New York: Oxford University Press.

Heclo, H. (2000). Campaigning and governing: A consensus. In N. J. Ornstein & T. Mann (Eds.), *The permanent campaign and its future* (pp. 1–37). American Enterprise Institute and The Brookings Institution.

Hefetz, A., & Warner, M. E. (2012). Contracting or public delivery? The importance of service, market, and management characteristics. *Journal of Public Administration Research and Theory, 22*(2), 289–317.

Hirschman, A. O. (1970). *Exit, voice, and loyalty: Responses to decline in forms, organizations, and states.* Harvard University Press.

Honadle, B. W. (1981). A capacity-building framework – A search for concept and purpose. *Public Administration Review, 61*(5), 575–580.

Huber, J. D., & McCarty, N. (2004). Bureaucratic capacity, delegation, and political reform. *American Political Science Review, 98*(3), 481–494.

Hupe, P. L., & Hill, M. J. (2014). Delivery capacity. In M. Lodge & K. Wegrich (Eds.), *The problem-solving capacity of the modern state* (pp. 25–40). Oxford University Press.

IHME. (n.d.). *COVID-19 models FAQs.* http://www.healthdata.org/covid/faqs. Accessed 12 Sept 2020.

Joaquin, M. E., & Greitens, T. J. (2009). Presidential policy initiatives and agency compliance: Organizational adaptation to A-76. *Administration & Society, 41*(7), 815–849.

Joaquin, M. E., & Greitens, T. J. (2012b). The ARRA websites through the lens of digital account-ability and citizen engagement. In A. Manoharan & M. Holzer (Eds.), *E-Governance and civic engagement: Factors and determinants of E-Democracy* (pp. 1–24). IGI Global.

Joaquin, M. E. (2009). Bureaucratic adaptation and the politics of multiple principals in policy implementation. *The American Review of Public Administration, 39*(3), 246–268.

Joaquin, M. E., & Greitens, T. J. (2012a). Contract management capacity breakdown? An analysis of U.S. local governments. *Public Administration Review, 72*(6), 807–816.

Johnston, J. M., Romzek, B. S., & Wood, C. H. (2004). The challenge of contracting and account-ability across the federal system: From ambulances to space shuttles. *Publius. The Journal of Federalism, 34*(3), 155–182.

Kagan, E. (2001). Presidential administration. *Harvard Law Review, 114*(8), 2245–2385. https://harvardlawreview.org/wp-content/uploads/pdfs/vol114_kagan.pdf. Accessed 15 Jan 2021

Kamarck, E. (2021, February 10). Building an agile government for an era of megachange. *The Brookings Institution.* https://www.brookings.edu/research/building-an-agile-government-for-an-era-of-megachange/. Accessed 17 Mar 2021.

Katz, E. (2021, January 21). Here's who is leading federal agencies as Biden nominees await confirmation. *Government Executive.* https://www.govexec.com/management/2021/01/heres-who-leading-federal-agencies-biden-nominees-await-confirmation/171512/. Accessed 28 Jan 2020.

Kelleher, C., & Yackee, S. W. (2008). A political consequence of contracting: Organized interests and state agency decision making. *Journal of Public Administration Research and Theory, 19*(3), 579–602.

Kettl, D. F. (2015). From intergovernmental to intersectoral. In M. E. Guy & M. M. Rubin (Eds.), *Public administration evolving: From foundations to the future* (pp. 18–37). Routledge.

Knott, J. H., & Miller, G. C. (1987). *Reforming bureaucracy: The politics of institutional choice.* Prentice-Hall.

Kweit, M. G., & Kweit, R. W. (1984). The politics of policy analysis: The role of citizen participation in analytic decision-making. *Policy Studies Review, 3*(2), 234–245.

Lane, L. M. (1992). The office of personnel management: Values, policies, and consequences. In P. W. Ingraham & D. H. Rosenbloom (Eds.), *The promise and paradox of civil service reform* (pp. 97–120). University of Pittsburgh.

Lartey, J. (2017, January 25). Trump bans agencies from 'providing updates on social media or to reporters'. *The Guardian*. https://www.theguardian.com/us-news/2017/jan/24/epa-department-agriculture-social-media-gag-order-trump. Accessed 10 Nov 2019.

Light, P. C. (2015a). A cascade of breakdowns: How government daydreams become nightmares, and how to wake up. American Political Science Association. New York University. https://wagner.nyu.edu/files/faculty/publications/rba15-A_Cascade_of_Breakdowns.pdf. Accessed 6 June 2020.

Light, P. C. (2015b, December). *Vision + action = faithful execution: Why government daydreams and how to stop the cascade of breakdowns that now haunts it*. The Volcker Alliance. Accessed 4 Sept 2020.

Light, P. C. (2020c, October 14). The six government reforms we need in 2021. *The Brookings Institution*. https://www.brookings.edu/blog/fixgov/2020/10/14/the-six-government-reforms-we-need-in-2021/. Accessed 30 Oct 2020.

Light, P. C. (2020d, October 15). Trump said 'I alone can fix' government. He failed. *Government Executive*. https://www.govexec.com/management/2020/10/trump-said-i-alone-can-fix-government-he-failed/169289/. Accessed 30 Oct 2020.

Lodge, M., & Wegrich, K. (Eds.). (2014). *The problem-solving capacity of the modern state*. Oxford University Press.

Long, N. N. (1949). Power and administration. *Public Administration Review, 9*(4), 257–264.

Mason, J., & Holland, S. (2021, January 21). Fauci credits Biden for letting 'the science speak' as the new administration puts focus on the virus. *Reuters*. https://www.reuters.com/article/us-usa-biden/fauci-credits-biden-for-letting-the-science-speak-as-new-administration-puts-focus-on-virus-idUSKBN29Q15Y. Accessed 25 Jan 2021.

Merriam-Webster. (n.d.-a). "capacity". https://www.merriam-webster.com/dictionary/capacity. Accessed 1 Mar 2019.

Merriam-Webster. (n.d.-b). "deconstruct". https://www.merriam-webster.com/dictionary/deconstruct. Accessed 1 July 2019.

Mervosh, S., Baker, M., Mazzei, P., & Walker, M. (2021, February 12). Without a national strategy, U.S. states were left to battle the virus on their own. *The New York Times*. https://www.nytimes.com/live/2021/01/18/world/covid-19-coronavirus?type=styln-live-updates&label=coronavirus&index=1&action=click&module=Spotlight&pgtype=Homepage#without-a-national-strategy-us-states-were-left-to-battle-the-virus-on-their-own. Accessed 2 Mar 2021.

National Academy of Public Administration (NAPA). (n.d.). Grand challenges in public administration. Washington, DC. https://napawash.org/grand-challenges/the-12-grand-challenges. Accessed 17 Dec 2020.

O'Leary, R. (2006). *The ethics of dissent: Managing guerrilla government*. Sage.

O'Leary, R. (2015). From silos to networks. In M. E. Guy & M. M. Rubin (Eds.), *Public administration evolving: From foundations to the future* (pp. 85–100). Routledge.

Parks, M. (2019, September 4). Cyber experts warn of vulnerabilities facing 2020 election machines. *NPR*. https://www.npr.org/2019/09/04/755066523/cyber-experts-warn-of-vulnerabilities-facing-2020-election-machines. Accessed 18 Oct 2019.

Partnership for Public Service. (2021, January). Resilient: Keeping your WITS – Workforce, innovation, technology, security – About you. [PDF File] https://ourpublicservice.org/wp-content/uploads/2021/01/Resilient_.pdf. Accessed 26 Nov 2020.

Pelley, S. (2020, November 30). Fired director of U.S. cyber agency Chris Krebs explains why President Trump's claims of election interference are false. *60 Minutes*. https://www.cbsnews.com/news/election-results-security-chris-krebs-60-minutes-2020-11-29/. Accessed 30 Nov 2020.

Peters, B. G. (2015). Policy capacity in public administration. *Policy and Society, 34*(3–4), 219–228. https://doi.org/10.1016/j.polsoc.2015.09.005

Pierson, P. (2004). *Politics in time: History, institutions, and social analysis*. Princeton University Press.

Piotrowski, S., & Liao, Y. (2012). The usability of government information: The necessary link between transparency and participation. In H. L. Schachter & K. Yang (Eds.), *The state of citizen participation in America* (pp. 77–100). Information Age Publishing.

Rampell, C. (2020, November 30). Trump lays the groundwork for a massive government purge on his way out the door. *The Washington Post*. https://www.washingtonpost.com/opinions/trump-lays-the-groundwork-for-a-massive-government-purge-on-his-way-out-the-door/2020/11/30/2 80519ac-333d-11eb-a997-1f4c53d2a747_story.html. Accessed 1 Dec 2020.

Roberts, A. S. (2019a). Bridging levels of public administration: How macro shapes meso and micro. *Administration & Society, 52*(4), 631–656.

Roberts, A. S. (2019b). *Strategies for governing: Reinventing public administration for a dangerous century*. Cornell University Press.

Rohr, J. A. (1986). *To run a constitution: The legitimacy of the administrative state*. University Press of Kansas.

Romzek, B. S., & Johnston, J. M. (2002). Effective contract implementation and management: A preliminary model. *Journal of Public Administration Research and Theory, 12*(3), 423–453.

Rosenbloom, D. (2015). The public context. In M. E. Guy & M. M. Rubin (Eds.), *Public administration evolving: From foundations to the future* (pp. 3–17). Routledge.

Rosenbloom, D., & McCurdy, H. (2007). Introduction. In D. Rosenbloom & H. E. McCurdy (Eds.), *Revisiting Waldo's administrative state: Constancy and change in public administration* (pp. 1–14). Georgetown University Press.

Rubin, I. S. (2006). *The politics of public budgeting: Getting and spending, borrowing and balancing* (5th ed.). CQ Press.

Salamon, L. M. (2002). *The tools of government: A guide to the new governance*. Oxford University Press.

Samuels, B. (2021, March 15). White House would welcome Trump urging supporters to get vaccinated. *The Hill*. https://thehill.com/homenews/administration/543252-white-house-would-welcome-trump-urging-supporters-to-get-vaccinated. Accessed 21 Oct 2020.

Seidman, H. (1970). Politics, position, and power: The dynamics of federal organization. New York: Oxford University Press.

Selin, J. (2020, June 8). How the Constitution's federalist framework is being tested by COVID-19. *The Brookings Institution*. https://www.brookings.edu/blog/fixgov/2020/06/08/how-the-constitutions-federalist-framework-is-being-tested-by-covid-19/. Accessed 16 June 2020.

Shick, R., & Weikart, L. A. (2009). Public organizations undergoing change: A study in urban contracting. *Public Administration Quarterly, 33*(1), 72–117.

Silverman, C. (2020, November 16). This analysis shows how viral fake election news stories outperformed real news on Facebook. *BuzzFeed News*. https://www.buzzfeednews.com/article/craigsilverman/viral-fake-election-news-outperformed-real-news-on-facebook. Accessed 29 Nov 2020.

Simonsen, W., & Robbins, M. D. (2000). *Citizen participation in resource allocation*. Westview.

Skowronek, S. (1982). *Building a new American state: The expansion of national administrative capacities, 1877–1920*. Cambridge University Press.

Skowronek, S., Dearborn, J. A., & King, D. (2021). Phantoms of a beleaguered republic. The deep state and the unitary executive. Oxford University Press.

Stivers, C. (2008). *Governance in dark times: Practical philosophy for public service*. Georgetown University Press.

Suleiman, E. N. (2005). *Dismantling democratic states*. Princeton University Press.

Sunstein, C. R., & Vermeule, A. (2020). *Law and leviathan: Redeeming the administrative state*. Belknap Press. https://www.hup.harvard.edu/catalog.php?isbn=9780674247536&content=toc. Accessed 5 May 2020

Terry, L. D. (2003). *Leadership of public bureaucracies: The administrator as conservator*. M.E. Sharpe.

The Economist. (2021, January 2). The Senate will be worse off without Lamar Alexander. https://www.economist.com/united-states/2021/01/02/the-senate-will-be-worse-off-without-lamar-alexander Accessed 2 Feb 2021.

Thomas, J. C. (2012). *Citizen, customer, partner book: Engaging the public in public management.* Routledge.

US House of Representatives. (2019, January 14). H.R.4174 - Foundations for evidence-based policymaking Act of 2018. https://www.congress.gov/bill/115thcongress/house-bill/4174/text?q=%7B%22search%22%3A%5B%22HR+4174%22%5D%7D&r=1.

U.S. Government Accountability Office (GAO). (1995, February). High-risk series: An Overview. [PDF file]. https://www.gao.gov/assets/hr-95-1.pdf. Accessed 16 May 2020.

U.S. Government Accountability Office (GAO). (2012, July). Food safety: FDA's food advisory and recall process needs strengthening. [PDF file] https://www.gao.gov/assets/gao-12-589.pdf. Accessed 13 Nov 2020.

U.S. Government Accountability Office (GAO). (2019, March). High-risk series: Substantial efforts needed to achieve greater progress on high-risk areas. GAO-19-157SP. Washington, DC.

U.S. Government Accountability Office (GAO). (2021, March). High-risk series: Dedicated leadership needed to address limited progress in most high-risk areas. [PDF file] https://www.gao.gov/assets/gao-21-119sp.pdf. Accessed 13 Nov 2020.

Weiss, J. A. (2002). Public information. In L. M. Salamon (Ed.), *The tools of government: A guide to the new governance* (pp. 218–252). Oxford University Press.

White, L. D. (1954). *Introduction to the study of public administration* (4th ed.). The Macmillan Company.

Wilson, J. Q. (1989). *Bureaucracy: What government agencies do and why they do it.* Basic Books.

Wood, D. B. (2010). Agency theory and the bureaucracy. In R. F. Durant (Ed.), *The Oxford handbook of American bureaucracy* (pp. 181–206). Oxford University Press.

Yang, K., Hsieh, J. Y., & Li, T. S. (2009). Contracting capacity and perceived contracting performance: Nonlinear effects and the role of time. *Public Administration Review, 69,* 681–696.

Chapter 4
Capacity and Reform Movements

*To tug at the bureaucratic lynchpin is to the challenge the way
government officials gain and maintain their positions, the way
they relate to each other within and across institutions, and the
way they relate back to social and economic groups.*

Stephen Skowronek (1982, p. 291)

*The ultimate problems of the federal service are political
problems, capable only of political solution and
guidance...Convulsions and violence characterize the entire
political world. As varies the political whole so does the use of
public office, the instrument, and often the basis, of
political power.*

Paul Van Riper (1958, p. 564)

4.1 Capacity and Reformism in the Administrative State

In the preceding chapter, we developed a nuanced conceptualization of *capacity*. Its
core dimensions – problem-solving, management, engagement, administrative conservatorship, and accountability – represent what is expected of an administrative
system in a democratic setting. In this chapter, we frame the dynamics of capacity
change over time to arrive at our notions of decline and decay. To get there, we
discuss the ecology of political actors and their roles, the obvious as well as
the imperceptible power shifts, the lessons lost and learned, and the business, academic, and civic nexus with bureaucratic reforms. Capacity's ebb and flow is fundamentally presented in this book using knowledge from the American political
development (APD) literature and the various ways scholars have made sense of the
forces that have shaped bureaucracy throughout history. Capacity is conceptually
wobbly without anchoring it to a consistent feature of the American political system – the need to control the bureaucracy through reform and the inculcation of
long-term beliefs about what the government can properly do and the means to do
it (Wilson, 1887). Our framework looks to bureaucracy's beginnings marked by
institutional struggles and stalemates among the branches of government and

© Springer Nature Switzerland AG 2021
M. E. Joaquin, T. J. Greitens, *American Administrative Capacity*,
https://doi.org/10.1007/978-3-030-80564-7_4

political parties (Skowronek, 1982). This section discusses how such struggles were portrayed in the literature.

Reformism is a staple of the American government system. Some reforms made more rational sense than others. For example, many reforms in history were said to be oddly similar (Ingraham & Rosenbloom, 1993, p. 285), cyclical (Romzek, 2007, p. 153), recycled (Koppell, 2010, p. 129) or, as Gerald Caiden (1994) noted long ago, "compromised out of recognition from their original intentions" (p. 124). But what is also important is that we can now look back at the development of the administrative state and examine it for clues as to how capacity seemed to have degraded in the modern era.

Metaphors of reform movements are rich in insight. The patterns that make sense from a long view are aptly captured in the analyses of scholars such as Herbert Kaufman, Paul Light, and Jonathan Koppell. Elements of their frameworks allow us to see capacity's decline due to a *shift in the political ground* after the New Deal, a move that has prioritized executive control over a balanced approach (the traditional controls), such that it is now so much harder to arrest capacity's decline or reconstitute capacity from decay. In history, capacity responds to the complex combination of reform values and goals, as they balance or take turns like tides or waves, pushing and pulling, reacting and counter-reacting. Underneath, slow but persistent "tectonic" shifts move the administrative state in directions hidden by the cycle of reforms or tides. Stephen Skowronek described one such pattern in early reform movements, in which capacity evolved amid *executive advance, congressional reaction, a confrontation or crisis of authority, and then stalemate.* Presidents would initiate reforms to make the bureaucracy politically responsive, Congress would mount a counteroffensive, and over time one branch would triumph – but not always in a linear or neat fashion. The two repeat the dynamic, with the judicial branch and the administrative class also staking out their positions. As the American state developed in response to industrialization and global contests, political parties, judicial, and business interests sought their opportunities to recast institutional power relationships. The electoral incentives, political interests, and legal constraints confronting these principals molded the bureaucracy's role, power, and capacities for promoting the economy and public welfare (Skowronek, 1982, pp. 165, 291). But while Skowronek depicted the early bureaucracy as evolving between executive advances and legislative reactions, Kaufman described the historical arc of American administrative institutions in terms of the three values pursued by the reformers: representativeness in government, neutral competence, and executive leadership to arrest the fragmentation in the growing administrative state (1956). Each value was pursued successively, though the quest for each did not really wane, and none was fully supplanted by another. Dilemmas from each reform period often led to the pursuit of other values.

Reforms come and then recede, with a cyclicality reflecting the values and mood shifts about government and its operations (Romzek, 2007, p. 153). The well-known depiction is Light's tides of reforms to make government work in the four decades after World War II: he clustered the initiatives around scientific management, war on waste, the watchful eye, and liberation management. Adding to the metaphor, Koppell used geological dynamics to represent the permanent shifts that occur almost imperceptibly underneath the tides of reform. Such efforts to make sense of the development of the administrative state led Durant to coin the term "tidetonic" – combining the tides and massive shifts witnessed over the last hundred years of administrative history (Light, 1997; Koppell, 2010; Durant, 2010). If you refer back to Fig. 3.1 in the previous chapter, the shifts under the core dimensions of capacity represent those movements. An example here involves the rampant contracting out of government work and the emphasis on performance measurement with an eye to business principles. As part of the large-scale, bureaucratic retrenchment and privatization that took off in the 1980s, a tectonic move transformed public administration from a hierarchy-based regime to a market-based service delivery system. But within each sphere of change, one also sees tidal movements, as when emphasis in reform moved from efficiency to accountability and back.

Such ebbs and flows reflect how capacity is not merely a managerial construct within the agencies but a product of conscious choices and relationships within political processes over time. Strategies at the highest level dictate the capacity that gets built at the sub-levels of the administrative apparatus. As Alasdair Roberts explained, the macro-level is where leaders determine the broad architecture of the state. Their governing strategies are carried out by renovating bureaucracy: "dismantling obsolete capabilities, building new capabilities, shifting agency operations to emphasize different values" at the meso-level of public administration, tides that reflect the leaders' momentary preoccupations (Roberts, 2019a, pp. 631, 633–634). Using the literature above, we can imagine the dimensions of capacity that rise or decline with reform values, rituals, and political development. Capacity is controlled through *traditional* and *transactional* approaches in pursuit of the *energetic executive*. Decline occurs as the dimensions are unbalanced or ignored, and controls are amassed in the *unitary executive*.

4.2 Two Approaches to Controlling Capacity

Having recognized those macro-political elements, we assume that the different dimensions of capacity rose and fell in history as the political branches vied for control of the federal bureaucracy. This battle was manifested by two approaches, which we call traditional and transactional, each embodying definitive periods, reform politics, theoretical underpinnings, and reform tools. Each was an approach of reformers to "control capacity" – identifying or articulating what capacity was needed, how it would be built or sourced, and what reform might accomplish that vision. The traditional approach operated as the administrative state rose, while transactional approaches emerged to develop capacity in new ways that presidentialized administration (see Table 4.1).

Table 4.1 Two approaches to controlling capacity

	Traditional	Transactional
Period of reform involved	Seeded at the birth of the administrative state but most influential during: The Republic's founding to New Deal: • Capacity mapping period • Capacity buildup period • Capacity consolidation period	Seeded at the birth of the administrative state but most influential during: Post-New Deal to present: • Capacity dilution period • Concealed decline period • Deconstruction period
Brief definition	An approach in which administrative capacity is formed within a system defined by the Constitution that allows for the building of such capacity in the executive branch while putting checks on executive power	An approach in which control of the administrative capacity concentrates in the executive and capacity is externalized through various reforms that make it easier for the president to directly control
Representative reforms	• The Constitution • Brownlow Committee • Spoils system	• Civil service reform • National Performance Review • President's Management Agenda • Devolution • Schedule F
Description within the context of political development	Traditionally known as the orthodox approach, professional capacity replaces politicized capacity of the pre-administrative state; an energetic capacity in the executive is under control by all the political branches; the structure and incentives of political control influence reform as administrative state expands in size and scope, leading to executive-legislative rivalry	Congress and presidents vie for control of capacity; politicization of the civil service; efficiency considerations become linked with externalized notions of capacity; legislative incapacity advantages the executive and business interests; symbolic reformism; decline and decay of capacity as unitary executive thesis leads to administrative deconstruction
Dimensions of capacity emphasized and impacted	All core dimensions of capacity built up, incrementally; efficiency in management and accountability to political branches pursued, later followed by development of administrative conservatorship, problem-solving, and engagement capacities	Dimensions of capacity increasingly becoming tools caught between the power rivalries; accountability, management efficiency, and engagement emphasized by different tides of reform; management dimensions emphasized for the president's use; problem-solving capacity decays with weakened administrative conservatorship
Role of the parastate and operating theories of administration	Weberian bureaucratic notions to energize the executive branch; politics-administration separation to promote neutral competence; academic theory was seen relevant to debates and source of ideas for legislation and presidential reform initiatives	Administrative theory weaned off political grounding, leaned toward market-inspired ideas; decoupling from political context left theory unable to explain capacity issues; academic contributions increasingly sidelined as executive leans on the consulting industry for capacity reform ideas

(continued)

Table 4.1 (continued)

	Traditional	Transactional
Role of the private sector and political parties	During the era of the compensatory capacity, business aided the young nation; as progressive movement erected regulations, conservative party-business alliance forms to influence future design and reform of government operations	Era of a "constitutional coup" in privatizing traditionally governmental functions; an expansive executive sidelines Congress; anti-government movement rises as state gets "submerged"; separation of parties dominates separation of powers; failure of the democratic bargain
Role of the public/citizens	Orthodox theory calls for educational role of reformers to create an informed public; greater role in civil service out of the spoils system; control of bureaucracy through notice and commenting; citizen participation in decision-making	Citizens retreating, unable to comprehend government functions amid contracting; polarization; loss of sense of a shared fate with competent bureaucracy; distrust deters necessary attention to capacity and pressures on Congress to rebuild capacity

4.2.1 Traditional Approaches

The periods of capacity mapping out, buildup, and consolidation were attended by the traditional approaches to capacity. Administrative capacity was formed within a system defined by the Constitution that allowed for the building of such capacity in the executive branch while putting checks on its power. The milestones in political development that represent this approach are those following the establishment of the Constitutional "joint custody" over the bureaucracy, the spoils system of Jacksonian democracy, and the reforms espoused by the Brownlow Committee.

Under this approach, which we describe in Chap. 5, the administrative system was built up in all of its dimensions of capacity, from the preadministrative state to the 1940s. The blueprint for the creation of capacity was the Constitution itself, with "energy in the Executive" (unity, duration, adequate provision of support, and competent powers) (Hamilton et al., 2008) drawn up, and corresponding checks to be provided by other branches of government. The administrative state embodied all three branches; control or oversight aimed at a balance between the legislative and executive branches, with Congress – the First Branch – in a more dominant, designer role. Political control over the bureaucracy was ensured through partisan influence, first, and then through progressive professionalization.

As capacity professionalized, government's role became more positive over time, with experts and academics edging out political machines in configuring the emerging administrative landscape. The role of citizens in public administration was addressed in theory and in practice at this time, and schools and networks of public affairs built upon their municipal reform roots. The political parties yielded to civil service reformers in the 1880s once they reached a critical mass. Private sector energy and resources compensated (Eisner, 2001) for the young nation's budding capacity before the twentieth century. This would lay the seed for corporations to appear as an ally of professional bureaucracy. "Occupying the field" before others allows an actor to shape the path of policy. Businesses in that way were able to position themselves, acquiring privileged access over later debates on how to reform the bureaucracy (Robertson, 2010, p. 38; Durant, 2010, p. 167).

4.2.2 Transactional Approaches

Transactionalism is an approach in which control of the administrative capacity became concentrated in the executive and capacity was externalized through various reforms that made it easier for the president to wrest further control of capacity from Congress (see Chap. 6). The consolidation of capacity continued until the Great Society of the 1960s just when transactional approaches started becoming dominant. They would gradually usher in a period of *capacity dilution and decline* at the dawn of the deconstruction era. It happened as the constellation of forces influencing federal bureaucracy shifted and agencies moved gradually away from legislative and toward public-private nexus. As societal conditions and demands grew in complexity in the 1960s, the traditional approach weakened. Administrative tinkering became more strategic in advancing unilateral, executive initiatives. Representative of such reforms are the Civil Service Reorganization Act of 1978, the National Performance Review, and the 2001 President's Management Agenda. Transactionalism enabled entrepreneurialism in the management dimension of capacity. When national prosperity started becoming insecure in the 1970s, politicians outdid themselves in promoting solutions that scapegoated the bureaucracy and rather favored third-party government. The political parties regained the influence they lost from the civil service reform era and reawakened their business alliances in eyeing bureaucratic transformations. Setting the tone of bureaucratic reform, transactionalism refocused or shifted capacity increasingly out of the traditional bureaucracy. The resulting "neo-administrative state" pushed federal government responsibilities "upward to international bodies, downward to state and local governments, and outward to private and nonprofit actors" (Durant, 2007, p. 181), for which both Democratic and Republican presidents took credit. Proponents of outsourcing often emphasize the problem of control of the bureaucracy, but not as much its invisible or layered components in the "shadow" bureaucracy. Privatization, the twin of starving the beast, according to GAO has increased governing complexity, systemic risks, and communication problems and reduced the government's ability to better manage uncertainty, tailor policies, and allocate scarce resources (2018). In this new milieu, in-house management capacity could hardly keep up with the shift (Joaquin & Greitens, 2012). Nor could administrative law or theories (Rosenbloom, 2015).

Transactionalism, like traditionalism, allowed politicians to make promises and grab credit; but unlike the latter, it promoted solutions that were less direct, avoiding the appearance of bureaucratic bloat. Efficiencies from entrepreneurial reforms were achieved in the short run but contributed to long-term issues in the other dimensions – accountability, problem-solving, civic engagement, and agency conservatorship. This spurred frequent calls to revisit the traditional elements that worked for the administrative state (Olsen, 2006). Outside the Beltway, the downward push of responsibilities to the states in the name of federalism made state bureaucracies function as engines of inequality (Kettl, 2020). Creating what we call the *concealed decline period* in American political development, transactionalism expanded capacity under the thumb of the president, overall, but imbalanced it and rendered it incapable of addressing changing national problems efficiently and accountably. How did it happen?

Congress became a party to this transactionalist approach. Problems of administration were automatically assumed as problems to be resolved within the ambit of the presidency. When Congress acquiesced to executive streamlining and other de-professionalization strategies in the name of making agencies accountable and cost-efficient, hollowing out raised lesser and lesser alarm: privatization became normalized. The ground shifted, putting overall capacity on a long road to decline as transactionalism bred approaches to capacity that catered mainly to the unitary executive. In Metzger's analysis of modern presidential politics, the solution that some reformers sought might have made administration worse:

> those fearing unaccountable power often advocate greater presidential control over government administration. But from an aggrandized power perspective, such a response may simply worsen the problem, adding the President's popular authority and political leadership to the mix of executive, legislative, and adjudicatory powers agencies wield on their own. (Metzger, 2017, p. 37)

Ever since the New Deal era pushed for a bureaucratic anatomy that would enhance executive control, rather than a shared authority with the branches (Newland, 2015, p. 45), arguments for enhancing presidential resources kept emerging, whichever party controlled the White House (U.S. House of Representatives Committee on Government Reform and Oversight, 1995). The Democrats followed Reagan by cutting down the workforce and enlarging the third sector and creating tools that consequently Republican presidents would use for more extreme measures later on. Putting all the elements of the framework together, capacity's decline may be understood as being concealed amidst the reforms whose primary outcome was to accumulate executive power at the expense of Congress. Eventually, transactionalism made capacity brittle and vulnerable to decay with the rise of "full-throated presidentialism" (Skowronek et al., 2021, p. 23).

4.3 Executive Dominance and the Broken Branch: The Tectonic Shift

Reforms that camouflaged the slow erosion of capacity did not attract public attention in history because most were glued to the rhetoric of the different tides of reform, but not as much to the forces beneath the tides. Referring back to Fig. 3.1 in the previous chapter, macro-tectonic plates can be found beneath the meso-tides of reform, and over time, it became the president, rather than Congress, that controlled the tides. Despite congressional intent, the control levers gradually converged in the hands of a unitary actor, the executive. Before Franklin Roosevelt, public administration operated on an assumption of bipartisan legislative oversight of the bureaucratic apparatus. Losing that assumption has helped weaken public administration as a field (Newland, 2015, p. 46). It also clouded the public's grasp of the administrative system. Indeed, ever since the Brownlow Committee used the term "the executive branch" to refer to the bureaucracy, many forgot that Congress was the first branch of the government, and it became customary to think that the administrative system belonged to the White House (Radin, 2012, p. 78). As president, Roosevelt was said to have used the agencies as if they were "pawns in a chess game, moving them wherever it would best strengthen his position" (Seidman, 1970, p. 69). The expansion of the administrative state enabled this president and his successors to create their own national political constituency, independent institutional tools, and escape from the impositions of a locally based party state on the national leadership. Moreover, the New Deal imagery of the president as the "steward of the nation," who would protect the public within the government and lead public opinion on reform (Skowronek, 1982, p. 172; PCAM, 1937), were key developmental outcomes in the history of the administrative state. The echoes of such presidentialized administration would be heard fiercely a generation later in the deconstructive agenda of an insurgent president, leading federal bureaucracy to the brink of disaster.

Congress was, itself, declining to notice how much of administration was slipping from its control and being molded into the policy shop of whichever party controlled the Oval Office. The chambers neglected maintaining their institutional abilities to restrain executive ambitions of sole administrative command and execution of the laws as the president saw fit. The reason? The legislature retreated on the premise that the executive branch alone was bestowed a national constituency by the Constitution (Skowronek et al., 2021). Proponents justify this muscular theory by harking all the way back to the populism of the Jacksonian era, even though the world has changed a lot since then. As Skowronek explained:

> The democracy that ratified the creation of the presidency is not the same as the democracy that politicized central administration in the Jacksonian era, nor is it the same as the democracy that nationalized governmental power in the Progressive era. By some unstated transitive property of construction, however, the original act of ratification now provides democratic sanction to unbridled presidential control over the vast powers that have accumulated in the executive branch. (Skowronek, 2009, p. 2020)

As Congress forfeited some of its powers to the White House, the thinning of administrative conservators was occurring at the same time, subjecting the bureaucracy even more to "slicing and dicing" by the unitary executive. The decline of the bond between Congress and the administrative apparatus is therefore intertwined with the enlarged scope of personnel and budget under executive OMB's control. Transactionalism would prove conducive to the executive's permanent campaign to control the bureaucracy relative to the "clumsy collective manager," that is, Congress, despite its vast powers in statute making, fiscal control, and investigation (Kettl, 2020).

One such demonstration of this tectonic shift was seen in the Department of Homeland Security's (DHS) behavior under Trump. The twilight of checks and balance and the legislative failures in agency design crippled the capacity of the agency to perform and perform accountably. One of the last administrative reforms in history, the creation of DHS was supposed to address the deficit in problem-solving capacity that had led to the September 2001 terrorist attacks. A consequence of its design was a weakness in the new agency's capacity to respect democratic norms and the bounds of authority.

First, in 2020, on the heels of reports of atrocious federal agent actions against families detained at the border (Armus, 2020), congressional Democrats suggested dismantling or at least reorganizing DHS. The clamor arose against Trump's draconian "zero tolerance" policy at the border. The president was trying to convince the public that immigration was a problem that Congress was unable to solve and only solvable by a unitary executive. The White House control over the focal agency's capacity – tweaking the DHS mission to go after sanctuary cities and documented immigrants, beefing up its staffing, appointing agency leaders that Senate would not confirm, declaring a national emergency so that parts of the DOD budget could be reprogrammed toward the border wall program, fast-tracking construction contracts despite disputes over the land to build them on, contracting out private prisons and detention centers in anticipation of a surge of arrests, granting concessions to the DHS unions to determine how to carry out their mission (Foer, 2018), and so on – demonstrates Alasdair Roberts' (2019b) point about the macro governing strategies molding the capacity that gets built, or degraded, at the meso- and micro-levels. At DHS, enhancing its problem-solving capacity in promoting the president's immigration vision was traded off with the dimensions of effective management, democratic engagement, and accountability.

Second, when DHS deployed unmarked agents in Portland during anti-racism protests in the summer of 2020, the crisis it brewed was reminiscent of Nixon's law-and-order campaign messaging that Trump seemed to have adopted for his second presidential campaign (Crespo, 2020; Koerth & Mazumder, 2020). The clamor to reform DHS only grew stronger. Demonstrating how the executive could wield an agency beyond its statutory mission, Senator Barbara Boxer pointed to Congress' failure in agency design as that of neglecting a balanced regard for each of the dimensions of capacity, especially accountability. Reflecting, the lawmaker said:

I made a mistake in 2002 when I voted to create the Department of Homeland Security…
There was no protection built into this bill to stop a power-hungry president from misusing
a powerful federal police force, hidden in disparate agencies, controlled by one agency head…

When we debated the DHS bill, I sided with 27 other senators on an amendment by Sen.
Robert Byrd (D-W.Va.) to delay the merger of the 22 organizations included in the department for three years and set up checks and balances as well as robust congressional oversight. We lost that fight, but…I voted for the final, imperfect, vulnerable product, and I
admit my mistake.

When we write laws, we must think harder about how they might be misused. I can't get
my vote back, but Congress can act to both condemn this gross tyranny and then restructure
the department so that no president, now or ever again, can have a private police force and
menace the people he or she swears to protect. (Boxer, 2020, para. 10–11)

The original design of DHS demonstrates that the macro-political values or context,
in this case national security, drives administrative reforms and actions. It also
shows that short-term political expedience, one of the factors behind congressional
decline, drowns out a careful incorporation of the elements of capacity (Ornstein &
Mann, 2006). Both parties in Congress rushed to create an agency to assuage a terrified nation after the September 2001 terrorist attacks. The Bush administration
also favored it as a way to deflect criticism that the intelligence community could
have prevented the attack had it managed better the information it already possessed
(Lind, 2015). Within a few years of DHS' creation, in the hands of the executive, the
loopholes in the agency's design became glaring.

By 2006, a decade and a half before the coronavirus pandemic, Congress was
pronounced "broken:" indifferent to its history, identity, or independence; devoid of
interest in institutional well-being, maintenance, or reform; and neglectful of the
heritage of asking the tough questions and using its power to hold the executive
accountable. Failures of oversight were particularly crushing. Unified party government further disincentivized restraining a president of the same party (Ornstein &
Mann, 2006).

4.4   Capacity Decline and the Separation of Parties

Partisan unity may be as much to blame as partisan conflict for congressional debil-
ity. Extreme partisanship has distracted leaders and polarized voters' attention away
from capacity – "owning the libs" according to some critics, being "the whole pointless point" of running government the way the 45th president had, for example
(Lyons, 2019). A capacitated bureaucracy requires a capacitated Congress exercising its institutional prerogative. But partisanship consumes leaders to leave durable
political consensus or movements as their legacy at the expense of the Constitution's
requirement for one branch of government to act as a restraint on the other. Though
this is nothing but a continuation of the battles from the Progressive era, modern
presidents like George W. Bush and Donald Trump have fostered a zero-sum mentality that heightened the stakes for owning the power levers and leaving their
stamp in Washington, DC, but not necessarily for solving the nation's problems.

Perhaps nothing could provide more durable conservative political legacy than the deconstruction of the administrative state and the long-term control of the judiciary, which the modern Republican Party successfully engineered out of party unity – the fruit of a movement cultivated over decades, waiting for the window of opportunity that Trump had recently provided. The speed with which Trump was able to undo Obama's administration also was nothing less than impressive (Mashaw & Berke, 2018, p. 551). Party unity explains how Republican Mitch McConnell's Senate leadership was one of support for as long as possible to a twice-impeached president, right until the president's supporters in 2021 became an existential threat to Congress itself. Conversely, the Republican lawmakers' fierce stance against Obama in his time owed more to unified partisanship against the Democratic president than the constitutional vision for the legislature.

Given such dynamics, Daryl Levinson and Richard Pildes argued that "separation of parties," not separation of powers, is the more realistic framework for understanding the mechanisms of control. It explains the inability of lawmakers to exert measurable restraint over the executive in times of unified government and their tendency to exercise the chambers' prerogatives in divided eras. The Constitution's framework of separated powers is more like a "paper partition between the branches" that is easily overwhelmed by ideological partisanship. When the same party controls both branches, as what happened over the last few years, Congress sides rather than competes with the White House. When government is divided, partisan animus drives Congress more than its institutional identity. Separation of parties, not powers, therefore explains one more avenue through which the executive could dominate the administrative landscape and extend his power into another branch of government (Levinson & Pildes, 2006, pp. 2314–2315). But as Kettl (2017) observed of partisanship, in modern history, there might have been "neglect" of capacity from the political left, but from the right, it had been nothing less than an "assault," undermining the agencies that must carry out the law and confidence in government itself.

Congressional weakness out of partisanship inevitably breeds executive opportunism in administration. This can be seen in the broken budgeting system that frequently invites shutdowns and, therefore, high-risk government and allows presidents to bifurcate government agencies and programs (see Chap. 7). It drives presidents to get more creative through OMB's transactionalist controls over the agencies' budget and management systems, rake in any political credits, and point the blame for any problem toward Congress. Lawmakers, to their discredit, have gotten used to creating *ad hoc* exceptions to the constraints they encounter, rather than finding ways to rationalize the budget process (J. Justice, personal communication, August 23, 2019). The modern practice of passing omnibus appropriations also indicates this lost vitality of the first branch. In the last contentious budget session of the Trump presidency, for example, Representative Alexandria Ocasio-Cortez likened the mere 2 hours they were given to consider the 5593-page bill – the longest in congressional history – to hostage-taking. Between 1983 and 2005, the ReadtheBill.org Foundation found that it would have been impossible for 13 of the 14 omnibus appropriations bills to have been read by lawmakers before they were debated (*The Economist*, 2020). Failures at the budget design phase only serve to empower OMB once the ball gets back to its court.

Congress is also known to wrap the agencies in oversight theater and yet is unable to prevent a leadership vacuum in the agencies or check the president's appointment power. Trump, with the Senate in Republican control, found it too easy to sidestep the "advice and consent" role of the chamber in the nomination and confirmation process as required by law. When agencies drifted for years without adequate leadership and collided with various crises during his presidency, Brookings put the blame on Congress:

> amidst this massive leadership vacuum... the institution that could do the most about this problem has mostly remained silent...but it appears to be of little concern, raising important questions about government performance and our system of checks and balances. (Tenpas, 2021, para. 2)

Unlike the energetic executive, the unitary executive can more easily sever the ties between Congress and the bureaucracy. Incentivizing long-serving bureaucrats to leave *en masse* makes it easier to bend the agencies' legislatively granted missions, reduce their visibility to Congress, and increase the influence of business as a source of policy information (Rampell, 2019; Young & McMahon, 2020). Like George W. Bush, the Trump administration harnessed known and even some dormant powers of the executive (Wagner, 2020; Shane, 2009) to work around Congress. As political scientists Frank Baumgartner and Bryan Jones noted long ago, these wounds were self-inflicted. Congress' dramatically diminished information processing capacity over the past generation has led to lawmakers losing power to the executive and public servants losing their capacity to third parties, in turn (Baumgartner & Jones, 2018).

4.5   Capacity Decline, Belief Making, and Reform Theater

Administrative reform in a complex system is necessarily chaotic despite the rationality that reformers might ascribe to their actions. Given that, reform failures can be explained rationally from all sides. Constant political wrestling in federal administration affects the ability of reformers to design and execute reform well and anticipate the long-run effects of their actions, subjecting the bureaucracy and its capacity to instability. Baseline capacities, agency variations, sunk costs, and lessons from previous reforms can get lost in reform theater. For instance, former EPA Chief William Ruckelshaus' sentiment below describes the pendulum swings that arise from hyper-partisanship that, in turn, imbalance capacity:

> The new Congress may believe that it is the vanguard of a permanent change in attitude toward regulation, but unless the past is no longer prologue, the pendulum will swing back...What is wrong with this picture? Are not such changes in emphasis part of the fabric of democracy? Yes, but in the case of environmental policy, these violent swings have had an unusually devastating–– perhaps a uniquely devastating – effect on the executive agency entrusted to carry out whatever environmental policy the nation says it wants. (Ruckleshaus, 1995, p. 229)

Like any organizational change, some of the most crucial things that get overlooked in politicized reforms are the baseline capacities and variations among the agencies, even within the agencies. When reforms are applied across the board, the inability of reformers to create meaningful distinctions between the agencies can lead to pushing square pegs on round holes, risking further degradation of the ability of the agencies to carry out their mission (Joaquin, 2009). In public bureaucracies, starting size matters a lot in transactional games. "Employees in small organizations often feel change, uncertainty, and stress more deeply and personally" (Ogrysko, 2019).

Failures in reforming capacity also result from an inability to learn from past reforms (Radin, 2012). Some reforms disregard sunk costs by abandoning relationships and other resource investments made in previous reforms or fail to build upon the gains of the previous reforms. They ignore goal contradictions, such as promising "better, cheaper, and faster" government as simultaneous results of reform. Contradictions and nonrationalities may also characterize reform, as when advocates require performance information through executive mandate, when the ability to couple it with budgetary incentives lay within congressional power (Moynihan, 2008), or when massive amounts of (compliance) information are sought, yet are not used in decision-making (Cohen et al., 1972).

Despite practical shortcomings, movements can take shape. Earlier, we noted the desire of political parties to leave long-lasting legacies. The endurance of the reform mindset despite constant drawbacks is a testament to the power of beliefs. John Kamensky, who has overseen reforms big and small since the Clinton-Gore era, noted that reformers were not so much launching a program as inspiring a movement (J. Kamensky, personal communication, March 10, 2019). This echoes the ideas propounded by administrative theorists James March and Johan Olsen, how meanings and symbolism suffuse reformism, though failures often mark the effort. Reforms are as much symbolic as they are tangible platforms in a ritual that has characterized American politics throughout history – the persistent effort to convey that change is possible through bureaucratic reform – like a cultural "rite of assent" that celebrates even minor reforms to preserve a self-image of freedom and ability to improve the future (Rana, 2016, p. 52). This, despite the *realpolitik* that prevents attainment of purported goals. An atmosphere of cyclicality and uniformity pervade this reform theater, where voters reward reformers for simply launching an initiative; execution need not be complete nor successful, because the politics is psychological – the gradual inculcation of beliefs (for instance, about the role of government or the private sector) in a society where participants suffer from cognitive or attention limits (March & Olsen, 1983).

Small government and anti-statist solutions are a product of such a belief movement and have, for decades, been searching for problems to solve. From the early "deep state" views of the Nixon administration to the administrative presidency of Ronald Reagan, through Newt Gingrich's Contract with America, to the Tea Party movement, and, more recently, to Trump-Bannon's deconstructionism, these movements that are decades apart created beliefs and effects that outlasted their proponents' hold on power or their policy measures that were abolished on paper. Conceptions of the administrative state endure and linger, like the proverbial policy soup from which the elements stew until a window of opportunity opens up for them to join the decision fray (Cohen et al., 1972). But also, due to these cognitive dynamics, unplanned adaptations can occur; capacity building may sometimes look like a one-step forward, two-step backward process; except, fundamental shifts do happen, and in the case of American public administration, the cumulative impact of various reforms over the past decades has been away from rationalizing in-house capacity and toward externalizing capacity as befits the executive's power objective.

4.6 Capacity Decline and "Agency X"

The dissipation of American administrative capacity cannot be regarded apart from the decline of the parastate – academics and good government coalitions – in influencing leaders' designs for government or breaking through the political logjam to build capacity in the long term. Bureaucracy's condition, while traceable to the actions of those fighting at the helm, is partly due to the inability of the field of public administration to keep up with the challenges of the times (Fukuyama, 2018) and the displacement of political analysis by business precepts in coming up with ideas to repair government capacity. The nexus between practice and theory got severed long ago. One reason is that government fragmentation and privatization have rendered old notions of administration incapable of solving the juggernaut that is the blended state.

The field has also gotten sidetracked. Academia's influence reached its peak with the New Deal and has ebbed since Carter's personnel system reorganization in 1978. As positivism began to dominate academic analysis, Dwight Waldo had decried public administrators' preoccupation with the superficial, trying to "solve immediate problems without reflecting on deeper dimensions" (Stivers, 2008, p. 75). This was part of a colorful period in the field's history when its most influential thinkers debated the types of questions asked and the rigor with which they were pursued (Simon et al., 1952). More recently, Roberts (2019b) lamented that public administration scholars have stopped asking, and publishing, and teaching about the grand challenges in the field – the *what* and the *how* of government – or strategies to adjust government to the facts of the modern world (Lippmann, 1914). As institutions of liberal democracy get assaulted from multiple fronts, the field was failing in the task of crafting blueprints of the capacities that are needed for the state to govern effectively. The discipline, just like the administrative state examined here, has lost its capacity to interrogate the reason for a state's existence, its design, and path of development (Roberts, 2019b).

Roberts attributed this to the self-consciousness of the profession's officers and academic journal editors since the 1980s. Their quest for methodological purity, when the "public management" approach became popular paid greater emphasis on performance management and related techniques to find efficiencies and ways of serving "customers" better. Academic pressure to focus on those subject matters heightened just as governments came under fire from groups who preferred the tasks of the administrative state to be neatly divided between "inherently governmental" functions and the rest that are available for outsourcing. Market ethos blended with the field's desire to improve its reputation for being empirical, at the expense of some important research questions. Thinkers in the field got trapped in a silicon cage where their intellectual creativity was suppressed by employers, publishers, commercial providers of ancillary services, and brokers of academic business intelligence data that monitored and regimented scholarly work (Roberts, 2020). Scholarship in the field turned toward quantitative-statistical methods to pursue research questions at the "meso-" and "micro"-levels, instead of the "macro," where the most important questions are lodged. A rediscovery of the grand questions is necessary, in his view:

> In moments of strategic collapse, the question of whether Agency X is operating with optimal efficiency is not of foremost importance. Rather, we are concerned with the architecture of government as a whole and whether it is designed to achieve national priorities, given the prevailing conditions. (Roberts, 2019b, p. 138)

In the Progressive era, with the likes of Luther Gulick and Louis Brownlow, public administration stalwarts were the architects of the renewed administrative state. Even when Woodrow Wilson talked about a science of administration in 1887, he kept the grand picture in focus when he wrote that the state "is the conscience of administration" (p. 201). Public administration scholars parted from the grand questions inherent in Waldo's view of bureaucracy in democracy. Rather, research and teaching have dwelled on the meso-capacities or:

> on problems of policy design, management within public organizations, and the implementation and evaluation of programs. When prospective managers and analysts are encouraged to take a wider view, to look upward and outward, it is often with the purpose of understanding …the constellation of actors in the immediate neighborhood of the agency or program that have a direct influence on its behavior. (Roberts, 2019b, p. 128)

While these studies are important, their dominance helped the field neglect analysis of the shifting plates on which administrative affairs stood.

4.7   Decline and Citizen Attitude Toward Capacity

Seeing the bureaucracy as the door to power, presidents, Congress and their allies in the economy have driven the political game and built an almost anti-capacity dynamic (B. Cook, personal communication, March 9, 2019) that has contributed to disillusionment among citizens. Generations of politicians have all too easily made their mark by convincing the public that failure is never a result of politics and success is often achieved from some infusion of market-like efficiency or stringent controls over some "rogue" agencies.

Such beliefs have led to the opposite of the value chain created when people trust in government. Robert Durant's (2010) analysis of American political development found that both the tectonic and tidal processes in governmental evolution are influenced by citizens' perceptions of the bureaucracy. Their beliefs shape contemporary assessments and their support for bureaucracy itself. That support became shaky when the nation started confronting steep fiscal conditions after the 1970s and bureaucrats were lumped with the so-called tax eaters (Rubin, 1998) in the eyes of the public. The conservatives' success in promoting this claim may be rooted in an earlier time when businesses worked with the young government to professionalize capacity. That collaboration helped the government shake free of the political machines in order to focus on the economy. That compensatory capacity (Eisner, 2001) positioned business well for future debates about the government's reach and how to build (or source out) its capacity. Once business' power was threatened by the continued expansion of administrative institutions post-New Deal, the former sought the latter's retreat. By mid-twentieth century, that campaign evolved to convince the public that privatization was better for the sake of the citizen-turned-consumer.

Privatization as a movement added third parties into the capacity discussion and weakened the bonds between the national bureaucracy and the public. During the Progressive era, the ideal citizen was cast as "endowed with the capacity to absorb, evaluate, and act upon information, and to make rational choices based on what she knew" (Jasanoff, 2016, p. 388). Modern politics destroyed this framework as citizens became customers to be regaled with cost-saving advertisement that enriched vendors. With third parties positioned between them and the agencies, the public got to know less and less about administrative institutions and their underlying issues. It became easy, amid polarization and mistrust, to forget that institutions needed people's support and investment of public resources to keep them vibrant. Instead, both citizens and institutions suffered from what may be called a mistrust spiral. Once Washington started causing disillusions in the 1970s, public suspicions of government developed. Durant (2010) explained how this only drove politicians to bash government itself, compete among themselves in overpromising, and find cleverer ways of pleasing voters outside traditional bureaucratic mechanisms. Instead of focusing on the issues of capacity to solve national problems, elections simply divided people culturally. Citizens retreated from meaningful participation in administration, their avenues for input blocked by procedural complexity. Their appreciation for the role of government was preempted by misinformation and the so-called submerged state (Mettler, 2011). People could no longer coherently define the connection between their demands and the government's capacity to achieve them. In time, the complexity of governmental action, the overreliance on contractors, and the incessant bashing of bureaucracy weakened the identification and public support that was necessary to make Congress act and remedy bureaucratic capacity (Durant, 2010, p. 163).

Unfortunately, as political scientist Mordecai Lee (personal communication, March 9, 2019) expressed to us before the pandemic:

The public is naïve about how much of government touches their lives. A tectonic event has to happen first for them to clamor for funding professional government. Public opinion will want to bring back big bureaucracy if and when they directly experience the problems of a hollowed-out government.

4.8 Capacity Decline and Decay

Based on the preceding analysis, various elements have set the stage for the demise of capacity. Capacity *decline* is indicated by the breakdowns in the different dimensions of capacity. Problem-solving, management, accountability, and engagement capacity declines are indicated by "resource shortages, bloated hierarchies, miscommunication, bad decisions, organizational confusion, ethical misconduct, and failure to track potential problems" (Light, 2015, p. 7), such as new infectious diseases abroad. Erosion in administrative leadership and engagement capacities is reflected in citizen mistrust of agency expertise and pandemic data. The dominance of business-backed ideas in the marketplace of public management reform ideas over the last several decades also indicates dissipation in administrative conservatorship. Finally, decline has occurred when agencies are deprived of sufficient autonomy, expertise, and cohesion around their mission.

Decay may be defined as a continuous decline or regression in administrative capacity. Earlier we referenced the work of GAO in identifying how agencies could move from the list of high-risk areas in government. GAO has noted a "regression" in certain agencies' capacities for budget and staffing, leadership, action planning, monitoring, and demonstration of problem-solving over the last 2 years of the Trump administration. Regression means the agency in the past had met the GAO criteria for improvement in those dimensions, but then the agency recently failed to make any improvements or has even gotten worse. These areas of regression are in regard to some of the most neglected, delegitimized, or controversial programs of the 4 years under Trump: the US Postal Service's financial viability, the conduct of the decennial census, ensuring the nation's cybersecurity, strategic human capital management, and the EPA's process for assessing and controlling toxic chemicals (GAO, 2021, p. 1).

In essence, within the context of social, economic, and political development, national administrative capacity decline and decay are rooted in executive dominance, congressional hyper-partisanship, privatization, weaknesses in administrative theory, and the loss of civic identification with a capacitated bureaucracy. In sum, decline and decay are driven by:

- The dominance of the executive, supplanting a balanced control of the bureaucracy with Congress. Trump declaring "I alone can fix" the nation's problems (Light, 2020, para. 1) is the culmination of the unitary executive theory that links back to the managerial presidency of the 1990s and the growth of presidential power throughout the twentieth century.

- The inability of reformers to balance the different dimensions of capacity and pursue the imperative of resilience in finding ways of addressing national problems.
- The fraying of the connection between Congress and the bureaucracy and the erosion of congressional capacities, as individual lawmakers face incentives that clash with their party's own goals (Norris, 2021) and partisan incentives that clash with Congress' institutional identity and goals.
- Hyper-partisanship that sees national politicians manipulating federalism for partisan wins and the weakening of the capacities below rather than fixing capacity at the federal level (Kettl, 2020; Selin, 2020).
- The de-professionalization of federal agencies and the thinning of administrative expertise, which serves as the repository of institutional memory and resilience.
- The perennial poking and failure of reform (Light, 2019), symbolic reformism, and reform theater that squander agency resources, energy, and public trust.
- The decline in public administration's grounding in political development and in the field's waning focus on the bigger questions of capacity.

As the succeeding chapters will show, different administrative reforms unintentionally set capacity on the road to decline, weakening the bonds between bureaucracy and civil society, while enhancing the power of the president to manipulate capacity. In confluence with antagonistic forces in society, such enhanced powers would eventually enable a president to gain more political support the more his government failed.

References

Armus, T. (2020, October 21). The parents of 545 children separated at the border still haven't been found. *The Texas Tribune.* https://www.texastribune.org/2020/10/21/donald-trump-immigration-parents-children-separated/. Accessed 13 Dec 2020.

Baumgartner, F. R., & Jones, B. D. (2018, March 1–2). *Why congressional capacity is not enough.* The State of Congressional Capacity Conference.

Boxer, B. (2020, July 25). Barbara Boxer: DHS was a mistake. I regret voting for it. *The Washington Post.* https://www.washingtonpost.com/outlook/2020/07/25/barbara-boxer-regret-dhs/. Accessed 28 July 2020.

Caiden, G. E. (1994). Administrative reform- American style. *Public Administration Review, 54*(2), 123–128.

Cohen, M. D., March, J. G., & Olsen, J. P. (1972). A garbage can model of organizational choice. *Administrative Science Quarterly, 17*(1), 1–25.

Crespo, A. (2020, July 25). Unpacking DHS's troubling explanation of the Portland van video. *Lawfare.* https://www.lawfareblog.com/unpacking-dhss-troubling-explanation-portland-van-video. Accessed 28 July 2020.

Durant, R. F. (2007). Institutional values and the future administrative state. In D. Rosenbloom & H. E. McCurdy (Eds.), *Revisiting Waldo's administrative state: Constancy and change in public administration* (pp. 179–202). Georgetown University Press.

Durant, R. F. (2010). Herbert Hoover's revenge: Politics, policy, and administrative reform movements. In R. F. Durant (Ed.), *The Oxford handbook of American bureaucracy* (pp. 153–178). Oxford University Press.

Eisner, M. A. (2001). *From warfare state to welfare state: World War I, compensatory state building, and the limits of the modern order*. The Pennsylvania University Press.

Foer, F. (2018, September). How Trump radicalized ICE. *The Atlantic*. https://www.theatlantic.com/magazine/archive/2018/09/trump-ice/565772/. Accessed 22 Mar 2019.

Fukuyama, F. (2018, August 13). The decline of American public administration. *The American Interest*. https://www.the-american-interest.com/2018/08/13/the-decline-of-american-public-administration/. Accessed 10 May 2019.

Hamilton, A., Jay, J., & Madison, J. [1788] (2008). *The federalist papers*. Oxford University Press.

Ingraham, P. W., & Rosenbloom, D. H. (1993). *The promise and paradox of civil service reform*. University of Pittsburgh.

Jasanoff, S. (2016). A century of reason. In S. Skowronek, S. M. Engel, & B. Ackerman (Eds.), *The progressives' century: Political reform, constitutional government, and the modern American state* (pp. 382–404). Yale University Press.

Joaquin, M. E. (2009). Bureaucratic adaptation and the politics of multiple principals in policy implementation. *The American Review of Public Administration, 39*(3), 246–268.

Joaquin, M. E., & Greitens, T. J. (2012). Contract management capacity breakdown? An analysis of U.S. local governments. *Public Administration Review, 72*(6), 807–816.

Kaufman, H. (1956, December). Emerging conflicts in the doctrines of public administration. *American Political Science Review, 50*(4), 1057–1073.

Kettl, D. F. (2017, February 28). The clumsy war against the administrative state. *Government Executive*. https://www.govexec.com/management/2017/02/clumsy-war-against-administrative-state/135733/. Accessed 22 May 2019.

Kettl, D. F. (2020). *The divided states of America: Why federalism doesn't work*. Princeton University Press.

Koerth, M., & Mazumder, S. (2020, August 5). What happened in Portland shows just how fragile our democracy is. *FiveThirtyEight*. https://fivethirtyeight.com/features/the-federal-clampdown-on-portland-shows-just-how-fragile-our-democracy-is/. Accessed 8 Dec 2020.

Koppell, J. G. S. (2010). Metaphors and the development of American bureaucracy. In R. F. Durant (Ed.), *The Oxford handbook of American bureaucracy* (pp. 128–150). Oxford University Press.

Levinson, D. J., & Pildes, R. H. (2006). Separation of parties, not powers. *Harvard Law Review, 119*(8), 2311–2386.

Light, P. C. (1997). *The tides of reform: Making government work, 1945–1995*. Yale University Press.

Light, P. C. (2015, December). *Vision + action = faithful execution: Why government daydreams and how to stop the cascade of breakdowns that now haunts it*. The Volcker Alliance. Accessed 4 Sept 2020.

Light, P. C. (2019, April 18). *The coming shutdown over government reform*. The Brookings Institution. https://www.brookings.edu/research/the-coming-showdown-over-government-reform/. Accessed 4 Sept 2020.

Light, P. C. (2020, October 15). Trump said 'I alone can fix' government. He failed. *Government Executive*. https://www.govexec.com/management/2020/10/trump-said-i-alone-can-fix-government-he-failed/169289/. Accessed 30 Oct 2020.

Lind, D. (2015, February 17). The Department of Homeland Security is a total disaster. It's time to abolish it. *Vox*. https://www.vox.com/2015/2/17/8047461/dhs-problems. Accessed 4 June 2020.

Lippmann, W. (1914). *Drift and mastery*. Mitchell Kannerly.

Lyons, G. (2019, September 13). To Trump, 'owning the libs' is the whole pointless point. *Chicago Sun Times*. https://chicago.suntimes.com/columnists/2019/9/13/20864843/donald-trump-2020-election-liberals-republicans-twitter. Accessed 19 Jan 2020.

March, J. G., & Olsen, J. P. (1983). Organizing political life: What administrative reorganization tells us about government. *The American Political Science Review, 77*(2), 281–296. https://doi.org/10.2307/1958916

Mashaw, J. L., & Berke, D. (2018). Presidential administration in a regime of separated powers: An analysis of recent American experience. *Yale Journal on Regulation, 35*(2). https://digitalcommons.law.yale.edu/yjreg/vol35/iss2/5. Accessed 11 Feb 2021.

Mettler, S. (2011). *The submerged state: How invisible government policies undermine American democracy*. University of Chicago Press.

Metzger, G. E. (2017). The supreme court, 2016 term – Foreword: 1930s redux: The administrative state under siege. *Harvard Law Review, 131*(1), 1–95.

Moynihan, D. P. (2008). *The dynamics of performance management: Constructing information and reform*. Georgetown University Press.

Newland, C. A. (2015). From trust to doubt. In M. E. Guy & M. M. Rubin (Eds.), *Public administration evolving: From foundations to the future* (pp. 38–62). Routledge.

Norris, P. (2021, February 8). Why Republicans haven't abandoned Trumpism. *The Washington Post.* https://www.washingtonpost.com/politics/2021/02/08/why-republicans-havent-abandoned-trumpism/?fbclid=IwAR1S1Srs_5KYzeCgxFbNg0vslUwBURBVptzOEFn0-vPb4lCCkc72FQUrq8w. Accessed 11 Feb 2021.

Ogrysko, N. (2019, December 17). Agencies facing reorganization, relocation suffer major drops on best places to work rankings. *Federal News Network.* https://federalnewsnetwork.com/workforce/2019/12/agencies-facing-reorganization-relocation-suffer-major-drops-on-best-places-to-work-rankings/. Accessed 15 May 2020.

Olsen, J. P. (2006). Maybe it is time to rediscover bureaucracy. *Journal of Public Administration Research and Theory, 16*, 1–24.

Ornstein, N., & Mann, T. E. (2006). *The broken branch: How congress is failing America and how to get it back on track*. The Brookings Institution. https://www.brookings.edu/articles/the-broken-branch-how-congress-is-failing-america-and-how-to-get-it-back-on-track/. Accessed 14 May 2020.

Radin, B. A. (2012). *Federal management reform in a world of contradictions*. Georgetown University Press.

Rampell, C. (2019, August 8). Opinion: For Trump and his cronies, draining the swamp means ousting experts. *The Washington Post.* https://www.washingtonpost.com/opinions/trump-is-draining-the-swamp%2D%2Dof-needed-experts/2019/08/08/7ec457e4-ba12-11e9-a091-6a96e67d9cce_story.html. Accessed 21 Nov 2019.

Rana, A. (2016). Progressivism and the disenchanted constitution. In S. Skowronek, S. M. Engel, & B. Ackerman (Eds.), *The progressives' century: Political reform, constitutional government, and the modern American state* (pp. 41–64). Yale University Press.

Roberts, A. (2020). The third and fatal shock: How pandemic killed the millennial paradigm. *Public Administration Review, 80*(4), 603–609.

Roberts, A. S. (2019a). Bridging levels of public administration: How macro shapes meso and micro. *Administration & Society, 52*(4), 631–656.

Roberts, A. S. (2019b). *Strategies for governing: Reinventing public administration for a dangerous century*. Cornell University Press.

Robertson, B. D. (2010). Historical institutionalism, political development, and the study of American bureaucracy. In R. F. Durant (Ed.), *The Oxford handbook of American bureaucracy* (pp. 25–51). Oxford University Press.

Romzek, B. S. (2007). Business and government. In D. Rosenbloom & H. E. McCurdy (Eds.), *Revisiting Waldo's administrative state: Constancy and change in public administration* (pp. 151–178). Georgetown University Press.

Rosenbloom, D. (2015). The public context. In M. E. Guy & M. M. Rubin (Eds.), *Public administration evolving: From foundations to the future* (pp. 3–17). Routledge.

Rubin, I. S. (1998). *Class, tax, and power: Municipal budgeting in the United States*. Chatham House Publishers.

Ruckleshaus, W. D. (1995, November/December). Editorial: Stopping the pendulum. *Environmental Toxicology and Chemistry, 15*(3), 229–232.

Seidman, H. (1970). *Politics, position, and power: The dynamics of federal organization*. Oxford University Press.

Selin, J. (2020, June 8). How the Constitution's federalist framework is being tested by COVID-19. *The Brookings Institution.* https://www.brookings.edu/blog/fixgov/2020/06/08/how-the-constitutions-federalist-framework-is-being-tested-by-covid-19/. Accessed 16 June 2020.

Shane, P. M. (2009). *Madison's nightmare: How executive power threatens American democracy.* The University of Chicago Press.

Simon, H., Drucker, P., & Waldo, D. (1952). Development of theory of democratic administration: Replies and comments. *American Political Science Review, 46,* 494–503.

Skowronek, S. (1982). *Building a new American state: The expansion of national administrative capacities, 1877–1920.* Cambridge University Press.

Skowronek, S. (2009, October 29). The conservative insurgency and presidential power: A developmental perspective on the unitary executive. *Harvard Law Review, 122*(8), 2070.

Skowronek, S., Dearborn, J. A., & King, D. (2021). *Phantoms of a beleaguered republic. The deep state and the unitary executive.* Oxford University Press.

Stivers, C. (2008). *Governance in dark times: Practical philosophy for public service.* Georgetown University Press.

Tenpas, K. D. (2021, January). *Tracking turnover in the trump administration.* The Brookings Institution. https://www.brookings.edu/research/tracking-turnover-in-the-trump-administration/. Accessed 2 Mar 2021.

The Economist. (2020, December 29). *America's elephantine spending bills are becoming increasingly unreadable.* https://www.economist.com/graphic-detail/2020/12/29/americas-elephantine-spending-bills-are-becoming-increasingly-unreadable. Accessed 5 Feb 2021.

The President's Committee on Administrative Management (PCAM). (1937). *Report of the committee with studies of administrative management in the federal government.* United States Government Printing Office.

U.S. Government Accountability Office (GAO). (2018). *Trends affecting government and society: Strategic plan 2018–2023* (GAO-18-396SP). GAO. Accessed 12 Mar 2021.

U.S. Government Accountability Office (GAO)Government Accountability Office (GAO). (2021, March). *High-risk series: Dedicated leadership needed to address limited progress in most high-risk areas.* [PDF file]. https://www.gao.gov/assets/gao-21-119sp.pdf. Accessed 13 Nov 2020.

U.S. House of Representatives Committee on Government Reform and Oversight. (1995, December 21). Making government work: Fulfilling the mandate for change. House Report 104-435.

Van Riper, P. (1958). *History of the United States civil service.* Row, Peterson and Company.

Wagner, E. (2020, February 8). White House memo could end unionization at the Pentagon. *Government Executive.* https://www.govexec.com/management/2020/02/secret-white-house-memo-could-end-unionization-pentagon/162981/. Accessed 15 June 2020.

Wilson, W. (1887). The study of administration. *Political Science Quarterly, 2*(2), 197–222.

Young, R., & McMahon, S. (2020, February 4). Uncertainty, 'brain drain' plague USDA's economic research service after trump administration relocates agency, experts quit. *WBUR.* https://www.wbur.org/hereandnow/2020/02/04/usda-ers-kansas-city-trump-move. Accessed 7 Mar 2020.

Chapter 5
Traditional Approaches to Controlling Administrative Capacity

> *There is an idea, which is not without its advocates, that a vigorous executive is inconsistent with the genius of republican government. The enlightened well-wishers to this species of government must at least hope that the supposition is destitute of foundation; since they can never admit its truth, without at the same time admitting the condemnation of their own principles. Energy in the executive is a leading character in the definition of good government.*
>
> Hamilton (1788, p. 200)

> *The "spoils" system introduced by President Jackson, which is now stigmatized as the "American system," imperils not only the purity, economy, and efficiency of the administration of the government, but it destroys confidence in the method of popular government by party. It creates a mercenary political class, an oligarchy of stipendiaries, a bureaucracy of the worst kind.*
>
> Eaton (1880, p. v)

> *The president needs help.*
>
> President's Committee on Administrative Management (1937, p. 5)

5.1 Exploring the Formation of Administrative Capacity

The battle over the administrative state and its capacity is a political process grounded in history. To better understand the current debates surrounding the control and rebuilding of administrative capacity, this chapter examines the historical evolution of administrative capacity within the federal government's executive branch. We regard the past with a special emphasis on the development of tools that influenced and controlled federal administrative capacity. These tools emerged as ideas at different points in American history. Some of them were based on the US Constitution and emerged at the founding of the country. Others emerged later and were based on political developments and an emergent parastate of professional experts from

© Springer Nature Switzerland AG 2021
M. E. Joaquin, T. J. Greitens, *American Administrative Capacity*,
https://doi.org/10.1007/978-3-030-80564-7_5

academia, government, and various research centers in the field of public administration. We label those ideas as traditional approaches to controlling administrative
capacity. We explore those ideas in this chapter by considering how each idea
emerged over time and how they were originally linked to the Constitution and then
later supplemented with administrative theories regarding control and efficiency.
From the founding era's constitutional framework that structured debate about the
presidency and the executive branch to the formation of a modern administrative
state during the midpoint of the twentieth century, policymakers have consistently
tried to both control administrative capacity and seek ways to improve it to meet
evolving governance challenges. However, such goals of control and improvement
were not always aligned in ways that resulted in effective responses to governance
challenges.

Administrative capacity within the federal government's executive branch greatly
expanded from the founding era to the formation of the modern administrative state
and went through periods in which capacity was mapped out, built up, and then
consolidated. Yet, during that expansion, administrative capacity was also controlled in ways that reflected concerns regarding the power and appropriate role of
unelected administrators in a democracy. Such concerns linked back to a long-
standing concern from the founding of the federal government about executive
branch power, namely, how can executive branch departments build sufficient
administrative capacity so that an "energetic executive" branch could form and provide services necessary for meeting existing governance challenges. At the same
time, the development of such capacity had to occur in ways that protected the
public from the worst tendencies of executives and their departments (e.g., the
amassing of unchecked power and the suppression of public liberty and welfare that
could result from that unchecked power). Initially at least, solutions to such concerns followed a more traditional approach to controlling administrative capacity.

In the traditional approach to control, departments expanded internally, and
elected policymakers controlled those departments through the competing constitutional interests of the president and Congress. Over time, the competition for control
could be observed in debates about (1) the power of presidential appointments, (2)
how best to reform federal administration, and (3) how to effectively reorganize the
federal bureaucracy. For example, as the founding era commenced, administrative
capacity within the executive branch formed within a system defined by the
Constitution that allowed for the *building of administrative capacity in the executive
branch while controlling for the excesses of executive power that often accompanied such developments through history*. Via the Constitution, Congress controlled
most aspects of administrative capacity within the executive branch through its
explicit powers of legislation, appropriations, and confirmation. In everyday practice, this allowed Congress to control capacity via legislation that provided for
departmental creation, personnel, budget, appointed positions, and programmatic
responsibilities. Presidential powers in relation to capacity, in contrast, were more
minor and focused more on the day-to-day administration of agencies. Presidents
had the power to nominate the leaders of departments, control the daily operations
of those departments, and influence legislation, but Congress ultimately enjoyed

more power over administrative capacity. Such congressional control mitigated the propensity of executive actors to abuse their power while still allowing a president enough power to effectively implement departmental programs and services. In this way, the tensions inherent in wanting an "energetic executive" branch while also protecting the public from unchecked executive power could occur through the sharing of power between Congress and the president.

Alexander Hamilton first emphasized this tension between "executive effectiveness," on the one hand, and "protection from unchecked executive power," on the other. His writings on this tension and the concept of executive power more generally in *Federalist nos. 70–77* shaped the formation of administrative capacity within the federal government and subsequent attempts at controlling it by presidents and Congresses. Hamilton's writings (along with James Madison and John Jay) in *The Federalist Papers* showed the public why the newly written Constitution should be ratified as a system of government and specifically explained how power, especially executive power, could be checked through multiple branches of government. When supplemented with a variety of political and administrative developments in the years after the adoption of the Constitution, the tension between "executive effectiveness" and "protection from unchecked executive power" helps to explain the evolution of administrative capacity in the federal government and the initial attempts at controlling it through constitutional means.

5.2   The Early Context of Administrative Capacity in the United States

The early context of administrative capacity was shaped by past experiences living under a colonial system of government before the Revolutionary War. Under the system, most of the colonies had strong governors who were appointed by the King of Great Britain (Sabato, 1978). Their powers were usually broad and included appointing judges and other civil officials, commanding the colony's armed forces, leading law enforcement, issuing pardons and reprieves, calling and dissolving legislative sessions, and vetoing acts passed by the legislature (Greene, 1898). After rebelling against the colonial rule of Great Britain and forming a new national government where colonies transitioned to state governments, executive power was weakened in both state governments and the national government.

Legislatures had much to do with it. After the Revolutionary War ended colonial rule, it was common for many state governments to limit the power of their elected executive (i.e., the governor). Most state governments put strict limits in place regarding executive power, from terms of office that lasted only 1 year to prohibitions against serving multiple terms to the formation of executive councils that could constrain and even overrule a decision made by the governor (Dodd, 1908; Kallenbach, 1966; Thorpe, 1909). This led to a system of weak governors and weak executive systems in the state governments. Additionally, the national government in operation during this time, based on the Articles of Confederation, had no real executive authority at all. Instead, the national legislature controlled all aspects of government. This then led a national system of government that had no direction and could take no timely actions, even in the times of extreme crisis (Sanders, 1935; Thach, 1923).

Such ineffectiveness was by design. The early government under the Articles of Confederation reflected the founders' deep distrust of executive power, a sentiment shared by most of the public and their respective state governments. Some of that distrust was due to that generation's understanding of history. After all, most of the individuals involved in government during that time had a deep knowledge of the tragedies experienced by the ancient democracies as they descended into tyrannical regimes, usually directly led by a person of executive authority seeking more power (Richard, 2008). However, distrust of executive power also manifested from their immediate past. They had first-hand experiences on the nature of unconstrained executive power under King George III and the colonial governors.

5.2.1 Fundamental Tension of Administrative Capacity

Thus, the founders had direct experiences with a fundamental tension of administrative capacity in democracies. This tension included figuring out how a lack of strong executive power could impair the ability of government to solve problems and provide needed services, while the presence of strong executive power could harm individual freedom and compromise the fundamental tenets of democracy. Consequently, as they wrote the Constitution to form a new national government to replace the Articles of Confederation, the founders knew that executives needed enough power and support to effectively lead the nation and their executive departments. However, the founders also knew that executives had to be constrained by other forces. Otherwise, ancient history and immediate experience indicated that executive power tended to grow in ways that eroded democracy.

Reconciling this fundamental tension, the founders designed the Constitution to allow for a president with increased executive power, steadied and balanced by legislative and judicial powers and even by state governments, through a federalized system of government. Predominant in opposition to the president was the legislative branch's Congress. From a technical perspective, Congress had more powers in the Constitution that could be linked back to administrative capacity because their legislative prerogatives included the design and funding of any executive department, as well as the confirmation of appointees to departmental leadership positions. The president's powers, in regard to administrative capacity, were less explicit but included nominating appointees to departmental leadership positions and leading the various departments in the executive branch. Informal powers of lobbying and political persuasion were implicit in presidential powers but otherwise left unstated in the Constitution. The more instructive principles, in terms of administrative capacity, that explained the founder's thinking regarding the power of the executive and the executive's departments were contained in *The Federalist Papers*, especially *Federalist nos. 70–77*.

5.2.2   Tempering Executive Power with Responsibility

To persuade the public that the newly written Constitution provided for a more effective government, Alexander Hamilton, James Madison, and John Jay wrote a series of arguments in favor of it. In these discussions, the first sentiments regarding administrative capacity in the federal government's executive branch emerged. In *Federalist no. 70*, Hamilton described the ingredients necessary for an effective executive administration. While explicitly structured in terms of executive power and the Constitution's office of the presidency, these ingredients also had pertinence for the entire executive branch, including the departments working under the president in the implementation of public services and the law (Arnold, 2011). Hamilton wrote that:

> Energy in the executive is a leading character in the definition of good government. It is essential to the protection of the community against foreign attacks; it is not less essential to the steady administration of the laws; to the protection of property against those irregular and high-handed combinations which sometimes interrupt the ordinary course of justice; to the security of liberty against the enterprises and assaults of ambition, of faction, and of anarchy. (Hamilton, 1788, p. 201)

Upon stating this fundamental characteristic of executive administration, Hamilton then identified the ingredients of "energy in the executive" as unity, duration, adequate provision of support, and competent powers (Hamilton, 1788). Given the vibrant debates about a unitary executive system versus a plural executive system that occurred during the design of the Constitution, Hamilton then used the remainder of *Federalist no. 70* to discuss how a unitary executive bred unity and helped to ensure stability with other ingredients necessary for an effective executive in a democratic government:

> Taking it for granted, therefore, that all men of sense will agree in the necessity of an energetic Executive, it will only remain to inquire, what are the ingredients which constitute this energy? How far can they be combined with those other ingredients which constitute safety in the republican sense? And how far does this combination characterize the plan which has been reported by the convention? (Hamilton, 1788, p. 201)

And later on, he noted that:

> The ingredients which constitute safety in the republican sense are, first, a due dependence on the people, secondly, a due responsibility. (Hamilton, 1788, p. 202)

Thus, Hamilton showed how the ingredients for effective executive administration became tempered with notions of responsibility to the public to ensure that the

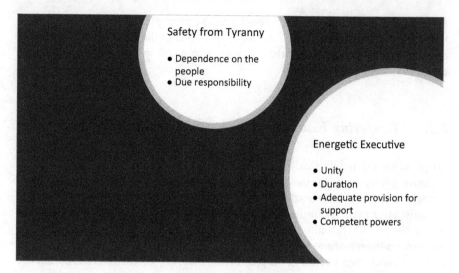

Fig. 5.1 Executive ingredients balanced in the federal system

power of executive administration did not overwhelm the processes of a democratic government. Followed by further discussions in *Federalist nos. 71–77* that explored the nature of executive power, how the Constitution limited excessive executive power, and how the executive served the public (Agranoff, 2011), the shaping of administrative capacity within the executive branch was clarified. That is, the effective executive was defined by a unity of command flowing from one executive (i.e., the president) who held office for a sufficient duration of time in order to execute the administration of government within the limitations of resources set by Congress, powers established through the Constitution, and responsibilities beholden to the public (see Fig. 5.1). In this sense, discussions on the "energetic executive" by the founders centered on the tension between ensuring that an effective executive administration could exist with the limits placed on that executive administration by the Constitution and the people.

From a theoretical perspective, Hamilton's ideals regarding the energetic executive also helped to explain the first notions of administrative capacity. To be effective in the federal government's system, the executive branch had to balance the power and skill of the executive with certain democratic values to keep executive power in check. Thus, executives and their federal departments needed to possess an administrative capacity powerful enough to implement services to the public while concurrently limited in terms of power to prevent a descent into executive-based tyranny. Congress, in turn, helped check executive power by ensuring support in terms of resources and more direct accountability back to the public.

5.3 Early Challenges of Administrative Capacity

After the federal government officially formed with the ratification of the US Constitution by the states, the complexities and challenges involved in actually operating federal departments emerged with significant implications for administrative capacity. First were concerns about personnel. While a healthy competition from a multitude of office-seekers existed for lower-level positions like clerks and collectors, higher-level positions often attracted little interest from the elites of society. Federal departments were new and untested, especially when compared to state governments that had longer traditions of service and a more elevated status among elites (White, 1948). Consequently, once he assumed the office as the first president, George Washington prioritized appointing people of prominence to higher-level positions in federal departments, especially former soldiers from the Revolutionary Army, to help improve the prestige of federal service to elites (White, 1948). Additionally, Washington filled at least some positions with Federalist supporters and tried to equalize such appointments by geographic location (Van Riper, 1958). As such, political priorities influenced the personnel development of federal agencies, and their requisite administrative capacities, from the start. But overall, Washington is best remembered for using his "rules of fitness" to try and pick people with the best character for the numerous positions emerging in federal administration (Van Riper, 1958).

Second, institutional tensions between Congress and the president emerged over the operation of federal departments within the president's cabinet. These tensions were written into the Constitution in a variety of clauses concerning appointments and the respective powers of the legislative and executive branches. Specifically, in Article II, Section 2, the Constitution gave the president the power to appoint a variety of ambassadorships, judges, and cabinet positions with the advice and consent of the Senate. Congress was allowed to vest the appointment of more inferior positions within the executive branch to the president or cabinet secretaries. However, the president could fill any such vacancy for a limited time when the Senate was in recess. Left explicitly unsaid in the Constitution was whether the president could unilaterally remove any appointed positions within the executive branch.

Clarity regarding the removal power emerged in 1789 when Congress gave the power to the president. Introduced by James Madison in the House of Representatives, this bill helped to enshrine in law the powers of the presidency over executive branch agencies and the nascent federal bureaucracy. Debates on the bill were intense, lasted close to 2 months, and reinvigorated many legislators' concerns about the power of the president. The bill ultimately passed the Senate with a tie-breaking vote from Vice President John Adams (Van Riper, 1958). But the debate regarding the removal power was far from over with Congress intermittently putting restrictions on the executive's removal power throughout the 1800s. Additionally, the removal power became infinitely more complex over time as Congress established more independent style government organizations that were insulated from politics in the late 1800s and 1900s.

The Constitution also created additional tension between Congress and the president regarding the administration of agencies. In Article I, Section 6, the Constitution prohibited members of Congress from holding dual appointments in government, including executive branch agencies. As stated in the Constitution:

> No Senator or Representative shall, during the time for which he was elected, be appointed to any civil office under the authority of the United States, which shall have been created, or the emoluments whereof shall have been increased during such time; and no person holding any office under the United States, shall be a member of either house during his continuance in office.

Often overlooked in discussions about the Constitution, this clause had significant impacts for administrative capacity in that it prevented legislators from also being the chief executives of departments and agencies (as seen in many European systems of government today). When combined with the president's appointment power guaranteed by the Constitution and removal power granted by statute in 1789, this clause helped to ensure that the president would ultimately have much authority in shaping the leadership of federal departments. However, Congress still had a constitutional role in managing the capacity of federal departments in terms of resources and mandates. Departmental resources were a significant problem at the beginning. Departmental expenditures rose quickly and Congress wanted to limit them. Additionally, under the direction of early presidents like Washington, the heads of departments were often given broad discretion on their operations. This helped to create a system whereby departments and the cabinet secretaries that led them directly lobbied Congress for additional resources, often with no direction from the president (White, 1948).

Lastly and perhaps most importantly in terms of the challenges of administration was the emergence of partisan politics. During the 1790s, the interests of Federalists favoring a more centralized role for the federal government and the interests of Republicans (as they were then known) wanting a more decentralized role for the federal government formed two divergent political factions. As the Federalist dominated administrations of George Washington and John Adams yielded to the Republican administrations of Thomas Jefferson, James Madison, and James Monroe, the specter of partisan politics on federal departments became more of a concern and gradually influenced administrative capacity.

For example, during Washington's tenure as president, the personnel in many positions within departments, especially lower-level personnel, rarely changed. While the politically appointed cabinet leaders of departments regularly experienced turnover, most other personnel within departments did not. When turnover in these positions occurred, it was usually due to mortality or personal resignation. This changed with the first Republican president, Thomas Jefferson. Wishing to better balance the Federalists in administration with Republicans, Jefferson did take steps to expel some Federalists from departments who publicly criticized the politics of his administration (White, 1948). But overall, such severe applications of the presidential removal power for political reasons were not widespread, at least for departmental personnel. Ultimately, Jefferson did not institute a complete transformation of the growing federal bureaucracy which primarily consisted of Federalist sympathizers. Instead, he just waited for Federalist personnel to resign or die and then replaced those individuals with personnel more aligned with Republican politics. While Jefferson did take steps to expel some Federalists from departments who publicly criticized the politics of his administration, such severe applications of the presidential removal power for political reasons were not widespread, at least for departmental personnel. Instead, Jefferson often sought to temper political demands for removal with more of an emphasis on other areas that would better justify removal. For example, the values of honesty, competence, and loyalty to the Constitution were used in many cases to justify removal, especially in the early years of the Jefferson administration (White, 1948).

Partisan politics was becoming important, but at least through the beginning of the 1800s, it was not used to dramatically transform the administration of departments after a presidential election. Instead, a perspective emerged that presidents could use their appointment powers to satisfy political demands, especially with their appointment of departmental leaders in the cabinet, but the active removal of lower level and mid-level departmental personnel for purely political reasons was usually avoided (White, 1951). Thus, a variety of departmental personnel with Federalist leanings who owed their appointment to Federalist policymakers remained in their positions throughout Jefferson's presidency. Sentiments like this continued into the successive administrations of James Madison, James Monroe, and John Quincy. Over time and into the 1810s and 1820s, this essentially formed a system of administration where presidents and their cabinet-level secretaries changed, but most of other personnel in departments remained the same.

New developments in politics and administration also occurred that lessened the influence of partisan politics on administration. For example, the Army and the Navy adopted formal examinations for professional personnel in 1814, presidents like John Quincy Adams began to abandon party affiliation in their appointment and reappointment of departmental personnel, and informal administrative norms about nepotism prohibitions, veteran's preferences, and geographic equality in administrative appointments gradually developed (White, 1951). In a real sense, the administration of departments began to disassociate itself from politics and focus on other professional values that could enhance capacity. Such a transformation in thought was directly influenced by the changing nature of partisan politics in the 1810s. With the end of the War of 1812, an "era of good feelings" swept through the nation and dissolved many of the long-standing partisan tensions between Federalists and Republicans. The Federalist Party itself even ceased to be a major political entity after 1816 with most of its members joining the Jeffersonian Republican Party.

Enlarged with new members, the Republican Party developed two different axes of support by the 1820s. One axis favored the tendencies of promoting a more centralized federal government, while the other axis wanted a more decentralized federal government. The axes split by the middle of the 1820s with a Whig Party that wanted a more centralized role for the federal government and a Democratic Party that favored decentralization. Other issues also defined each party's position, especially national economic development policies. But for administration and administrative capacity, the centralized/decentralized debate that had long plagued the old Federalists and Jeffersonian Republicans of the late 1790s reemerged and began to plague the newer Whigs and Democrats. Except this time, the ultimate impact of this political debate would have dramatic consequences on administrative capacity.

5.4   Politicized Administrative Capacity

The election of Andrew Jackson as president in 1828 forever changed administrative capacity within federal departments. It was at this juncture where the seeds of modern administrative contentions can be found. With Jackson's rise, the power of political parties grew, and they began to adopt a number of stances on governmental issues that previously were not discussed in explicit political terms. One of those issues was the problem of federal administration, specifically the personnel serving in federal administrative positions. According to Jackson and his Democratic Party, federal agencies had two major problems in terms of capacity: (1) they no longer served democratic ends, and (2) they were often incompetent (White, 1956). Such problems were specified by Jackson in his inaugural address:

> The recent demonstration of public sentiment inscribes on the list of executive duties, in characters too legible to be overlooked, the task of reform, which will require particularly the correction of those abuses that have brought the patronage of the federal government into conflict with the freedom of elections, and the counteraction of those causes which have disturbed the rightful course of appointment and have placed or continued power in unfaithful or incompetent hands.

> In the performance of a task thus generally delineated I shall endeavor to select men who diligence and talents will insure in their respective stations able and faithful cooperation, depending for the advancement of the public service more on the integrity and zeal of the public officers than on their numbers. (Richardson, 1905, p. 438)

Thus, the Jackson administration made reform of federal administration a central focus of their agenda. Jackson and the Democratic Party's idea of administrative reform was to make federal administration better through more direct political control by the president. Using the removal power given to the president by Congress decades before, Jackson implemented a "spoils system" where a newly elected president could replace existing personnel in executive departments with their own political supporters. Such replacements would make federal administration more representative of the people and keep administrators accountable to the public. Presumably, this would help make administration better and keep the tenets of "energetic executive" balanced against the forces of tyranny, just as Alexander Hamilton originally suggested in *The Federalist Papers*.

Such a change in the use of the removal power by the president was significant. While previous presidents had used the removal power and replaced some administrative positions with sympathetic political supporters, most notably Jefferson at the beginning of his presidency, its overall use and ultimate effect were minor in the presidencies before Jackson. In contrast, Jackson implemented a dramatic increase in the use of the removal power as a way to facilitate administrative transformation. While this change increased presidential control of administration, its effect on administrative capacity was negative.

For example, while federal departments in the 1820s did have problems, most famously with some federal administrators viewing their position as a type of aristocratic birthright (White, 1951), the overall performance of federal administration was often satisfactory. Administrative records from the time, while limited, indicate that common administrative positions such as clerks and accounting officers usually performed their tasks effectively and even adhered to an informal code of conduct with elements of professionalism (White, 1956). Other federal positions like postmasters and customs collectors were more prone to political and financial corruption, but overall, the capacity of federal administration seemed to meet the demands placed on it by a growing nation. That changed somewhat after the introduction of the spoils system by Jackson.

Primarily designed as a way to ensure that Jackson's notion of "common men" could participate in administration, the spoils system eventually produced a system of federal administration that accelerated corruption and routinely distracted presidents after Jackson (White, 1956). Political supporters were now rewarded with administrative positions with minimal consideration of their competence or abilities. However, during Jackson's presidency, the spoils system did not lead to a wholesale replacement of existing administrators with Jackson's political supporters. In total, approximately 25 percent of the federal workforce was replaced during the entirety of the Jackson presidency with many personnel replaced due to poor performance or through voluntary reasons and approximately 10 percent due to partisan politics (Eriksson, 1927; Maranto, 1998). While higher than previous presidents, these numbers show the limited scope of the spoils system on federal administration, at least initially. Subsequent presidents would keep on expanding the use of the spoils system in the years and decades following Jackson. This in turn led to a number of significant effects on administrative capacity in the following decades.

First, federal administration began to informally cleave into a dual system of administrative positions with one set of positions subjected to the spoils system and one set of positions left untouched by the spoils system. No matter which president implemented the spoils system, it usually focused on those upper-level administrative positions that were always considered a little more political than other administrative positions (Van Riper, 1958). For example, postmasters, customs collectors, and federal attorneys were positions often reserved for political supporters in the spoils system. In contrast, lower-level administrative positions, such as clerks, accounting personnel, and scientific officials, were usually left untouched by the spoils system (White, 1956).

Second, that cleavage eventually reinforced expectations of professionalism and expertise. With no qualifications necessary, positions considered a part of the spoils system were typically staffed by individuals with limited administrative abilities and a general ignorance of the administrative tasks that needed to be completed. Expertise and competence came to be associated with those lower-level positions that were not part of the spoils system, especially clerks, accountants, and staff in scientific positions (Van Riper, 1958). Such expertise and competence often resulted in those individuals directly lobbying Congress for more authority over administration and more protection from unqualified departmental leaders associated with the spoils system. This helped to lead Congress to the sanctioning of more independent bureaus and commissions, some within existing departments, so that the real work of administration could be completed without undue political influence from the president and the president's appointees. Caring about the services they provided, implementing a quasi-professional approach to administration, and helping to activate Congress in discussions on administrative capacity, these administrators and their newly formed bureaus and commissions helped sustain administrative capacity during the era of the spoils system.

Lastly and perhaps most significantly, the spoils system did eventually lead to a more corrupt state of federal administration, especially in the decades after Jackson. Later presidents from both political parties, especially during the 1840s and 1850s, expanded the use of the spoils system by increasing the number of administrative positions awarded to political supporters (White, 1956). Many of these positions were located outside of Washington, DC, and included positions that could both influence and be influenced by the specific politics within a state (White, 1956). With more positions filled by individuals with limited administrative qualifications and with more of those positions having direct linkages to the realities of state politics in individual states, administrative corruption consistently increased from the 1830s to the 1880s.

5.5 Professionalized Administrative Capacity

As the "spoils system" changed the nature of bureaucracy throughout the 1800s, a countervailing force emerged from within bureaucracy itself to ensure that administrative capacity survived and continued to increase. Another tectonic shift – the Progressive movement – would alter the path of capacity and whose echoes would be heard clashing with that of Jacksonian administration ideas in the future eras. Tiring of the partisan games and the havoc they were starting to create within many federal departments, some administrators began to lobby Congress for the creation of specific bureaus and commissions located within federal departments that could implement specific administrative services with minimal interference from the partisan politics of the presidency. Such bureaus and commissions performed services firmly in the middle-tier range of bureaucracy and became noted for their professionalization and effectiveness (White, 1956). These entities, driven by administrators and to a certain extent the legislators that supported them, allowed administrative capacity to survive the more negative effects of the spoils system. Along with congressional acts like the "Simple Clerical Classification Acts" of the 1850s (Van Riper, 1958), they provided the blueprint for the most extensive idea influencing administrative capacity since the spoils system: a commitment to professional administration.

Professional administration coalesced as a political force in reaction to the numerous political and administration scandals of the Johnson and Grant presidencies in the 1860s and 1870s, as well as rampant corruption in most state and local governments. Most notable at the federal level was the Credit Mobilier scandal which essentially involved bribery of federal officials in the passage of legislation benefiting the Union Pacific railroad company and the use of shell companies by Union Pacific to facilitate more profit from government contracts in the construction of rail lines from Missouri to California (Crawford, 1880). Although most aspects of the scandal occurred in the 1860s in the Johnson administration, the scandal became a media sensation in the mid-1870s and forever became linked to the Grant administration due to the fact that members of Grant's administration were heavily involved in it. The Grant administration had its own share of responsibility in the administrative scandals of the time. Specifically, the Grant administration had direct involvement in a number of other scandals involving access to the nation's gold supply, tax collection improprieties, international fraud committed in England and Brazil by official governmental staff, and the apparent stealing of federal tax revenues associated with distilled whiskey by a number of staff in the Treasury Department and the White House (Van Riper, 1958).

By the mid-1870s, these scandals had caused great concern from the public on the status of governmental administration in a society that was quickly urbanizing due to the industrial revolution. Consequently, administrative reform became a policy concern, and to help implement it, policymakers looked at previous attempts of administrative reforms occurring in the previous decade.

Initial reforms aiming for a more professional administration originated in Congress after the Civil War and initially focused on ways to limit the appointment powers of the president (Van Riper, 1958). Such reforms were debated by Congress in the decade before the Civil War but never implemented as law. Instead, after the Civil War, Congress passed the Tenure of Office Act of 1867. That Act limited the removal power of the president and specifically required presidents to obtain Senate approval for removing federal administrators that were confirmed by the Senate. While the Tenure of Office Act led to the impeachment, but not conviction, of President Andrew Johnson for his attempts to remove the Secretary of War without Senate approval, its actual impact on administrative capacity was quite limited. Most federal administrative positions were not subjected to it, and by 1869, Congress passed amendments to the Act that significantly narrowed its scope (Van Riper, 1958). However, in a larger sense, the Act signaled a new era of administrative reform where Congress began to examine a number of ways to make administration less beholden to the politics of the presidency. These efforts helped to reassert congressional control over administration and began in a significant way in the House of Representatives with the work of Representative Thomas Allen Jenckes from Rhode Island.

By the late 1860s, Representative Jenckes became concerned with the sheer increase in patronage-based positions within federal administration as well as its power over policymaking. As chair of Congress' Joint Select Committee on Retrenchment, Jenckes helped publicize the idea of administrative reforms that had recently occurred in Britain to Congress with a written report. The British reforms emphasized the utility of professionalized administration based on merit rather than politicized administration based on patronage (U.S. House, 1868). While Jenckes' report had no real impact on reform within Congress at the time, it did capture the attention of both the media and the public. As a result, from that time onward, administrative reform became of interest to both the Democratic Party and the Republican Party. Reflecting some of this interest, the first congressional reform that made it to statute was a minor provision in an 1871 Act that allowed the president to develop rules regarding federal administration that would promote ideals of efficiency. As noted in the Act's Section 9:

> That the President of the United States be, and he is hereby, authorized to prescribe such rules and regulations for the admission of persons into the civil service of the United States as will best promote the efficiency thereof, and ascertain the fitness of each candidate in respect to age, health, character, knowledge, and ability for the branch of service into which he seeks to enter; and for this purpose the president is authorized to employ suitable persons to conduct said inquiries, to prescribe their duties, and to establish regulations for the conduct of persons who may receive appointments in the civil service. (Sundry Civil Expenses Appropriations Action, 1871)

Ulysses Grant, who was president in 1871, had already supported ideals of administrative reform. And with this Act, he now had the means to implement it. The fact that he actually did this, given the number of patronage linked scandals that plagued his administration, was somewhat surprising at the time (and remains so to this day). Grant appointed an advisory commission, often called the Grant Commission but more accurately named the Advisory Board of the Civil Service, of seven individuals to design the rules of administrative reform that could generate the efficiency, and ultimately nonpartisan ideals, apparent in the 1871 Act. With minor funding from Congress, the commission used the British Civil Service as a guide, and informed by reformers like George William Curtis, who also served on the commission, the group of seven individuals eventually wrote a series of recommendations for administrative procedures that could guide federal administration away from patronage and more toward efficiency (Murphy, 1942). These recommendations included reforms like new terminology that allowed positions to be classified by duties performed with specific positional grades for promotion, a merit-based system of examination for entry-level positions as well as promotions within grade, and a board of examiners within federal administration that would implement the examination process.

However, the commission did not last. By 1873, Congress withdrew its small amount of funding needed for the commission to keep meeting. Additionally, the commission did not really have a significant impact on federal administration. Before they lost funding, the commission's new nonpartisan rules were applied to notorious bastions of partisan-based corruption, such as the New York post office and the New York custom house, but ultimately became inconsequential due to partisan lobbying (Van Riper, 1958). Indeed, Grant himself abandoned the cause of the commission due to disappointment over the loss of congressional funds, but also due to the intense lobbying against the commission by his political supporters who were heavily invested in patronage. By 1875, Grant even revoked the rules issued by the commission and stopped all notions of competitive examination into administration (Van Riper, 1958). Nonetheless, the concern over patronage continued even after the commission was abandoned. President Rutherford B. Hays, who became president after Grant in a contested election, showed continued interest in administrative reforms. Further, in 1877, Hayes commissioned a report on administrative reforms, commonly referred to as the Eaton report, and submitted the report to Congress. The Eaton report showcased the possibilities of administrative reforms that embraced a more professionalized view of administration and even suggested that patronage-based administration could be unconstitutional given the Constitution's barring of acts of nobility and the similarities between patronage-based administration in the United States and nobility in Europe (Eaton, 1880).

However, the real turning point for administrative reform came with the assassination of the president after Hays, President James Garfield, in 1881. Garfield was assassinated on just the 90th day of his administration by Charles Guiteau. Guiteau, who seemingly had a troubled history with psychological problems, inaccurately viewed his political support of Garfield as essential to Garfield's winning of the presidency in 1880. Demanding a diplomatic position in payment for his political support, Guiteau then shot Garfield when no position was awarded. Garfield died 79 days after the shooting and directly led to increasing calls to reform federal administration, especially the spoils system.

Eventually, the Pendleton Civil Service Reform Act of 1883 was passed. This Act replicated much of the work of the Advisory Board of the Civil Service a decade before and focused on ways to ensure a merit-based, professional, public service. Old ideas from the advisory board like an objective classification system and merit-based exams were included in the Pendleton Act along with a new empowered non-partisan entity, the US Civil Service Commission. As expressed in the Act, the Civil Service Commission had responsibilities for promulgating rules necessary for the civil service and investigating occurrences when they were not followed, implementing competitive exams as a mechanism of the merit-based selection of civil service employees, and communicating reports annually to the president and Congress that explained the commission's activities (Civil Service Act, 1883).

The commission itself was led by three commissioners appointed by the president with no more than two of the commissioners being from the same political party. The Act also mandated just around 10% of the current federal workforce to be classified into the civil service, and these were mainly clerks (Van Riper, 1958). The rest of the federal workforce was identified as "unclassified." It then permitted the president to classify more positions into the federal civil service over time via executive orders. The only positions where this could not occur was laborers and positions requiring Senate consent (Van Riper, 1958). While initially only applied to a small number of federal positions, merit-based appointments continued to expand in scope into the twentieth century.

The 1883 Act and the formation of a professionalized civil service within federal administration increased administrative capacity in two significant ways. First, professional administration became a reality that continued to grow in scope into the twentieth century. With merit as the central focus of administration, the sheer ability of federal administrators to efficiently and effectively complete their daily work tasks increased. Second, the Act incentivized the president to categorize positions into the civil service during their tenure in office. Thus, presidents were able to essentially reward supporters with patronage-based positions in the "unclassified" federal workforce and then ensure their positions into the future by classifying them as part of the civil service. As these supporters retired or left federal administration, such presidential behaviors ensured that a growing number of administrative positions would be part of the merit-based civil service over time. This greatly increased presidential influence over federal administration and placed Congress into more of an oversight role. That oversight role would be informed with a variety of administrative studies emphasizing efficiency. These studies, and their influence over both the president and Congress, would ensure that business-based ideals of efficiency were used within federal administration.

5.6 Congressional Attention to Efficient Administrative Capacity

After the emergence of the professionalized civil service at the federal level with the Pendleton Act, policymakers continued their efforts to ensure administrative capacity by focusing on efficiency. These efforts were showcased through a variety of congressional commissions in the late 1800s. Reflecting the momentum of the Progressive movement, which was at its highest point during this time, these commissions analyzed how to make agencies more efficient and perhaps more importantly in terms of administrative capacity how to ensure that quality public services continued to be delivered to the public. Even more than that, many of these commissions responded to a changing external environment for federal agencies as private businesses grew in power, the nation added more population and public services, and a mass media emerged willing to sensationalize accounts of administrative failings.

5.6.1 Early Ideas in Performance Management

The first of these efforts was in 1887 with a Senate established committee to examine how best to reform administration in federal agencies to meet these changes. Named after Senator Francis Cockrell, a Democrat from Missouri who first introduced a resolution to support such efforts, the Cockrell Committee primarily focused on why many federal agencies experienced delays in implementing daily services, especially regarding land transactions in the General Land Office and the payment of pensions and other expenses in the Treasury Department (Kraines, 1951).

To investigate these views and the origins of the delays, the Cockrell Committee went to every department, and the bureaus and divisions within each department, to request data on how these organizational units processed their daily service transactions. Additionally, the committee requested from these units information such as their organizational design, annual number of transactions, average number of employees, and performance of each employee in terms of number and quality of transactions (Kraines, 1951). Through their investigation, the committee determined that many federal departments, along with their component bureaus and divisions, were bogged down by excessive and duplicative clerical routines that prevented the processing of daily transactions that led to effective service delivery. This was especially true for financial routines and record-keeping (U.S. Senate, 1888).

The committee eventually concluded that most of the delays investigated could be linked to outdated management practices (or in the vernacular of the day, outdated business practices) and the performance of unneeded, useless, and often duplicative work (Weber, 1919). Of particular importance to the committee was the finding that many departments focused their efforts on copying records, leading to an overwhelming glut of records in most departments (U.S. Senate, 1888). Such a focus on duplicating records then led to delays in processing the daily transactions needed to implement services. To help resolve this problem, the committee recommended a process for the disposing of records. And this recommendation was eventually passed by the Congress.

While best remembered today as a committee focused on record keeping that had few tangible outcomes on improving administration, the Cockrell Committee is noteworthy in terms of administrative capacity for a variety of reasons. First, the committee established the concept that Congress had a role to play in the investigation into the performance of public agencies and the capacity of departments to fulfill their service demands. This was a relatively new concept in terms of administrative accountability and suggested that the work of departments and their ability to implement services in the expanded nation were becoming more important.

Second, the committee performed administrative analyses that had direct implications for capacity. For example, as the committee's investigation into delays progressed, many letters were written directly to the committee from bureaucrats in the departments trying to explain why their departments could not process transactions in a timely manner. Most of these letters blamed the delays on either a lack of adequate personnel or a lack of adequate compensation, such as a pension, for employees. However, the committee disagreed with such notions and suggested that the daily work hours of the bureaucrat be increased to 8 hours at no increase in salary, that employees performing at a suboptimal level be terminated, and that bureaucrats be prevented from engaging in proxy work, whereby the bureaucrat hired an outsider to perform their work, often at a lower wage than was paid to the bureaucrat (Kraines, 1951). Perhaps more interestingly in terms of administrative reforms, the committee recommended that departments coordinate their efforts with other departments by holding interdepartmental exchanges to develop new ideas and new processes that could eliminate duplicative work and improve service delivery to the public (U.S. Senate, 1888). Additional forward thinking ideas from the Cockrell

Committee suggested that each department should develop their own internal commission that would continually focus on ways to improve work processes and engage in administrative reform, although the committee only formally requested that the departments of Treasury and War implement such a commission (U.S. Senate, 1888).

Third, the committee's implicit values of efficiency and economy, modeled on private sector businesses, started a process that firmly linked administration and administrative capacity issues in the public sector to private sector ideals. Or as shown by the committee's conclusions:

> The business of the departments should be conducted in the same prudent, careful, and economical manner in which the business people of this country conduct their personal business affairs. In civil life persons are employed and paid to perform services, and are not retained or placed upon a retired list or allowed a pension when they are no longer, for any cause, able to perform the services for which they are to be paid. The same rule should be enforced in the departments, and if enforced, there might not be such accumulations of undisposed of business and so much delay in its transaction. (Kraines, 1951, p. 605)

5.6.2 Systematic Analysis of Capacity

Left unstated in such conclusions was how administration arrived at this point to begin with. When examined from today's perspective, the growth of duplicative efforts, the prevalence of suboptimally performing employees, and massive delays in processing transactions seem like a natural outcome of an administrative system that was only starting to get out from under the politics of the spoils system established some 60 years before the Jackson administration.

To further examine how a professional system of administration could be implemented, the Dockery-Cockrell Commission was formed by Congress in 1893. The Dockery-Cockrell Commission, officially named the "Joint Commission to Inquire into the Status of the Laws Organizing the Executive Departments," continued and expanded upon the work of the Cockrell Committee from the decade before. In many ways, it was a more systematic analysis of administration in executive departments and made more substantial recommendations into administrative processes that were later passed as statue in the Dockery Act of 1894. Such outcomes were more substantial than that of the Cockrell Committee.

Of particular interest for discussions on administrative capacity was the Dockery-Cockrell Commission's decision to analyze every department and independent bureau and commission in the executive branch. Through such an analysis, tailored recommendations could be provided to each organizational entity that would help solve their specific challenges and dysfunctions discovered by the commission. The most significant findings were linked to the Treasury Department. Building on the latest developments from the private sector, the commission recommended that new accounting and auditing procedures be used to ensure that financial transactions remained efficient and effective (Kraines, 1954). This was the first time that researched financial management principles were implemented in executive agencies. Additionally, the commission made noteworthy recommendations that eliminated numerous clerks in most departments who performed duplicative functions (Kraines, 1954). These recommendations later were passed into the Dockery Act of 1894.

Overall, the work of the Dockery-Cockrell Commission revealed the continued power of Congress over federal administration.   While presidents controlled many aspects of federal administration, ultimate accountability rested with Congress. Indeed, Congress had the power to investigate federal administration within the executive branch and reorganize administration based on the findings of such investigations. This helped to ensure that federal administrative capacity remained current with the times and the evolving practices of administration.

5.7   Presidential Attention to Efficient Administrative Capacity

Further analyses of federal administration occurred in subsequent years, primarily led by President Theodore Roosevelt who assumed the presidency in 1901. However, Roosevelt's investigations into federal administration were not sanctioned by Congress. From 1905 until the end of his presidency in 1909, Roosevelt used a series of six commissions to explore ways to improve federal administration. These commissions consisted of federal administrators working voluntarily in interdepartmental groups via endorsement of the president and signaled a shift toward more presidential activity in administrative reforms. The first commission explored how scientific work could be made more efficient in federal administration and made recommendations on the consolidation of existing administrative groups performing such work into one department (Kraines, 1970). Congress ignored those recommendations. Undaunted, Roosevelt formed a second commission, commonly known as the Keep Commission after its chairperson Charles Keep, assistant secretary of the Treasury, which would ultimately have more long-lasting effects on administrative capacity. Later commissions used by Roosevelt (i.e., the third through sixth commissions) focused on specific policy issues ranging from conservation to public lands and waters.

5.7.1   Capacity Building in Management, Engagement, and Administrative Leadership

The Keep Commission focused their efforts on improving federal administration and, by extension, federal administrative capacity. Urged on by Roosevelt who had a history of leading anti-corruption efforts throughout his career, the commission investigated a variety of current scandals plaguing federal administration, from improper contracting in the Government Publishing Office to manipulating the price of agricultural commodities in the Department of Agriculture (Kraines, 1970). The commission reports on such scandals led to the firing of federal administrators involved in the corrupt practices. Additionally and perhaps even more importantly in terms of administrative capacity, the commission used a series of questionnaires to explore and analyze administrative inefficiencies. While both the Cockrell Committee of 1887 and the Dockery-Cockrell Commission of 1893 had used some types of questionnaires in their exploration of administrative inefficiencies, the Keep Commission's use of questionnaires was more extensive and had greater implications for administrative capacity. As part of their analytical efforts, the Keep Commission distributed a questionnaire to all federal agencies. The questionnaire was extensive, with 107 questions focused on administrative areas like personnel, purchasing, accounting, filing, and organizational management, and it supplemented ongoing investigations by individual commission members on the administrative affairs of departments (Kraines, 1970).

Overall, the Keep Commission made a number of significant recommendations. These recommendations, some of which took decades to achieve, eventually led to the enhancement of administrative capacity within departments. First, the commission recommended the use of advisory committees as a way for agencies to promote interdepartmental cooperation. Primarily envisioned as a way to improve coordination and reduce duplication across departments, advisory committees were adopted by Roosevelt via executive order but de-emphasized in the succeeding presidency of Taft (Kraines, 1970).

Second, the commission made a number of recommendations on personnel management and the uniform classification of positions. These recommendations urged departments to move away from department-specific classification processes and toward a more comprehensive and more uniform system that could be applied within the entirety of federal administration (Kraines, 1970). Such a revision was desperately needed. Administrative clerical positions were still classified according to plans passed by Congress in 1853 and 1854. Such classifications were outdated by the early 1900s and no longer reflected the administrative realities and commensurate salaries needed in these positions.

Third, the commission recommended administrative engagement with the public. The commission wanted to record federal administrative acts like executive orders, contracts, civil service exam notices, and other significant administrative actions in a centralized publication (Kraines, 1970). This would help keep the public informed on all administrative actions and presumably keep federal administration accountable in their actions to the public. While recommended by the commission, this was not implemented by the federal government until 1935 with *The Federal Register* and the beginnings of the modern administrative state.

Lastly, the Keep Commission considered ways to directly enhance administrative capacity. For example, the commission considered a new class of executive assistants within each department and agency that would analyze administrative processes and offer ways to continually improve on them (Kraines, 1970). While never formalized as an official recommendation, this idea served as an important element in the formation of Bureau of Efficiency from its establishment in 1913 until its end in 1933, the Bureau of the Budget (today's Office of Management and Budget (OMB)) formed in 1921, and even a number of future administrative changes made by future presidential commission, the Hoover Commission, in 1947.

Yet, the Keep Commission did not directly lead to a comprehensive reorganization of federal administration. Many of the recommendations were either never adopted or adopted only temporarily. In many ways, the real impact of the Keep Commission was more implicit in that it signaled to Congress that administrative issues were becoming more of a concern of the president rather than Congress. Congress viewed the Keep Commission as a threat to their power over federal administration and never even formally acknowledged the Commission's work during Roosevelt's presidency. Indeed, in 1909, Congress even explicitly prohibited the use of federal monies by any commission, council, board, or similar entity in any analysis of administration unless authorized by Congress (Hobbs, 1953). When Congress eventually accepted the significance of the Keep Commission's work years later, the power of the presidency over federal administration was all but ensured. This was confirmed in the next presidential exploration on administrative reform, the Commission on Economy and Efficiency.

5.7.2   Solidifying Executive-Oriented Capacity in Theory and Practice

William Howard Taft, Roosevelt's presidential successor, endorsed the Commission on Economy and Efficiency. However, unlike Roosevelt, Taft sought congressional support and endorsement for the establishment of the commission. Part of this stemmed from the new law Congress had recently passed that prohibited the use of federal funds in such reform-minded commissions without authorization from Congress. But part of this also stemmed from politics. While garnering media attention and authoring a number of administrative reform recommendations that would have influence in the decades to come, the immediate impact of Roosevelt's Keep Commission was actually quite limited. As a result, Taft involved Congress in the creation and operation of this new commission. Congress responded with an appropriation for administrative inquiry in 1910.

With funding secured, the commission's work commenced in three distinct phases: an initial investigation phase lasting from July to September of 1910, an investigatory phase lasting from September 1910 to March 1911, and a commission phase lasting from March 1911 until the end of the commission at the conclusion of the 1913 fiscal year (Glenn, 1958). In the initial investigation phase, Taft empowered his secretary, Charles Norton, to lead all initial investigations. Norton then implemented an immediate survey of administrative conditions throughout the federal government and also began to contact experts in the private sector and government to help shape the investigation. Through this work, Frederick Cleveland became known and was eventually asked to lead the commission's investigations. Working directly with President Taft and using his past work on efficient administration in the New York Bureau of Municipal Research as a guide, Cleveland then directed each department to form investigatory committees and subcommittees that would conduct administrative research within each department. Cleveland worked to shape the objective collection and analysis of data in these investigations. In the final commission phase, the actual Commission on Economy and Efficiency was formed. The commission was chaired by Cleveland and included members such as Frank Goodnow and William Willoughby who were beginning to be influential within the public administration community.

Overall, the commission had two primary charges. First, and perhaps most famously, the commission focused on reforms to the federal budgeting process. Second and echoing the earlier Keep Commission, the Commission on Economy and Efficiency studied ways to make federal administration more efficient. Most of the commission's efforts focused on budgetary reform and eventually led to the formal executive-based budgeting process adopted by Congress in 1921. But the commission's work on reforms for a more efficient federal administration were also noteworthy in terms of administrative capacity.

For example, the commission heavily involved professionals from the nascent field of public administration. Frederick Cleveland, one of the significant early scholars embraced by the discipline, helped create and direct the highly influential New York Bureau of Municipal Research and led the initial investigations of the commission. Other scholars directly involved in the commission were Frank Goodnow and William Willoughby, both of whom produced scholarship that influenced the discipline of public administration in significant ways. Thus, the commission embraced the early work of public administration scholarship, as the field of public administration continued to grow and mature. Notions of administrative reform, efficient administration, and professional administration now had an emergent academic discipline behind them.

Additionally, the commission analyzed explicit problems of organizational design, personnel, and administrative processes (Dahlberg, 1966). Such analysis continued the quest for more efficient administration that was the focus of the Keep Commission and the earlier Cockrell Committee and Dockery-Cockrell Commission. Such analysis also showed that efficient administration was now the dominant approach used by policymakers to control administrative capacity. With the emergence of the civil service in the 1880s and its slow growth into the 1900s helping to decrease the power of the spoils system, policymakers from both the executive branch and legislative branch were now using concerns over efficient administration to control and shape administrative capacity. Such political concerns were essentially validated within the developing academic discipline of public administration. As the discipline evolved in the years after the Commission on Economy and Efficiency, early Progressive-minded scholars like Cleveland abandoned other areas of emphasis like public engagement to focus more on the value of efficient administration (Lee, 2011). This, in turn, influenced future collaborations between government and the discipline and ensured that the parastate of actors surrounding administrative capacity focused more on efficiency rather than other tenets of administrative capacity.

Finally, the commission set the precedent for legitimate presidential involvement in administrative reforms. To be sure, Congress still controlled the funding for any commission studying administrative reforms. But the acts of commission, especially with its strong endorsement of an executive-based budgeting process, signaled a strong presidential role in all administrative affairs. This precedent was controversial. As the commission entered 1912, Taft caused resentment in both the legislative and executive branches through his advocating of new estimate methods for the budget (Mansfield, 1970). This led to the commission losing support in Congress. Congress significantly curtailed the commission's funding and redirected its efforts to analyzing administrative processes in the Patent Office (Glenn, 1958). Additionally, the budgetary process envisioned by the commission only became a reality with Congress's passage of the Budget and Accounting Act in 1921. That Act also established new organizational entities like the Bureau of the Budget (today's OMB) and the Government Accounting Office (today's Government Accountability Office (GAO)) that played important roles in the formation of the modern administrative state.

5.8 Capacity in the Modern Administrative State

The passage of the Budget and Accounting Act of 1921 was a landmark event that signaled a new chapter in the federal government's long-standing debates on administration. Reflecting some of the tenets of efficient administration observed by public administration scholars and grounded in the recommendations of the Commission on Economy and Efficiency, the Act elevated presidential responsibilities over the budget. But the Act also considered newer ideas that helped form the modern administrative state. For example, with the passage of the Act, presidents worked with their departments to submit a unified budget proposal to Congress. Congress then adapted this proposal as it deliberated appropriation bills for each departmental service area. To assist in these endeavors, the Act created two new agencies to enhance administrative capacity: the Bureau of the Budget (today's OMB) located in the Department of the Treasury and under the control of the president and a more independent Government Accounting Office (today's GAO) associated with Congress. The Bureau of the Budget helped the president implement and coordinate the executive-based budgeting process, while the Government Accounting Office reported to Congress their investigations into administration to ensure that proper budgetary and administrative processes were being followed. This showed that while efficient administration remained a concern, newer reforms were now being implemented that directly enhanced administrative capacity in ways that formed the modern administrative state.

The modern administrative state dramatically enlarged the scope and size of federal administration. In some ways, it formally commenced with the presidential administration of Franklin D. Roosevelt and the creation of a variety of new agencies and programs to mitigate the crisis of the Great Depression through the 1930s. But in other ways, it can be traced to the civil service reforms emphasizing professional administration passed all the way back in 1883. For example, since that 1883 Act, presidents and Congresses endorsed a variety of laws that significantly increased the capacity of the federal government to do more acts than simple record keeping or revenue collection. These included laws that established independent agencies such as the Interstate Commerce Commission in 1887 to regulate aspects of interstate commerce, the Federal Reserve System in 1913 to better control monetary policy, and the Federal Trade Commission in 1914 to enforce antitrust law. But these instrumentalities would later attract the attention of coalitions that disfavored an expansive administrative state. These entities and others like them were unique in administration in that they performed a variety of substantive administration actions including the enforcement of law and the promulgation of rules that had the same practical impact as law passed by Congress. Consequently, they were structured as independent agencies with boards of commissioners appointed by the president and confirmed by the Senate. These boards were designed to de-emphasize politics with commissioner terms lasting longer than presidential terms and board composition rules preventing one political party from having a super majority. But even without these independent agencies, the size of federal administration kept expanding through the 1800s and into the 1930s with a greater number of personnel, departments, and agencies.

Thus, by the late 1930s, an unwieldy bureaucracy had emerged with increasing amounts of administrative capacity. Federal administrators were now doing more things that directly impacted more segments of the public and the economy. A variety of presidents and Congresses had long tried to control that growing capacity since the founding of the country. A spoils system of political patronage was used to ensure that capacity remained accountable to the public. That system led to corruption and scandal that impaired administrative capacity and the original tenets of the "energetic executive" as envisioned by Hamilton and the drafters of the Constitution. As a result, a more professionalized civil service was implemented to correct those deficiencies and to embrace merit, rather than political influence, as the dominant force in administrative selection.

Partisan politics still remained with the political appointments of agency and departmental leaders. However, a merit-based federal administration grew in scope with increasing numbers of federal administrators being classified as part of the civil service (Commission on Organization of the Executive Branch of Government, 1955). To counter such growth, presidents and Congresses used efficiency as a guiding principle in a series of investigations to ensure that administrative capacity remained controlled and beholden to some value. But even then, administrative capacity of departments and agencies continued to grow. By the 1930s, new control reforms for administrative capacity emerged. These reforms would further legitimate the administrative state while also offering new ways to control administrative capacity.

One focus of these reforms was greater presidential control of departments and agencies. Such control had already been given over the budget, and now that control expanded to focus more on administrative matters. In 1932, Congress delegated part of their control over administrative agencies by giving presidents the power of reorganization authority. This allowed presidents to propose reorganizations of executive agencies in the name of increased efficiency with Congress having to actively disapprove of the reorganization, via the so-called legislative veto, if they wanted to stop it. During the ensuing decades, reorganization authority was not always allowed, and Congress constantly changed its requirements to match current political realities. But by the time the US Supreme Court ruled the legislative veto unconstitutional in 1983's *Immigration and Naturalization Service v. Chadha* case and Congress let presidential reorganization authority to lapse for good in 1984, presidents had submitted over 100 reorganization plans to Congress with over 70% of the plans being successfully adopted (to some degree) (Congressional Research Service, 2012).

Additionally, in 1937, the President's Committee on Administrative Management, known as the Brownlow Committee, issued a set of recommendations that reorganized federal administration and helped to consolidate administrative capacity within the presidency. Most famously, the committee recommended expanding staff surrounding the president, the creation of a management-based office that would help improve the president's control of the executive branch's federal administration, the expansion of the merit system, and a number of significant administrative reorganizations that would help improve efficiency (President's Committee on Administrative Management, 1937). These recommendations showcased the then dominant views within the public administration discipline that favored efficiency and strong executive control over administration. Such views directly emerged from the committee's members who were Louis Brownlow, Charles Merriam, and Luther Gulick. At the time, all three were significantly involved in the public administration discipline with Gulick's ideals of administrative efficiency and agency design being pillars of the discipline.

However, the recommendations were controversial in Congress since they gave more power to the president over administrative areas. Congress only adopted some of the committee's recommendations when it passed the Reorganization Act of 1939, but the Act did allow the president to create an Executive Office of the President (EOP) and shift a number of more managerial-focused agencies, like the Bureau of the Budget, into it. With the Executive Office of the President, the president now had direct access to institutional staff with expertise on federal administration (Patterson, 2000). This significantly increased the power of the presidency over federal administration and its capacity and weakened congressional control over it.

The other focus of reform emphasized administrative rulemaking and reflected a growing concern that federal administration was becoming too powerful. No matter which political party controlled Congress or the presidency, federal administration continued to grow with the number of federal agencies doubling from the early

1900s to the early 1930s (Shepherd, 1996). Such concern often manifested with congressional attempts to control administrative acts. For example, in 1929, Senator George Norris proposed new legislation that would allow for greater appeals and greater accountability over administrative actions (Shepherd, 1996). While never formalized as law, Norris' bill is viewed as the opening salvo in a 17-year debate on administrative power that would culminate with the passage of the Administrative Procedure Act (APA) in 1946 (Shepherd, 1996).

The legislative history surrounding the APA is complex with most of its debates dominated by partisan concerns about the New Deal and its legacy, Franklin D. Roosevelt's use of executive power, the US Supreme Court's changing views on the delegation doctrine, and the tendency of administrative orders to be left unchecked by other branches of government (McCubbins et al., 1999). But by the time of its passage in 1946, the APA had codified a system of administrative decision-making that simultaneously protected the power of administrators to make substantive decisions while also keeping that power accountable to the public, the courts, and policymakers. Overall, the APA codified a system of administrative rule-making that (1) mandated the publicization of administrative procedures and rules to the public, (2) provided for the public to participate in administrative rulemaking via public comments, (3) created standardized processes for formal rulemaking and adjudication, and (4) clarified the scope of judicial review of administrative rules (U.S. Department of Justice, 1947). The APA's impact on administrative capacity was significant as it codified into statute processes for administrative decision-making on substantive policy concerns ranging from the economy to social welfare to the environment. This helped signal a need for continued investment in administrative capacity through future presidents and Congresses. But in an even larger sense, it showed that the modern administrative state, with all of its requisite capacities, had fully arrived. When combined with presidential powers of appointment, the implementation of reforms, and reorganization authority, the traditional approach to controlling and influencing federal administrative capacity had also arrived.

5.9 Consequences of Traditional Controls on Administrative Capacity

Responding to political, economic, and societal changes, federal administration grew significantly from the founding of the federal system in the late 1780s to the modern administrative state of the 1940s. During that time, the bureaucracy evolved from a rudimentary cadre of administrators mainly focused on clerical work and the collection of tariffs and duties to an expansive administrative state that included professionals and specialists making a variety of substantive policy decisions. At a basic level, such growth in the size and scope of federal administration indicates that a significant increase in administrative capacity occurred during that time.

In the early history of administrative reform, concerns about the control of federal administration and its capacity were always present. As shown in this chapter, traditional approaches to controlling administrative capacity were used during that time as leaders debated emphasizing administrative removal powers, patronage-based appointments, a merit-based administration, concerns over efficiency, and the utility of increasing power to the president and administrators to meet the needs of a modern society in an economic crisis. Such debates were decidedly piecemeal in nature but significant in terms of their impact on administrative capacity. They allowed departments to expand while relying on the constitutional competition between the president and Congress over federal administration to check any potential abuses of administrative power that concerned Hamilton's idea of the "energetic executive."

By the 1940s, these debates had helped to produce a modern administrative state with sufficient capacity to implement complex programs efficiently and effectively. And with the passage of the APA, the administrative state possessed sufficient accountability and engagement with the public to ensure that capacity sustained itself within the constitutional framework. Ultimately, federal administrative capacity was forged in the cauldron of continuous administrative reform that was more about controlling federal administration rather than increasing administrative capacity. But through those reforms, administrative capacity grew as it progressed through a capacity mapping out period defined by the Constitution, to a buildup of capacity abetted by new ideas throughout the 1800s, to a consolidation of capacity under the presidency in the 1930s and beyond. Perhaps as a reflection of changing politics, or perhaps as a reaction to a society moving through the industrial era, administrative capacity usually increased when traditional controls were debated. However, the growth in administrative capacity during this time eventually turned into deterioration in the later decades of the twentieth century.

References

Agranoff, R. (2011). Federalist no. 44: What is the role of intergovernmental relations in federalism? *Public Administration Review, 71*, s68–s77.

Arnold, P. E. (2011). Federalist no. 70: Can the public service survive in the contest between Hamilton's aspirations and Madison's reality? *Public Administration Review, 71*, s105–s111.

Civil Service Act of 1883, Ch. 27, 22 Stat. 403 (1883).

Commission on Organization of the Executive Branch of Government. (1955). *Personnel and civil service: A report to congress*. Government Printing Office.

Congressional Research Service. (2012). *Presidential reorganization authority: History, recent, initiatives, and options for congress*. Congressional Research Service.

Crawford, J. B. (1880). *The credit Mobilier of America: Its origin and history, its work of constructing the Union Pacific Railroad and relation of members of congress therewith*. C. W. Calkins and Company Publishers.

Dahlberg, J. S. (1966). *The New York Bureau of Municipal Research*. New York University Press.

Dodd, W. F. (1908). The first state constitutional conventions, 1776–1783. *American Political Science Review, 2*(4), 1545–1561.

Eaton, D. B. (1880). *Civil service in Great Britain: A history of abuses and reforms and their bearing upon American politics*. Harper and Brothers Publishers.

Eriksson, E. M. (1927). The federal civil service under President Jackson. *Mississippi Valley Historical Review, 13*(4), 517–540.

Glenn, B. (1958). The Taft commission and the government's record practices. *The American Archivist, 21*(3), 277–303.

Greene, E. B. (1898). *The provincial governor in the English colonies of North America, volume 7*. Longmans, Green, and Company.

Hamilton, A. (1788/2009). Federalist no. 70. In A. Hamilton, J. Jay, & J. Madison (Eds.), *The federalist papers* (pp. 199–204). Palgrave Macmillan.

Hobbs, E. H. (1953). *Executive reorganization in the national government*. University of Mississippi Press.

Kallenbach, J. E. (1966). *The American chief executive: The presidency and the governorship*. Harper and Row.

Kraines, O. (1951). The Cockrell committee, 1887–1889: First comprehensive congressional investigation into administration. *Western Political Quarterly, 4*(4), 583–609.

Kraines, O. (1954). The Dockery-Cockrell commission, 1893–1895. *Western Political Quarterly, 7*(3), 417–462.

Kraines, O. (1970). The president versus congress: The keep commission, 1905–1909, first comprehensive presidential inquiry into federal administration. *Western Political Quarterly, 23*(1), 5–54.

Lee, M. (2011). History of U.S. public administration in the progressive era. *Journal of Management History, 17*(1), 88–101.

McCubbins, M. D., Noll, R. G., & Weingast, B. R. (1999). The political origins of the Administrative Procedure Act. *Journal of Law, Economics, and Organization, 15*(1), 180–217.

Mansfield, H. C. (1970). Reorganizing the federal executive branch: The limits of institutionalization. *Law and Contemporary Problems, 35*(3), 461–495.

Maranto, R. (1998). Thinking the unthinkable in public administration: A case for spoils in the federal bureaucracy. *Administration & Society, 29*(6), 623–642.

Murphy, L. V. (1942). The first federal civil service commission: 1871–1875. *Public Personnel Review, 3*, 29–39.

Patterson, B. H. (2000). *The White House staff: Inside the west wing and beyond* (Rev. ed.). Brookings Institution Press.

President's Committee on Administrative Management. (1937). *Administrative management in the government of the United States*. Government Printing Office.

Richard, C. J. (2008). *Greeks and romans bearing gifts: How the ancients inspired the founding fathers*. Rowman and Littlefield.

Richardson, J. D. (Ed.). (1905). *Messages and papers of the presidents*. Bureau of National Literature and Art.

Sabato, L. (1978). *Goodbye to good-time Charlie: The American governor transformed, 1950–1975*. Lexington Books.

Sanders, J. B. (1935). *Evolution of executive departments of the Continental Congress*. University of North Carolina Press.

Shepherd, G. B. (1996). Fierce compromise: The Administrative Procedure Act emerges from new deal politics. *Northwestern University Law Review, 90*(4), 1557–1683.

Sundry Civil Expenses Appropriations Act of 1871, Chapter 114, 16 Stat. 514 (1871).

Thach, C. C. (1923). *The creation of the presidency, 1775–1789*. Johns Hopkins University Press.

Thorpe, N. (1909). *The federal and state constitutions, colonial charters, and other organic laws of the states, territories, and colonies*. Government Printing Office.

U.S. Department of Justice. (1947). *Attorney general's manual on the Administrative Procedure Act*. Government Printing Office.

Van Riper, P. P. (1958). *History of the United States civil service*. Row, Peterson, and Company.

Weber, G. A. (1919). *Organized efforts for the improvement of methods of administration in the United States*. D. Appleton and Company.

White, L. D. (1948). *The federalists: A study in administrative history*. The Macmillan Company.

White, L. D. (1951). *The Jeffersonians: A study in administrative history, 1801–1829*. The Macmillan Company.

White, L. D. (1956). *The Jacksonians: A study in administrative history, 1829–1861*. The Macmillan Company.

U.S. House. (1868). *Civil service of the United States* (H.R. Rep. No. 40–47). Government Printing Office.

U.S. Senate. (1888). *To inquire into and examine the methods of business and work in the executive departments* (Senate Rep. No. 50–507). Government Printing Office.

Chapter 6
Transactional Approaches to Controlling Administrative Capacity

I think we can drain the swamp. We can take on the Washington system. We can change from remote control to personal control of our lives.

Ronald Reagan quoted in Dickinson (1976, p. 6)

We are dominated by cheap and easy answers, and reorganization plans that tinker with the mechanism of government.

Adlai Stevenson III quoted in Kaiser (1979, p. 11)

The era of big government is over.

Bill Clinton quoted in Clinton (1996, p. 258)

6.1 New Conceptualizations of Capacity

The steady, but piecemeal, buildup of administrative capacity in federal agencies observed since the founding of the country reached a zenith during the presidential administration of Franklin D. Roosevelt. Responding to the economic crisis of the Great Depression, which in turn contributed to burgeoning societal and political crises, the Roosevelt administration and a Congress controlled by members from the Democratic Party invested heavily in administrative capacity. A variety of new federal agencies and programs, with new administrative personnel, were established in attempts to mitigate the effects of the Great Depression. With those new programs and personnel, agencies experienced a significant increase in administrative capacity that expanded even more during the years of World War II. Consequently, they also experienced significant increases in administrative power. Recognizing this and hoping to protect the Roosevelt legacy on federal administration while also ensuring that administrative power remained accountable to the public, Congress passed the Administrative Procedure Act (APA) in 1946. This Act helped to ensure more transparency and public accountability over administrative decisions and rule-making while enshrining the scope of administrative power that had grown in the Roosevelt administration.

© Springer Nature Switzerland AG 2021
M. E. Joaquin, T. J. Greitens, *American Administrative Capacity*,
https://doi.org/10.1007/978-3-030-80564-7_6

However, by 1947, the Republican Party had taken control of both chambers of Congress for the first time since the early 1930s. Concerned about the significant growth in federal administration witnessed during the Roosevelt administration, Congress began a new push to transfer administrative capacity from federal agencies and programs to other entities such as state governments and private companies. This push would eventually transcend politics and lead to Democrats and Republicans, in both Congress and the presidency, to advocate for a new vision of federal administrative capacity. In this new vision, the ideals of an "energetic executive" branch were better achieved by leveraging capacity through intergovernmental and intersectoral transactions controlled by the president, rather than by increasing administrative capacity within agencies. Such a vision was influenced by politics as well as emergent academic research on the realities of administration occurring in fields like economics, political science, and public administration.

Research of the time revealed that many federal agencies, including those created during the Great Depression, often possessed a type of politicized administration concerned with clientele and policymaker support (Selznick, 1949). This violated idealistic notions of apolitical administration that had long defined the field of public administration and a variety of reforms to federal administration since the Pendleton Act. Research increasingly revealed the obvious, that administrative capacity was politicized even in a structure dominated by a nonpartisan civil service. Worse, the incentives within that administrative structure seemingly favored suboptimal decisions in ways that promoted personal self-interest above organizational goals (Simon, 1947). By the latter part of the twentieth century, such findings would become integrated in a *laissez-faire* approach to economics that showed how free market entrepreneurialism could both keep federal administration accountable to the public while maximizing capacity in the private sector to ensure effective public service delivery. These ideals, combined with significant increases in the capacity and influence of private companies and the free market after World War II, eventually coalesced into political views suggesting the federal government, with its corresponding administrative capacities, did not yield the most effective administration and often compromised fundamental tenets of democracy. Thus, to provide the best services possible in ways that ensured democracy and protected the public from tyranny, a measure of capacity had to be sourced from nonfederal administrative entities.

Such transactional approaches to capacity coevolved with greater presidential control over capacity. While presidents always enjoyed a great deal of control over federal administration, the reforms of the Budget and Accounting Act of 1921 and the Brownlow Committee of the late 1930s expanded those powers. Increasingly, presidents now had more direct control over administrative capacity in ways not witnessed since the days of the spoils system. When coupled with the transactional approaches based on entrepreneurial models starting to dominate politics and academia in the 1980s, presidents could increasingly control and shape federal administrative capacity in new ways. Attending this new conceptualization of capacity, the presidency evolved during the latter part of the twentieth century and the early decades of the twenty-first century: from a managerial presidency enabled by the reforms adopted from the Brownlow Committee to an administrative presidency more concerned about how to ensure political control over administration to a unitary presidency that could command more levers of power on administration and even Congress.

6.2 Transferring Capacity from the Federal Government

Republicans became a majority in Congress during the election of 1946. One of their chief aims was to reexamine and reform the federal administrative state that had expanded since the start of the Great Depression. At least as initially designed, this was an attempt to weaken the administrative state that evolved under Roosevelt and was recently enshrined in the APA. Somewhat surprisingly though, this first attempt at a transactional approach to controlling administrative capacity ended up just validating the old traditional approach to capacity.

Created by statute (Public Law 80-162; 61 Stat. 246) in 1947, the Commission on the Organization of the Executive Branch of the Government, more commonly known as the First Hoover Commission, had specific goals aimed to make federal administration more efficient. For example, Section 1 of the statute enabling the commission specifically included goals linked to (1) decreasing governmental expenses, (2) stopping the duplication of federal programs and services, (3) consolidating similar administrative functions across agencies, (4) deleting administrative processes that were obsolete, and (5) limiting the scope of federal administration within the executive branch (Commission on Organization of the Executive Branch of Government Act, 1947). In that way, the First Hoover Commission had much in common with previous administrative reform endeavors that went back as far as the Cockrell and Dockery-Cockrell Committees of the late 1800s. However, Republicans in Congress also enacted the First Hoover Commission with the implicit goal of starting the deconstruction of the administrative state crafted under Roosevelt (Pemberton, 1986).

6.2.1 A Deconstruction that Enhanced the Administrative State

Unlike the Brownlow Committee and the reform endeavors in the presidential administration of Franklin Roosevelt, the First Hoover Commission was designed to be bipartisan and included active sets of interests from both Congress and the president. Specifically, it included four appointees each from the president (a Democrat), the speaker of the House (a Republican), and the president pro tempore of the Senate (also a Republican). In their appointments, the president, speaker, and president pro tempore had to appoint two Republicans and two Democrats with two of those appointees originating from the private sector and the other two coming from their respective branch of government. Thus, the commission had equal representation between the parties and between the government and the private sector. Additionally, both the legislative and executive branches were represented. Speaker of the House Joseph Martin included as one of his appointees former President Herbert Hoover, who as the president before Franklin Roosevelt, led a relatively limited governmental response to rapidly expanding problems manifesting from the Great Depression. As its most high-profile appointee, the commission quickly become associated with Hoover and become widely known as the Hoover Commission.

Leading the commission, Hoover used 24 task forces to make a series of recommendations for federal administration from 1947 to 1949. However, the 1948 federal elections changed the political dynamic surrounding the commission. As Democrats regained control of Congress and unexpectedly remained in control of the presidency, the Hoover Commission's recommendations readjusted to focus more on efficiency rather than broader recommendations reducing the role and size of the administrative state. Nonetheless, with its 1949 report, the commission could rightfully claim some degree of success by noting how a number of their recommendations were adopted. These included the adoption of program budgeting (identified by the commission as a type of performance budget), empowering political appointees (rather than bureau chiefs) within departments with more responsibility over program implementation, and centralizing more administrative functions and responsibilities in the executive branch within the direct control of the president.

Centralizing control within the presidency was arguably the most significant recommendation from the First Hoover Commission. With that recommendation, the theme of increased presidential control of administration was reemphasized and expanded. Such control had already expanded under the Budget and Accounting Act of 1921 and had been recommended without Congressional endorsement by the Brownlow Committee of 1939. But with the Hoover Commission recommendations, those trends accelerated. The committee even suggested that Congress should stop micromanaging administrative programs and services with legislation. Instead, more discretion should be given to federal administrators to ensure greater executive accountability and presumably more effective service delivery, with the president given more direct control over those programs (Lederle, 1949).

From a theoretical perspective, this further legitimated the managerial presidency as first noted by the Brownlow Committee, allowed opponents of Brownlow and Franklin Roosevelt's administrative state to embrace the managerial presidency, and allowed for the idea of an "energetic executive" to be fully equated with a managerial presidency (Arnold, 1976). Perhaps more importantly, these recommendations suggested that administrative capacity could erode without accountability. And to achieve accountability, federal administration needed a powerful executive with clear lines of authority and without the interdepartmental and intradepartmental divisions often caused by congressional micromanagement.

Although the commission was originally designed as a mechanism for deconstructing the power of the administrative state, its recommendations ultimately increased the power of the presidency and the administrative state surrounding the presidency. Additionally, its recommendations established the importance of executive-based accountability in terms of administrative capacity. In the end, the First Hoover Commission made recommendations more aligned with a traditional approach to administrative capacity. However, the original transactional goals of the First Hoover Commission were ultimately recommended by the Second Hoover Commission just a few years later.

6.2.2 Shrinking Public Sector Capacity

With the election of 1952, the Republicans gained control of Congress again and assumed control of the presidency for the first time in two decades with the election of Dwight Eisenhower. Consequently, another attempt at deconstructing the administrative state occurred. The Second Commission on the Organization of the Executive Branch of the Government, popularly known as the Second Hoover Commission, was enabled by Congress in 1953 (Public Law 83-108; 67 Stat. 142). Once again, the commission would include 12 appointees with 4 members appointed by the president, 4 by the speaker of the House, and 4 by the president pro tempore. 50% of the appointees had to come from government, and 50% had to come from the private sector. However, in a definite change from the First Hoover Commission, notions of bipartisanship were abandoned. With the Republicans controlling the presidency and Congress, there was no requirement in the Second Hoover Commission to ensure an equal mix of Democrats and Republicans.

Hoover was appointed and led this commission as well, and so the commission quickly became known as the Second Hoover Commission. In an attempt to realize the goals of shrinking or even deconstructing the federal administrative state, the Second Hoover Commission focused on policy and specifically analyzed which governmental functions competed with the private sector. Essentially, the Second Hoover Commission explored whether federal administrative functions should exist and, if they should exist, how best to implement them with either private or public means.

The difference in the two commissions can best be seen by comparing their enabling statutes. Specifically, Section 1 of the statute enabling the First Hoover Commission states the following:

It is hereby declared to be the policy of Congress to promote economy, efficiency, and improved service in the transaction of the public business in the departments, bureaus, agencies, boards, commissions, offices, independent establishments, and instrumentalities of the executive branch of the government by –

(1) limiting expenditures to the lowest amount consistent with the efficient performance of essential services, activities, and functions;
(2) eliminating duplication and overlapping of services, activities, and functions;
(3) consolidating services, activities, and functions of a similar nature;
(4) abolishing services, activities, and functions not necessary to the efficient conduct of government; and
(5) defining and limiting executive functions, services, and activities. (Commission on Organization of the Executive Branch of Government, 1947)

In contrast, Section 1 of enabling statute of the Second Hoover Commission restates many of the same themes from the First Hoover Commission while also adding new ones. It states the following:

> It is hereby declared to be the policy of Congress to promote economy, efficiency, and improved service in the transaction of the public business in the departments, bureaus, agencies, boards, commissions, offices, independent establishments, and instrumentalities of the executive branch of the government by -

(1) recommending methods and procedures for reducing expenditures to the lowest amount consistent with the efficient performance of essential services, activities, and functions;
(2) eliminating duplication and overlapping of services, activities, and functions;
(3) consolidating services, activities, and functions of a similar nature;
(4) abolishing services, activities, and functions not necessary to the efficient conduct of government;
(5) eliminating nonessential services, functions, and activities which are competitive with private enterprise;
(6) defining responsibilities of officials; and
(7) relocating agencies now responsible directly to the president in departments or other agencies. (Commission on Governmental Operations Act, 1953)

Note how the fifth point specifically mentions competition with private enterprise. Having lost in their efforts to deconstruct the administrative state via reorganizing capacity in the First Hoover Commission, policymakers forming the Second Hoover Commission now looked for ways to transfer capacity to other areas, specifically the private sector.

Overall, the Second Hoover Commission recommended the end of many governmental programs and services that directly competed with the private sector. The commission discovered approximately 3000 programs and services, almost all within the military, that were competitive with the private sector and that should be ended (Divine, 1955).

The commission also made a surprising number of other recommendations that could improve administrative capacity. These ranged from recommendations showing the value of interdepartmental committees to recommendations suggesting how a "senior civil service" of superior administrators could be formed to allow for administrators to easily transfer across departments to solve problems and crises (a recommendation that was only implemented in a future wave of administrative reforms in the late 1970s). Nonetheless, the Second Hoover Commission is best remembered for its attempts on shrinking government and transferring capacity to the private sector. These attempts were ultimately not successful, but they helped to shape future reforms and debates and administrative capacity occurring into the future. As noted in media reports of the time:

> The main substantive thread that runs through the report reflects Mr. Hoover's statement to *U.S. News World Report* that in his opinion "the government is too big." As the *Wall Street Journal* points out, "most of the important recommendations of the commission ... propose that the government stop doing something it is doing. And most of the things it is supposed to stop doing involve the type of 'social welfare' activity that the government has been carrying on for many years and that large groups of voters have come to expect the government to carry on." The *Journal*, which is certainly no foe of the Hoover Commission, reluctantly

concludes that, "most of the important recommendations of the Second Hoover Commission aren't going anywhere." (Divine, 1955)

However, the ideals expressed in the second Hoover Commission eventually influenced administrative capacity with a series of new developments more narrowly focused on a micro approach to administrative reform rather than grand ideas of administrative reorganization. One of these developments was the use of concepts like "commercial activities" and "inherently governmental activities" (first used and defined in the late 1970s) as policy instruments designed to help shrink the size of the administrative state and fundamentally transform the nature of federal administrative capacity. Such concerns about the size of the administrative state had been building for over a decade within the Republican Party and had only accelerated after the 1940s.

Notions of "commercial activities" and "inherently governmental activities" as policy instruments of control begin in 1955 with the publication of Bulletin 55-4 by President Eisenhower's Bureau of the Budget. That bulletin started a long-term process within the president's Bureau of the Budget (and later the president's Office of Management and Budget) that led to significant outsourcing trends within federal agencies. By the 1980s and 1990s, this would result in the leveraging of more private sector organizations in public service delivery. At a technical level, such trends allowed the president to better control administration through the crafting of short-term, transactional relationships with nongovernmental vendors. If the vendor provided ineffective or inefficient services, then the president could leverage the powers of the free market to find a better replacement. In some ways, this would better help achieve the goals of the "energetic executive" by ensuring more flexibility and even weakening administrative power. However, in other ways, such transactional relationships eroded the goals of the "energetic executive" by significantly weakening any notion of accountability or engagement.

But for the time being, Bulletin No. 55-4 began simply enough. It focused on those commercial activities that government provided itself and was careful to note that services provided to the public should not be included as part of this new policy. For example, it stated:

> It is the general policy of the administration that the federal government will not start or carry on any commercial activity to provide a service or product for its own use if such product or service can be procured from private enterprise through ordinary business channels. Exceptions to this policy shall be made by the head of an agency only where it is clearly demonstrated in each case that it is not in the public interest to procure such product or service from private enterprise. (U.S. Bureau of the Budget, 1955, p. 1)

Thus, the goal of outsourcing those commercial activities which government provided itself was noted in the bulletin. However, the bulletin also noted important limitations on that goal. First, agency leaders could allow exemptions to the outsourcing of such activities when it was not in the public interest. Second, the policy only applied to inward facing services and products that government provided itself. Outward-facing services and products provided to the public were not a part of the policy. For example:

'Activities...for its own use' will include the activities of producing a service or product primarily for the use of the government (whether the same agency or other agencies), even though some portion of the product or service is sold or given to the public. The coverage will include activities which are to provide a service or product for the use of a government agency in its official duties, even though the agency is engaged in carrying out a service to the public (e.g., it will include the manufacture of mail bags or the generation of power at a government institution). However, the coverage will exclude the activities of producing a service or product primarily to be sold or given to the public (e.g., it will exclude the generation of power for sale to the public). (U.S. Bureau of the Budget, 1955, p. 2)

Additionally, the bulletin specifically restricted activities from outsourcing that were not commercial in nature. For example:

There will be excluded from coverage as noncommercial, however, those functions which are a part of the normal management responsibilities of a government agency or a private business of comparable size (such as accounting, personnel work, and the like). (U.S. Bureau of the Budget, 1955, p. 2)

These restrictions helped the new policy emphasize accountability, administrative problem-solving, and flexibility in the leveraging of capacity from the private sector in service delivery. However, over time, the policy evolved and those restrictions were gradually removed. This moved the policy from one of leveraging administrative capacity from the private sector to transferring administrative capacity to the private sector. This gradual evolution can be seen in later revisions to the policy.

For example, the Bureau of the Budget revised the original Bulletin 55-4 in 1957 (Bulletin No. 57-7) and in 1959 (Bulletin No. 60-2). While the 1957 revision was relatively minor, the 1959 revision included an important update that limited the power of agency heads to exempt activities from outsourcing. It specifically noted that:

Compelling reasons for exceptions to the general policy include national security; relatively large and disproportionately higher costs; and clear unfeasibility. (U.S. Bureau of the Budget, 1955, p. 2)

While national security and cost were mentioned in general terms in the original bulletin from 1955 as reasons for exemption from the outsourcing policy, here they are reemphasized with a special emphasis on "large and disproportionately higher costs" and "clear unfeasibility." Essentially, this shifted the policy into more of a mandate, rather than a goal. Such shifts toward mandated actions regarding outsourcing would be even more significant in the decades to come as the policy was recrafted as Bureau of the Budget Circular A-76.

6.3   The Rise of Intergovernmental Capacity

Since at least the Great Depression, power-sharing between the federal government and state governments had been one way, with federal administration assuming greater ability and power on service delivery within states. Part of this stemmed from the twin crises of the Great Depression and World War II where only the federal government had the ability to meet the policy challenges of the day. But part of it also stemmed from incompetence and incapacity. Even as late as the 1940s, many state governments were administrative backwaters dominated by ineffective governors, borderline incompetent administration, and ineffective legislatures (Sabato, 1978). Thus, only the federal government truly had the capacity, ability, and authority to solve the national policy crises of the day, often through intergovernmental grant funding opportunities to state and local governments with significant requirements as a condition of funding.

The rise of such intergovernmental solutions from the federal government to state governments, often via policy mandates, prompted new concerns about the power of federal administration and how the federal administrative state fit into the constitutionally defined parameters of power-sharing between the federal and state governments. Over time, these concerns evolved to reflect changing political realities, which increasingly favored building administrative capacity within state governments. Ultimately, this gave presidents and Congress another tool to control federal administrative capacity: namely, they could transfer administrative capacity from federal administration to state governments and even local governments.

Increasing intergovernmental capacity, often at the expense of federal administrative capacity, had its origins in the later years of Roosevelt's presidency. The first efforts to analyze this concern were undertaken by the Council on Intergovernmental Relations. With origins in the late 1930s, the council led a series of well-publicized studies from 1943 to 1946 that analyzed how intergovernmental relations actually worked at the ground level of administration, especially as programs and services were implemented (U.S. House, 1958). The council was formed by the director of the Bureau of the Budget, Harold D. Smith, but was funded with nongovernmental resources, making it a unique public-private collaboration. With Smith leading as chairperson and with other members of the council coming from federal agencies, the American Municipal Association, the Council of State Governments, as well as academics like Luther Gulick, the council analyzed a variety of specific intergovernmental projects ranging from public health to agriculture that required effective collaboration between state and local governments, as well as the federal government (Lutz, 1949). In its most famous publication, the council stated a number of principles that showed their beliefs on intergovernmental relations. These included recognizing:

(1) That control over local affairs and local government has gradually been more and more centralized into the state and federal governments.
(2) That unless checked, this gradual drift will continue.
(3) That the rapid expansion of government has confused the minds of people at the 'grass roots' and there is no clear cut understanding as to what phases of government should properly and profitably be federal, state, or local.
(4) That unless clarified and the trend reversed, it may eventually undermine democratic government.
(5) That this gradual centralization of authority has been due in part to the feeling by those at the top and in control, that the people at the local level are not capable of handling the problems which arise.

(6) That the council does not believe this to be true. It believes that the feeling has arisen, not as a result of the incapacity of the people, but rather it is due to the absence of interagency coordination at the local level and a positive citizen interest and participation in the direction of 'our government.'

(7) That greater responsibility for operating and improving government services should rest in the hands of persons at the local level. (Council on Intergovernmental Relations, 1947, p. 8)

Interest in the council's work declined as World War II progressed. It ceased to be an operating entity by 1946. However, the principles espoused by the council quickly became part of the burgeoning policy discussion on intergovernmental relations and the power of federal administration relative to state and local administration. The First Hoover Commission also emphasized the importance of intergovernmental relations to the American system of administration in its final report. While most of its efforts centered on federal administration, it also made substantive recommendations to intergovernmental relations and the implementation of federal grant programs to state and local governments. Most notably, the First Hoover Commission recommended the creation of a new federal agency that would help ensure effective intergovernmental relations into the future (Colman, 1965).

While that recommendation was never adopted, it influenced the policy discussion on intergovernmental relations in the 1950s. With the Republican Party taking control of the presidency and Congress in the 1952 elections and with their party continually concerned about the power of the federal administrative state created in the presidency of Franklin Roosevelt, the Republicans created the Commission on Intergovernmental Relations in 1953. The commission, also known as the Kestnbaum Commission after its chairperson Meyer Kestnbaum, had two overarching goals: (1) to explore ways to prevent service duplication between federal, state, and local governments and (2) to improve the working relationship between those three levels of government (Conlan, 2006).

In operation from 1953 to 1955, the commission's final report recommended a number of significant administrative changes that could enhance intergovernmental capacity. These included recommendations that both aimed to improve the implementation of intergovernmental programs while also increasing the administrative capacity of the president to focus on intergovernmental relations. In terms of administrative capacity, the commission's most significant recommendations included a variety of new personnel and agencies that could analyze and solve problems associated with intergovernmental relations. These included a new executive branch agency, a new advisory board, new staff in the Executive Office of the President, new assistant secretaries for intergovernmental relations in a variety of executive branch departments, and a refocusing of the president's Bureau of the Budget on intergovernmental relations (Commission on Intergovernmental Relations, 1955).

The commission also crafted a number of recommendations to help improve the implementation of intergovernmental programs ranging from proposing standards for a federal presence in state and local affairs to specific recommendations on how to improve intergovernmental relations in a variety of specific policy areas

(Commission on Intergovernmental Relations, 1955). President Eisenhower adopted many of the Commission's recommendations including the hiring of staff within the Executive Office of the President and redirecting the Bureau of the Budget to focus on intergovernmental relations (Colman & Goldberg, 1990). Such a policy emphasis reflected the president's distrust of strong centralized power, informed by his experiences in Europe during War World II and influenced by various meetings with prominent Republican Senator Robert Taft during the 1952 Presidential election.

Since the late 1930s, Senator Taft helped lead Republican efforts to overturn the New Deal agenda of Franklin Roosevelt that created the modern administrative state. However, by 1955, with the presidency finally in Republican control and with the recommendations from the Kestnbaum Commission publicized, Senator Taft and the Republicans possessed a new policy tool to help accomplish their long-standing goal. When combined with efforts to transfer at least some elements of administrative capacity to the private sector (as stated in the original 1955 Bureau of the Budget Circular on commercial activities), this emphasis on intergovernmental capacity had the potential to fundamentally transform the existing federal administrative state. As President Eisenhower and Chairperson Kestnbaum noted in the final report of the Kestnbaum Commission:

> Leave to private initiative all the functions that citizens can perform privately; use the level of government closest to the community for all public functions it can handle; utilize cooperative intergovernmental arrangements where appropriate to attain economical performance and popular approval; reserve national action for residual participation where state and local governments are not fully adequate and for the continuing responsibilities that only the national government can undertake. (Commission on Intergovernmental Relations, 1955, p. 6)

By 1957, President Eisenhower successfully leveraged the National Governors' Conference to form a Joint Federal-State Action Committee with state governors and federal agencies. The joint committee had 7 federal members and 10 state governors. It had three goals: to identify federal activities that state governments could control and finance, to advocate for transfers of federal tax revenue to state governments, and to identify likely future activities that would require federal and state intervention (Joint Federal-State Action Committee, 1957). The joint committee worked from 1957 to 1959 and helped to identify some policy areas where states should exert more control, most notably in the use of atomic energy (Colman & Goldberg, 1990). It was then replaced by an independent federal agency that solely focused on intergovernmental relations, the Advisory Commission on Intergovernmental Relations (ACIR).

Congress created ACIR as an independent agency. And although Eisenhower eventually signed the ACIR legislation into law as public law 86-380, it was not without controversy. The major controversy was about congressional and presidential control of ACIR. As an independent agency, both Congress and the president could hold ACIR accountable. However, Eisenhower, backed up with a specific recommendation from the Kestnbaum Commission, wanted the agency as part of the Executive Office of the President with accountability controlled by the president.

Because of this, Eisenhower's Bureau of the Budget director advised a veto of the ACIR legislation. However, Eisenhower refused to veto the legislation because it enjoyed significant support in Congress (Colman & Goldberg, 1990). As a result, ACIR was created as an independent agency.

Reflecting its intergovernmental focus, ACIR had a diverse membership consisting of 4 state governors, 3 state legislators, 4 mayors, 3 county officials, 3 private citizens, 3 members of the federal government's executive branch, and 6 members of the US Congress. Throughout the next four decades, its focus consisted of building more administrative capacity in state and local governments so that the federal government could devolve more power and responsibilities to state and local governments. ACIR's work and cadre of experts helped implement ideas like general revenue-sharing, regionalism, and reforms to the federal grant-in-aid system for state governments (Conlan, 2006). In one sense, these efforts led to a decline in federal administrative capacity since presidents, and Congress now had a federal agency that could legitimate attempts to transfer more power, responsibility, and administrative capacity to state and local governments. In the coming decades, such transfers would be promoted by both Republican and Democratic presidents. But in another sense, these efforts improved overall capacity by creating new partners in program implementation.

6.4 Managing Capacity from the Executive Office of the President

After the 1950s came two decades of relative stability in terms of the development of new tools to control federal administrative capacity. Presidents, and to a certain extent Congress, now had the ability to control administrative capacity in five distinct ways. In more traditional approaches, controlling capacity involved appointments, reforms, and reorganizations that were all framed by the Constitution and changing political realities. And in more transactional approaches, control involved outsourcing and transferring administrative responsibilities to intergovernmental partners framed by administrative theories, political realities, and the Constitution.

With the powers of capacity control being established in the previous decades and the question of presidential and Congressional control over administrative capacity relatively settled, the 1960s witnessed large increases in federal administrative capacity with the progression of the Cold War, the new legislation on civil rights, and the beginning of the Great Society programs under President Lyndon Johnson. However, by the 1970s, those trends reversed, and retrenchment, excessive presidential control and corruption, and a reorganization of the civil service once again transformed the tools of capacity control and the very nature of federal administrative capacity.

6.4.1   The Rise of Competitive Sourcing

The first trend observed in this era was a focus on transforming the outsourcing power linked to capacity control. The original Bureau of the Budget bulletins on the outsourcing of commercial activities performed by the federal government were fairly limited in scope. For instance, the bulletins only called for the outsourcing of those commercial activities that the federal government provided to itself. Additionally, broad exceptions to the policies existed, although these became more limited as time progressed. Through it all, the bulletins also made special note to restrict outsourcing efforts for those services directly delivered to the public. However, by the 1960s, this policy was fundamentally transformed into a new A-76 policy on outsourcing that gradually broadened the scope of the original bulletins from the 1950s.

In 1966, the Bureau of the Budget produced Circular A-76. With a circular, the Bureau of the Budget could implement a more permanent policy as bulletins were generally viewed to be more temporary in nature (*Oversight on Issues Related to OMB Circular A-76*, 1981). Significantly, Circular A-76 defined commercial activities as:

> ...one which is operated and managed by an executive agency and which provides for the government's own use a product or service that is obtainable from a private source. (U.S. Bureau of the Budget, 1966, p. 1)

In the coming decades, this definition would continually expand. This enabled presidents to maximize their use of outsourcing power to transfer administrative capacity from federal agencies to the private sector. For instance, in 1979, the definition of commercial activities changed again. Now a commercial activity was defined as:

> ...one which is operated and managed by a Federal executive agency and which provides a product or service that could be obtained from a private source. (U.S. Office of Management and Budget, 1979, p. 20558)

At the same time, the 1979 update to Circular A-76 identified a definition for governmental functions that could not be outsourced. This included defining a "governmental function" as:

> ...a function which must be performed in-house due to a special relationship in executing governmental responsibilities. Such governmental functions can fall into several categories: (1) Discretionary application of government authority...(2) Monetary transactions and entitlements...(3) In-house core capabilities in the area of research, development, and testing, needed for technical analysis and evaluation and technology base management and maintenance. However, requirements for such services beyond the core capability which has been established and justified by the agency are not considered governmental functions. (U.S. Office of Management and Budget, 1979, p. 20558)

Thus, a tension was defined and set between "commercial activities" and "governmental activities." From the 1980s to the 2000s, the scope of governmental activities that could be subjected to outsourcing increased as new revisions to the A-76 occurred and presidents sought to use their outsourcing power to better control federal administrative capacity and respond to political pressures that valued smaller government.

6.4.2 Presidential Reorganization Authority: From Control to Abuse

The second trend observed during the 1960s and 1970s was the attempted expansion of the power of presidential reorganization. Congress delegated to the president reorganization powers beginning in 1932 but also continually revised the power and even sometimes let it lapse for a number of years. For example, Congress allowed the power to lapse from 1935 to 1939, 1941 to 1945, and for shorter periods of time throughout the 1940s and 1950s (Congressional Research Service, 2012a, b). While the scope and limits of the power changed with each revision and renewal, the general theme of this power gave presidents the power to reorganize executive branch agencies on their own, with Congress having to actively object to the reorganization if they disagreed (Congressional Research Service, 2012a, b). Thus, the power was based on ideas of streamlined executive power that had been building since the findings of the Taft Commission of the 1910s and the Brownlow Committee of the late 1930s as well as the growing discipline of public administration that favored streamlined executive power in organizations. With reorganization power, presidents could significantly reorganize federal agencies to maximize the impact of administrative capacity. But as seen during the 1960s and 1970s, presidents increasingly tried to use their reorganization power as tool to exert more political control over federal administration and to counter Congressional interest in reorganizing agencies.

All presidents from President Roosevelt to President Nixon used their delegated reorganization authority to varying degrees. Notably, President Eisenhower transformed it into a significant power in the modern managerial presidency by forming his own advisory committee on reorganization. The President's Advisory Committee on Government Organization (PACGO) issued a number of recommendations to Eisenhower on reorganization, and its work led to Eisenhower enjoying a significant record of reorganization success in his first 2 years as president, including a plan that created the Department of Health, Education, and Welfare (Arnold, 1998). Eisenhower used PACGO throughout his presidency, both as a way to make agencies more effective and as a way to contravene and control recommendations from the congressionally sponsored First and Second Hoover Commissions. With his own set of reorganization recommendations from PACGO, Eisenhower was able to shift congressional focus away from the Hoover Commissions and instead refocus Congress to supporting his own set of administrative based goals. This tactic especially worked on the recommendations from the Second Hoover Commission, which, by most accounts, were almost totally ignored (Arnold, 1998).

Building on such precedents of reorganization power, President Kennedy tried to use reorganization authority to establish a Department of Urban Affairs and Housing after legislation supporting its creation failed in Congress (U.S. House, 1962). Kennedy's reorganization efforts failed, and his use of the power was limited thereafter. However, his successor, President Johnson, used reorganization authority to focus on policy as the ultimate coordinating strategy between departments and policy analysis as the ultimate administrative capacity that could result in more cost-effective and successful program implementation. Johnson's use of reorganization centered on two presidential task forces.

In 1964, Johnson created the Task Force on Government Reorganization led by the dean of Harvard Kennedy School of Government, Don K. Price. The Price Task Force focused on analysis and evaluation as ways to achieve to increased administrative capacity, especially within the Executive Office of the President. It also recommended a variety of traditional reorganization endeavors including the formation of new departments for areas like transportation, education, and housing and community development as well as the merger of various programs and departments into mega-departments for economic development and natural resources (Redford & Blissett, 1981). While those reorganizations failed, the group's work on analysis and evaluation led to new capabilities forming in the President's Executive Office of the president. Ultimately, the task force is best remembered for its rather distant relationship with President Johnson. Unlike presidentially formed advisory groups observed in previous administrations, the Price group had no direct meetings with Johnson and instead relied on direct communications with the president's Bureau of the Budget director (Arnold, 1998). Perhaps adding to its isolation, the Price Task Force had more representation from academia and business rather than government. The power of the Bureau of the Budget over the task force was also significant. When the group completed its final report at the end of 1964, the Bureau of the Budget submitted its own analysis of the report, carefully serving as a gatekeeper on which recommendations would have the chance for actual implementation (Arnold, 1998).

In 1966, Johnson created another reorganization group named the Task Force on Government Organization, chaired by Railroad Executive Ben Heineman on the challenges of implementation, especially in regard to Johnson's Great Society programs. The Heineman group had more representation from individuals with government experience and generally had greater access to policymakers compared to the earlier Price group. In its focus, the Heineman group examined intergovernmental implementation challenges, the need for additional reorganizations, and whether a new office of coordination should exist in the Executive Office of the President (Arnold, 1998). In many ways, it is best remembered for its recommendations favoring massive departmental mergers to strengthen the president's ability to control executive branch agencies (Arnold, 1998). Ultimately, the recommendations from the task force came at a time when Johnson's presidency was fading under the strains of the Vietnam War. Thus, its recommendations were essentially ignored as the Johnson administration ended. However, they would influence the reorganization strategy of the next president, Richard Nixon.

Johnson's use of the reorganization power reflected a new trend to reemphasize presidential control over federal administration. During this time, attitudes regarding federal administration had started to shift with both academia and the public becoming ever more concerned with the tendency of administrators to amass power and ignore the will of the people and the elected president (Garvey, 1995). With the use of policy analysis as a type of coordinating mechanism, departments with similar policy responsibilities could be merged into super-departments. This would allow greater presidential control over administration while also promoting ideals of efficiency. In this way, administration could be better controlled by the president and become more effective as well.

President Nixon continued to use reorganization in this way when he assumed the presidency in 1969. During that year, he formed the Ash Council, officially known as the Advisory Council on Government Organization. Led by Roy Ash, who co-founded and led a major contractor for the Department of Defense, the Ash Council worked until 1971 on a variety of reorganization proposals. Recommendations from the Ash Council led to the formation of the Environmental Protection Agency and the National Oceanic and Atmospheric Administration. But perhaps more dramatically, the Council also recommended a dramatic reorganization of the Bureau of the Budget into an Office of Management and Budget (OMB) that would enhance its ability to focus on program management and ensure better control of the agency. Since at least the Eisenhower administration, the Bureau of the Budget had often been criticized as either being too powerful or not responsive enough to presidential priorities (Tomkin, 1998). Additionally, Nixon seemed to view the Bureau of the Budget with some suspicion, as he apparently did for most of the federal bureaucracy (Nathan, 1983). Consequently, the Ash Council recommended a transfer of policymaking capacity from the Bureau of the Budget to a newly established Domestic Council located within the Executive Office of the President and the use of political appointees to lead operating divisions within OMB, positions which had historically been held by careerist in federal administration (Arnold, 1998). This resulted in the Domestic Council focusing more on policymaking, with the new OMB focusing more on overseeing how effectively policies were implemented in the agencies (Tomkin, 1998). Congress eventually passed this reorganization plan, but the final outcomes as envisioned by the Ash Council were never achieved. Somewhat surprisingly, OMB eventually focused more on policymaking, while the Domestic Council, as expected, focused on implementation with specific monitoring of administrative tasks often on its agenda (Tomkin, 1998).

Overall, however, the emerging reality of the Nixon reorganization suggested a further evolution of presidential control, a long-standing concern of presidents (Lee, 2010). Except now, the implementation of policy was becoming viewed more and more as a partisan activity best controlled by the president rather than a nonpartisan civil service. This was seen in the most controversial idea that emerged from the Ash Council: the consolidation of almost all federal domestic programs into four super-departments – Natural Resources, Economic Affairs, Human Resources, and Community Development. The super-departments would allow the president to end existing constituencies that supported specific departments while also focusing administrative capacity on broad policy areas to better leverage resources and hopefully improve efficiency and effectiveness (Arnold, 1998). Such efforts at reorganization were not successful and perhaps not even realistic. Eventually these efforts were seen as a type of abuse of executive power, even though similar recommendations had been made in previous presidencies (Lee, 2010), and signaled the beginning of the end of reorganization authority as a practical presidential tool for controlling administrative capacity.

6.4.3 Reorganizing the Civil Service

The last significant use of presidential reorganization authority occurred in President Carter's administration in the latter part of the 1970s. Carter used the power to create two new departments in energy and education and also submitted a number of other reorganization proposals for minor administrative issues. His proposals for the Department of Energy and Department of Education simply transferred administrative capacities from existing programs into new departments. The proposals faced significant revisions from Congress (Arnold, 1998). In this way, Congress had increased its own power over executive reorganization authority.

Carter's use of reorganization power also coincided with the third major trend influencing administrative capacity during the 1960 and 1970s: the reform of the civil service. Working on dual tracks with congressional bills that reformed the civil service, Carter used reorganization authority to end the near century-old Civil Service Commission (CSC) and replace it with new entities. Concerns about the Civil Service Commission, and the civil service in general, had been building for years. Many of the reorganization efforts of Presidents Eisenhower, Johnson, and Nixon could even be interpreted as reactions against the federal civil service and their perceived lack of responsiveness to presidential priorities. As an example of this concern and even outright hostility to the civil service, the Nixon administration used its infamous Malek manual to describe various administrative tactics that could be used to make administrators in the civil service, as well as lower-level political appointees from previous administration, resign their positions (U.S. Senate, 1974). While not as severe in their outright hostility to federal administration, Carter also publicly shared a variety of concerns and frustrations about administrative responsiveness and efficiency present in federal agencies. Ultimately, his concerns helped shaped the Civil Service Reform Act of 1978 (CSRA). The Act passed for a number of reasons.

First, Carter had expressed frustration at the perceived slowness and inefficiencies of federal administration throughout his administration. In fact, it was one of the main points made during his political campaign for the presidency. Many of the new reforms passed in the CSRA, like the senior executive service (which was first proposed in the Second Hoover Commission), could at least theoretically alleviate some of those problems. Carter promoted this during the campaign. He often spoke of "removing the deadwood" from bureaucracy (Ingraham, 1984). He formed the PMP (personnel management project) once he became president to try and get buy-in from civil servants about the need for reform. But many civil servants viewed the reform as a return to the spoils system (Lynn & Vaden, 1979).

Second, and perhaps more importantly, the CSRA was also a reaction to Nixon's excessive politicization of federal administration. Specifically, Nixon's OMB used the federal political personnel manual (also known as the Malek manual) as a guidebook on how to actively politicalize federal administration, including the nonpartisan civil service. As a reaction to those abuses, the Civil Service Reform Act aimed to integrate more aspects of nonpartisan merit into federal administrative decisions.

Ultimately, the CSRA attempted to solve multiple problems (both real and perceived) with federal administration. Many of those problems went back to excessive politicization in administration – a problem that had been building since the administration of Franklin Roosevelt and that turned into corruption in the Nixon administration. But many of those perceived problems also went back to the CSC, and the first series of administrative reforms passed in the early 1880s. By the late 1970s, the CSC was often viewed as an excessive force that crafted rules to protect administrators, often at the expense of effectiveness and flexibility (Ink, 2000). Consequently, policymakers designed the CSRA to both establish new processes to protect administration from politicization and also abolish rigid administrative processes that prevented quick administrative solutions to emergent problems (Ink, 2000).

The reforms contained in the Act were significant. The CSRA, along with two complementary administrative reorganization plans, formally abolished the near century-old CSC. It was replaced with three new administrative units: the Office of Personnel Management (OPM), the Merit Systems Protection Board (MSPB), and the Federal Labor Relations Authority (FLRA). OPM and MSPB were the direct replacements for the CSC. OPM was designed as an independent agency under the president's control that had responsibility for designing personnel specific policies for federal administration. It would be led by a presidential appointee confirmed by the Senate with authority over the merit system and the crafting of policies and programs that impacted federal employees (Perry, 2008). The MSPB was designed as an independent agency with both appellate and investigatory powers. Notably, it included the presidential appointed position of the Office of Special Counsel (OSC) with investigatory and prosecutorial powers. At least as initially designed, this allowed MSPB to protect merit processes associated with the civil service and also act as a force of investigation when allegations of interference in merit rules occurred (Perry, 2008). The FLRA was an additional independent agency designed to assist in labor relations between the federal government and federal employees.

In the end, the CSRA accomplished many things. It allowed for two distinct administrative entities that could both protect the merit system and also act in accordance with presidential political directives regarding personnel; it established the senior executive service that created a high performing cadre of administrators that could go into different federal programs and essentially solve problems; it created significant protections for whistleblowers; and it helped to make federal administration more responsive and more accountable to the president and the public

(Ingraham, 1984). With accountability once again emphasized, the tenets of Hamilton's energetic executive could be realized.

Yet, the CSRA also created immediate problems that only grew over time. The MSPB was never fully embraced by either the president or Congress (Ink, 2000). In many ways, it never operated as intended and even came to be seen more as an advisory body rather than a true investigatory unit. Additionally, OPM gradually became a very ineffective administrative unit that was significantly downsized in subsequent administrative reforms in the 1990s. By 2018, the latter presidential administration of Donald Trump would propose merging OPM with the General Services Administration (GSA). The National Academy of Public Administration (NAPA) even agreed to analyze the proposed merger (Edwards, 2020). Thus, many of the goals of the CSRA were never achieved. Presidential control of administration still remained an issue, administrative effectiveness still remained a concern, and the faith in federal administrators even having sufficient ability to quickly solve problems and respond to new challenges was increasingly questioned. All these factors helped to accelerate more entrepreneurial approaches to administration that would fundamentally transform capacity in the decades after the 1970s.

6.5 Implementing Entrepreneurial Capacity

By the 1980s, the concept of federal administrative capacity and presidential approaches to it became intertwined with entrepreneurialism. Over time, the entrepreneurial approach depended heavily on outsourcing administrative capacity to external vendors (often in the private sector), increasing responsibilities to state and local governments, and instituting performance reforms on administration. Out of those, outsourcing became the dominant method used by presidents to transform and control federal administrative capacity.

The dominance of outsourcing began with further revisions to the A-76 policy in the early 1980s. Throughout the next few decades, the scope of commercial activities that could be outsourced would continually expand in numerous revisions to A-76. For instance, in the 1983 revision to the A-76 policy, OMB defined "commercial activity" as:

> ...one which is operated by a federal executive agency and which provides a product or service which could be obtained from a commercial source. A commercial activity is not a governmental function. (Congressional Research Service, 2012a, b, p. 8)

But by the 2003 revision to the A-76 policy, "commercial activity" was defined as:

> ...a recurring service that could be performed by the private sector and is resourced, performed, and controlled by the agency through performance by government personnel, a contract, or a fee-for-service agreement. A commercial activity is not so intimately related to the public interest as to mandate performance by government personnel. Commercial activities may be found within, or throughout, organizations that perform inherently governmental activities or classified work. (U.S. Office of Management and Budget, 2003, p. A3)

Such expansions to the A-76 policy, specifically, and the outsourcing power of the president, generally, reflected the shift in national and political moods surrounding governmental work. In some ways, this shift in mood had started as early as the 1960s as the field of public administration moved away from administrative solutions to governmental problems and became more focused on policy and political solutions to governmental problems (Garvey, 1995).

By the presidency of Ronald Reagan in the 1980s, such sentiments had become mainstream and began to fundamentally alter approaches to federal administrative capacity. As Reagan stated in his first inaugural address:

> The economic ills we suffer have come upon us over several decades. They will not go away in days, weeks, or months, but they will go away. They will go away because we, as Americans, have the capacity now, as we have had in the past, to do whatever needs to be done to preserve this last and greatest bastion of freedom.
>
> In this present crisis, government is not the solution to our problem; government is the problem. From time to time, we have been tempted to believe that society has become too complex to be managed by self-rule, that government by an elite group is superior to government for, by, and of the people. But if no one among us is capable of governing himself, then who among us has the capacity to govern someone else? All of us together, in and out of government, must bear the burden. The solutions we seek must be equitable, with no one group singled out to pay a higher price. (Reagan, 1981, p. 258)

After he assumed the presidency, Reagan implemented two large reforms to help implement his ideas on federal administrative capacity. First, his use of political appointees to lead agencies sometimes included individuals who did not fully believe in the mission of an agency. This was especially the case in agencies focused on environmental issues and even social issues like discrimination. Over time, these appointees clashed with civil service careerists over the direction of agencies, their mission, and how programs were implemented. Sometimes careerists were able to resist the efforts of appointees (as in the Environmental Protection Agency); other times they were not (as witnessed in the Equal Employment Opportunity Commission) (Wood, 1990). Clashes were especially severe in agencies focused on environmental and conservation issues (Kraft & Vig, 1984).

Second, the Reagan administration focused on privatization. Reagan formed the Private Sector Survey on Cost Control led by J. Peter Grace, a private sector businessman. The Grace Commission focused on catching waste and inefficiency in federal administration. It generated three conclusions which claimed to show how administrative inefficiency was promoted in the federal government: (1) inefficient administration still received increases in funding and personnel, (2) a lack of competition prevented administrative innovation, and (3) agency constituents often prevented innovation through lobbying (Grace, 1984). But overall, the work of the Grace Commission is best remembered as being overly political with a focus on changing social policies as a way to economize administration rather than focusing on actual reforms embracing business-like management innovation (Hayes, 1986). The work of the Grace Commission led to no immediate transformation in administration, but its political sentiments helped herald a new stage of presidential control of administrative capacity that favored outsourcing and competition as the best way to control federal administration.

Outsourcing also became more favored as two other powers associated with presidential control of federal administrative capacity began to fade. In 1983, the US Supreme Court ruled the legislative veto unconstitutional in the *Immigration and Naturalization Service v. Chadha* decision. The legislative veto had been an integral component of presidential reorganization authority by allowing Congress to overrule a presidential reorganization only with an active vote of disapproval. Now, with the legislative veto deemed unconstitutional and the ability of presidents to use reorganization authority to transform federal administrative capacity in significant ways becoming more difficult given the experiences of past presidents in the 1960s and 1970s, presidents had to increasingly utilize other tools to control the bureaucracy.

But by the mid-1990s, another one of these tools lessened in significance. In 1996, the Advisory Commission on Intergovernmental Relations (ACIR) was eliminated as a federal agency with bipartisan support from a Republican-dominated Congress and Democratic President Bill Clinton. The agency, like the civil service body, had entered a definite era of decline in the 1980s. Some politically appointed leaders of ACIR even actively lead efforts to delegitimize it as many congressional leaders became disinterested in serving on intergovernmental relations subcommittees (Conlan, 2006). Additionally, ACIR's capacity to engage in intergovernmental analysis had weakened significantly since the 1970s, with most of its efforts focused on political advocacy rather than intergovernmental analysis (Conlan, 2006). The end of ACIR in 1996 did not necessarily mean that intergovernmental relations were no longer a factor in federal administration. Quite the contrary, intergovernmental funding and policies remained significant forces in the federal government. Instead, the end of ACIR meant that serious analysis of ways to transfer federal administrative capacity to state and local governments was no longer being emphasized within the federal government, hurting the intergovernmental dimension of administrative capacity.

As the modern administrative system evolved, presidents increasingly had to rely on their transactional powers of outsourcing and their traditional powers of appointment and reform as approaches to controlling federal administrative capacity. These powers set the framework for understanding what happened to federal administrative capacity from the 1990s to the presidency of Donald Trump. For example, President Clinton and his Vice President Al Gore had spent the early part of their presidential term working on the National Performance Review (NPR). Publicized as a way to "reinvent government," the effort was a traditional approach to controlling administrative capacity through reform. It came in the context of increasing anti-government sentiment among citizens in the West and mounting fiscal crises that ushered conservative government regimes in the United States and Britain. While certain tenets of NPR were unique, such as its focus on decentralizing reform ideas using feedback from middle managers in government, its reliance on results-based performance measurement, and its emphasis on competition whereby governmental agencies could also compete with the private sector for service delivery (Gore, 1993), it also led to a number of negative effects on administrative capacity. Most notably, the NPR effort resulted in dramatic cuts to the Office of Personnel

Management (OPM) which would only exacerbate in significance in the coming decades. After NPR, OPM was left a weakened, hollowed-out agency with limited administrative capacity to fulfill its original vision as specified by the CSRA.

Second, NPR was sometimes viewed as being more of a marketing endeavor rather than a significant attempt at reforming federal administrative capacity (Pfiffner, 1997). The Clinton administration heavily promoted the achievements of NPR and how it significantly ended a number of unnecessary regulations and decreased the size of federal administration. Yet, such promotion might have actually hurt federal administration rather than helped. For instance, such communications often reiterated the failures of federal administration, sometimes in ways that avoided the complexities of governance (Arnold, 1995). This, in turn, helped to reinforce the perception that effective administration could only occur in the private sector. As a result, policymakers in both Congress and the presidency continued to embrace entrepreneurial approaches to administrative capacity in the succeeding years.

As NPR was implemented, Congress – wanting to respond as well as the president to citizen pressures to show how bureaucracy was being made more efficient – also embraced an entrepreneurial approach to reform and passed the Government Performance and Results Act (GPRA) in 1993. GPRA focused on performance measurement as a way to ensure administrative accountability to the public. It mandated three new performance systems on agencies: (1) a 5-year strategic plan, (2) annual performance plans, and (3) reports detailing annual programmatic performance (Government Performance and Results Act, 1993). Of note, GPRA specifically identified these new performance systems as inherently governmental activities that could only be performed by federal employees (Government Performance and Results Act, 1993). This showed the pressure agencies were now under to outsource all types of activities, something Congress wanted to specifically avoid with GPRA performance systems, an effort to stem presidential control over an increasingly shrunk administrative state.

GPRA flowed from the same ideals as NPR with many of its supporters noting how its performance regimen could be used to improve administration, justify cuts to administrative spending, or even legitimate an expansive increase in the outsourcing of federal administration (Frederickson & Frederickson, 2006). Like NPR, its historical legacy is somewhat uncertain with proponents noting how performance measurement often can result in good government while detractors viewing it as an unnecessary process that incentivized congressional micromanagement and had no substantive influence on administration (Schoen, 2008). This view was perhaps shared in the presidential administration of George W. Bush, which in 2001 started its own system of performance measurement distinct from GPRA. GPRA itself was updated in 2010 with new provisions requiring more frequent performance reporting requirements and new roles for OMB to help monitor performance and help agencies implement performance improvement plans when performance was deficient (GPRA Modernization Act, 2011). The update also formalized the use of program improvement officers, a practice that had been informal since the original GPRA passed in 1993 (Kamensky, 2011).

Viewed in a larger context, GPRA helped normalize the measurement of performance in ways that were not always beneficial to improvements in program management capacity. In the private sector, performance data were almost always tied to profit and thus necessary to justify entrepreneurial decisions. But in federal administration, performance data were messier. Programs whose outcomes were only achieved over a long span of time could have difficulty measuring their performance, data could be politicized, influences on outcomes could be uncertain, and even when performance data existed, policymakers might choose to ignore it in funding decisions (Radin, 2006). Nonetheless, a variety of performance-based reforms were also implemented in the administration of George W. Bush, the presidential successor to Bill Clinton.

President Bush implemented a number of reforms that embraced entrepreneurial approaches to capacity. As discussed earlier, his administration expanded the scope of the A-76 process and thus increased the use of outsourcing within federal administration. The Bush administration also embraced performance measurement in OMB-directed reforms like the President's Management Agenda (PMA) and the Program Assessment Rating Tool (PART).

The PMA focused on five management priorities in outsourcing, e-government, performance budgeting, financial accountability, and human capital (U.S. Office of Management and Budget, 2001). Using OMB and OPM, the administration implemented the PMA across federal agencies and used a traffic light scorecard to track progress on each priority every quarter (Breul, 2007). Similarly, the PART process was managed by OMB and focused on measuring the ability of federal programs to demonstrate results tied to:

> Program Purpose and Design: Reflecting whether the program had a clear purpose and if the program was designed to meet that purpose;
> Strategic Planning: Showing if the program's agency had established suitable annual goals and long-term goals for its programs;
> Program Management: Indicating whether the program had good management including appropriate financial oversight controls and program improvement methods;
> Program Results: Demonstrating if the program achieved performance results according to strategic planning goals. (U.S. Office of Management and Budget, 2006, p. 5)

Programs were divided into seven distinct categories that allowed specific questions from OMB to be tailored to programmatic type while also using more generalized questions that OMB asked of all programs.

Much like Clinton's NPR reform, PMA and PART were heavily promoted as ways to realize greater performance in federal administration. However, their ultimate impact was mixed. Academic research into both processes indicated an often subjective process, not clearly tied to actual budgetary decisions, which often showcased the complexities of bureaucratic politics between the president and agencies rather than actual performance (Joaquin & Greitens, 2009; Radin, 2006). In particular, agencies such as the Department of Agriculture (USDA) and OPM used excessive competitive sourcing to increase their scorecard ratings in ways that seemingly compromised capacity (Joaquin, 2009). Worse yet, PART performance scores often linked back to partisan politics (Greitens & Joaquin, 2010; Gilmour & Lewis, 2006). These findings perhaps induced the presidential administration of Barack Obama to de-emphasize performance measurement reforms for management and instead refocus such measurements on broad policy ideas, from healthcare implementation to educational outcomes (McGuinn, 2016; Rivers & Rivers, 2012). When the Obama administration engaged in attempts to influence administrative capacity, it focused on reorganization, efficiency, and, to a certain extent, outsourcing.

For example, President Obama wanted Congress to re-enable presidential reorganization authority that was last approved by Congress in 1984. In an effort framed as the Consolidating and Reforming Government Act of 2012, the administration wanted to use reorganization authority to consolidate programs with responsibility in business and trade into one department (Lawrence & Abramson, 2011). However, those efforts ultimately failed. With some aversion to expanding the use of outsourcing given how it had been increased during the Bush administration, the Obama administration ultimately focused on presidential reforms to influence federal administrative capacity. These reforms commenced at the start of the administration and coalesced into the Accountable Government Initiative which aimed to reduce waste, increase efficiency, and rescind some of the expansions to outsourcing witnessed during the Bush administration (U.S. Office of Management and Budget, 2010).

Thus, by the end of the Obama administration and the beginning of the Trump administration, presidents had limited reorganization authority but a powerful set of administrative tools to control and influence federal administrative capacity. These tools included their traditional power of appointment, which was constitutionally checked by Congress; their traditional power of executive-based reform, which had seemingly become hollow and more focused on publicizing and politicizing reform than achieving it; and the transactional power of outsourcing. During the Trump presidency, these powers would persist and be used in unique ways as Congress increasingly cedes its institutional prerogatives out of partisan motives.

The history of administrative reforms covered in this chapter demonstrates the increasing assertiveness of presidents relative to Congress in shaping the metes and bounds of the administrative state vis-à-vis the private sector and in requiring bureaucracy's political responsiveness to the White House. In Reagan's time, externalizing capacity was attended by a significant push to politicize greatly the upper ranks of agency leadership through appointment powers in an attempt to push presidential policy priorities and a symbolic effort to rein in the unelected bureaucrat (Nathan, 1983). Under Clinton, Congress became an accomplice in hollowing out capacity; under Bush, presidential signing statements would become a preeminent symbol of the rising theory of the unitary executive.

6.6 Consequences of Transactional Controls on Administrative Capacity

Transactional approaches to controlling administrative capacity, especially those linked to outsourcing, helped to fundamentally transform the administrative state that emerged after World War II. After the transactional transformation, capacity was more under the control of the president, more dependent on external partners, more devoted to performance measurement, and weaker in terms of civil service protections. Gains in efficiency and performance achieved via reforms and reorganizations were often short-lived, with new presidential administrations always changing the managerial focus of administrators. The consequences for administrative capacity were significant. Administrative capacity now focused on short-term realities often driven by the politics of presidential priorities. For ideals of the energetic executive, this ensured federal administration was accountable to the public but left ideas of administrative effectiveness and even administrative competence minimized.

A clear theme had emerged: all approaches to controlling administrative capacity were political approaches to controlling administrative capacity. In that sense, when viewed across the decades of successive presidential administrations, the control of administrative capacity appears more like a symbolic concept used by presidents to meet the political concerns of the day. And with the techniques of management science becoming secondary to political realities, administrative capacity declined and decayed over time.

Political realities also influenced the creation of the modern administrative state in the 1940s and the civil service system in the 1880s. But something changed during the transactional period: presidential power grew, informed by congressional reforms such as the Budget and Accounting Act of 1921, the adoption of recommendations from the Brownlow Committee in the late 1930s, and the ability of presidents to leverage outsourcing to control administration. Along with Congress delegating more authority over administrative decisions to the executive branch, a more powerful and more unitary approach to the presidency developed. Thus, administrative capacity became more of a political tool for an all-powerful president, rather than an administrative tool used to ensure efficiency, accountability, and effectiveness in solving national concerns.

References

Arnold, P. E. (1976). The first Hoover commission and the managerial presidency. *Journal of Politics, 38*(1), 46–70.

Arnold, P. E. (1995). Reform's changing role. *Public Administration Review, 55*(5), 407–417.

Arnold, P. E. (1998). *Making the managerial presidency: Comprehensive reorganization plan, 1905–1996* (2nd ed.). University Press of Kansas.

Breul, J. D. (2007). Three Bush administration management reform initiatives: The president's management agenda, freedom to manage legislative proposals, and the program assessment rating tool. *Public Administration Review, 67*(1), 21–26.

Clinton, W. J. (1996). State of the union 1996. *Vital Speeches of the Day, 62*(9), 258–262.

Colman, W. G. (1965). The role of the federal government in the design and administration of intergovernmental programs. *Annals of the American Academy of Political and Social Science, 359*, 23–34.

Colman, W. G., & Goldberg, D. C. (1990). The Eisenhower years and the creation of ACIR. *Intergovernmental Perspective, 16*(3), 19–23.

Commission on Governmental Operations Act, Ch. 184, 67 Stat. 142 (1953).

Commission on Intergovernmental Relations. (1955). *A report to the president for transmittal to the Congress*. Government Printing Office.

Commission on Organization of the Executive Branch of Government Act, Ch. 207, 61 Stat. 246 (1947).

Congressional Research Service. (2012a). *Presidential reorganization authority: History, recent initiatives, and options for Congress*. Congressional Research Service.

Congressional Research Service. (2012b). *Sourcing policy: Selected developments and issues*. Congressional Research Service.

Conlan, T. (2006). From cooperative to opportunistic federalism: Reflections on the half-century anniversary of the commission on intergovernmental relations. *Public Administration Review, 66*(5), 663–676.

Council on Intergovernmental Relations. (1947). *Grass roots: A report and an evaluation*. Council on Intergovernmental Relations.

Dickenson, J. R. (1976, March 12). Ford, Reagan philosophically close together. *Decatur Daily Review*, p. 6.

Divine, W. R. (1955). The second Hoover commission reports: An analysis. *Public Administration Review, 15*(4), 263–269.

Edwards, J. (2020, March 24). NAPA to study potential outcomes of OPM-GSA merger. *ExecutiveGov*. https://www.executivegov.com/2020/03/napa-to-study-potential-outcomes-of-opm-gsa-merger. Accessed 5 Mar 2021.

Frederickson, D. G., & Frederickson, H. G. (2006). *Measuring the performance of the hollow state*. Georgetown University Press.

Garvey, G. (1995). False promises: The NPR in historical perspective. In. D. F. Kettl & J. J. DiIulio Jr. (Eds.), *Inside the reinvention machine: Appraising governmental reform* (pp. 87–106). The Brookins Institution.

Gilmour, J. B., & Lewis, D. E. (2006). Does performance budgeting work? An examination of the office of management and budget's PART scores. *Public Administration Review, 66*(5), 742–752.

Gore, A. (1993). *From red tape to results: Creating a government that works better and costs less*. Government Printing Office.

Government Performance and Results Act of 1993, Pub. L. 103-62, § 3-5, 107 Stat 286 (1993).

GPRA Modernization Act of 2010, Pub. L. 111-352, § 6,9, 124 Stat. 3866 (2011).

Grace, P. J. (1984). *President's private sector survey on cost control: A report to the president, volume 1, the survey*. Government Printing Office.

Greitens, T. J., & Joaquin, M. E. (2010). Policy typology and performance measurement: Results from the program assessment rating tool (PART). *Public Performance and Management Review, 33*(4), 555–570.

Hayes, R. M. (1986). The president's private sector survey on cost control: An opinion essay on the Grace commission report. *Government Information Quarterly, 3*(1), 73–81.

Ingraham, P. W. (1984). The Civil Service Reform Act of 1978: Its design and legislative history. In P. W. Ingraham & C. Ban (Eds.), *Legislating bureaucratic change: Civil service reform act of 1978* (pp. 13–28). SUNY Press.

Ink, D. (2000). What was behind the 1978 civil service reform? In J. P. Pfiffner & D. A. Brook (Eds.), *Twenty years after the Civil Service Reform Act* (pp. 39–56). Johns Hopkins University Press.

Joaquin, M. E. (2009). Bureaucratic adaptation and the politics of multiple principals in policy implementation. *American Review of Public Administration, 39*(3), 246–268.

Joaquin, M. E., & Greitens, T. J. (2009). Presidential policy initiatives and agency compliance: Organizational adaptation to A-76. *Administration and Society, 41*(7), 815–849.

Joint Federal-State Action Committee. (1957). *Report of the joint federal-state action committee to the President of the United States and to the chairman of the governors' conference, progress report no. 1*. Government Printing Office.

Kaiser, R. G. (1979, February 9). Adlai III fed up, may run for president. *Akron Beacon Journal*, p. 11.

Kamensky, J. (2011). *GPRA Modernization Act of 2010 explained*. IBM Center for the Business of Government.

Kraft, M. E., & Vig, N. J. (1984). Environmental policy in the Reagan presidency. *Political Science Quarterly, 99*(3), 415–439.

Lawrence, P. R., & Abramson, M. A. (2011). Agency-level reorganization can work. *Public Manager, 40*(2), 19–21.

Lederle, J. W. (1949). The Hoover commission reports on federal reorganization. *Marquette Law Review, 33*(2), 89–98.

Lee, M. (2010). *Nixon's super-secretaries: The last grand presidential reorganization effort*. Texas A&M University Press.

Lutz, E. A. (1949). Intergovernmental relations at the grass roots. *Public Administration Review, 9*(2), 119–125.

Lynn, N. B., & Vaden, R. E. (1979). Bureaucratic response to civil service reform. *Public Administration Review, 39*(4), 333–343.

McGuinn, P. (2016). From No Child Left Behind to the Every Student Succeeds Act: Federalism and the education legacy of the Obama administration. *Publius: The Journal of Federalism, 46*(3), 392–415.

Nathan, R. P. (1983). *The administrative presidency*. John Wiley and Sons.

Oversight on issues related to OMB circular A-76: *Hearing before the Committee on Veterans' Affairs*, 97th Cong. 179 (1981) (testimony of Robert M. Gilroy).

Pemberton, W. E. (1986). Truman and the Hoover commission. *Presidential Studies Quarterly, 16*(3), 511–527.

Perry, J. L. (2008). The Civil Service Reform Act of 1978: A 30-year retrospective and a look ahead (symposium introduction). *Review of Public Personnel Administration, 28*(3), 200–204.

Pfiffner, J. P. (1997). The national performance review in perspective. *International Journal of Public Administration, 20*(1), 41–70.

Radin, B. A. (2006). *Challenging the performance movement: Accountability, complexity, and democratic values*. Georgetown University Press.

Reagan, R. (1981). Inaugural address: Putting America back to work. *Vital Speeches of the Day, 47*(9), 258–260.

Redford, E., & Blissett, M. (1981). *Organizing the executive: The Johnson presidency*. University of Chicago Press.

Rivers, D. L., & Rivers, K. T. (2012). The President Obama healthcare scorecard: The Affordable Care Act in real life. *National Social Science Journal, 38*(2), 73–79.

Sabato, L. (1978). *Goodbye to good-time Charlie: The American governor transformed, 1950–1975*. Lexington Books.

Schoen, M. S. (2008). Good enough for government work: The Government Performance Results Act of 1993 and its impact on federal agencies. *Seton Hall Legislative Journal, 32*(2), 455–484.

Selznick, P. (1949). *TVA and the grass roots: A study in the sociology of formal organization*. University of California Press.

Simon, H. A. (1947). *Administrative behavior: A study of decision-making processes in administrative organization*. Macmillan.

Tomkin, S. L. (1998). *Inside OMB: Politics and process in the president's budget office*. M. E. Sharpe.

U. S. Bureau of the Budget. (1955). *Commercial-industrial activities of the government providing products or services for governmental use* (Bulletin no. 55–4). Executive Office of the President.

U. S. Bureau of the Budget. (1959). *Commercial-industrial activities of the government providing products or services for governmental use* (Bulletin no. 60–2). Executive Office of the President.

U. S. Bureau of the Budget. (1966). *Policies for acquiring commercial or industrial products and services for government use* (Circular no. A-76). Bureau of the Budget.

U. S. House. (1958). *Federal-state-local relations: Federal grants-in-aid.* H.R. Rep. No.85-2533. Government Printing Office.

U. S. House. (1962). *Message from the President of the United States transmitting reorganization plan no. 1 of 1962.* H.R. Doc. No. 87-320. Government Printing Office.

U. S. Office of Management and Budget. (1979). Acquiring of Commercial or Industrial Products and Services Needed by the Government; Policy Revision, 44 *Fed. Reg.* 20558 (proposed April 5, 1979).

U. S. Office of Management and Budget. (2001). *President's management agenda*. Government Printing Office.

U. S. Office of Management and Budget. (2003). *Performance of commercial activities* (Circular no. A-76 revised). Office of Management and Budget.

U. S. Office of Management and Budget. (2006). *Program assessment rating tool guidance no. 2006-02*. Government Printing Office.

U. S. Office of Management and Budget. (2010). *The accountable government initiative: An update on our performance management agenda*. The White House.

U. S. Senate. (1974). *Final report of the select committee on presidential campaign activities* (Senate Report No. 93–981, Book 19). Government Printing Office.

Wood, D. B. (1990). Does politics make a difference at the EEOC? *American Journal of Political Science, 34*(2), 503–530.

Chapter 7
Decay and the Battle to Redefine Capacity

*Why is the inevitable so often surprising? Many people blame a
'failure of imagination.' That is true, but it does not get us closer
to a solution ... imagining things is the easy part. What is hard
is imagining future scenarios that are sufficiently believable to
spur one to act in advance, and find ways to persuade
others to act.*

– Peter Schwartz and Doug Randall (2007, p. 94)

*Trump is crashing the car before turning back the keys...Can
you simply fix the car? Perhaps, but (1) people will get hurt in
the crash, including the public and public servants; (2) you
can't use the car while it is getting fixed; and (3) not clear the
car will ever drive the same.*

– Max Stier quoted in Rampell (2020, para. 17)

We're going to do something very, very special.

– Donald Trump quoted in Katz (2017a, para. 16)

7.1   A Movement Accelerates

In 2017, as the Obama administration came to an end, many things needed fixing in
American federal administration. Experts who thought that human capital management was the fundamental element of administrative capacity were especially
alarmed. The GAO had long identified strategic human capital management as a
high-risk issue, with the silver tsunami of retirements from the baby boom generation among its countless concerns. The data breach that occurred at OPM years
before was the biggest theft of sensitive personnel data in history (Adams, 2016).
The incentive to get talent into government also did not seem to be there, as the mil-
lennials shunned bureaucracy. Government shutdowns, poor compensation, and a
reputation as a bad employer nagged the federal government. Donald Trump's capture of the Oval Office did not help: a *Government Executive* and Government
Business Council survey conducted immediately after his victory found that 60% of

© Springer Nature Switzerland AG 2021   153
M. E. Joaquin, T. J. Greitens, *American Administrative Capacity*,
https://doi.org/10.1007/978-3-030-80564-7_7

respondents thought his election contributed to a more negative public perception of the federal service (Daniels, 2017). It deepened the sense that there was nothing special or even particularly worthy about public service: "Government is…only one actor among many. The real action is elsewhere" (Stivers, 2008, p. 105).

Significant issues of capacity had been rumbling even before Trump's election. The civil service system was struggling despite a patchwork of reforms over the years or what the president of NAPA, the elite body of experts in government affairs, described to us as "bypasses over bypasses that gum up the machinery of the state" (T. Gerton, personal communication, March 11, 2019). These unsuccessful efforts to modernize management by conservatives and liberals alike proved the system was fundamentally broken (NAPA, 2017). Like NAPA, the Volker Association and other public interest groups sensed the dire level of capacity that the government could draw from were it to meet some kind of a man-made or natural catastrophe. "Has the U.S. federal government reached a point where critical operations might fail in stressful events that are likely to occur?" Professor Molly Jahn and the Senior Executives Association investigated years before the coronavirus pandemic. "Based on the data collected in this study, it appears the answer to these critical questions is yes" (Jahn et al., 2019, p. 1).

But for a short while in 2017, there was a sense within the parastate, 40 years after the last government reorganization, that the new Trump administration would be tackling things afresh. In fact, when Trump's OMB released its President's Management Agenda (PMA) that reproduced many of the elements of the Bush and Obama PMAs, experts were genuinely pleased. They called it "a world-class plan," "a powerful diagnostic for what ails it," promising "greater mission effectiveness," and "appealing" as it concentrated on "mission, service, and (fiscal) stewardship" (NAPA, 2019, para. 1–3). Alas, those promising avenues of meso-level reforms were overpowered by the personalization of executive power converging with the ascendant theory of the unitary executive among Republican and Democratic presidents alike. The outcome, which is now known to all, was catastrophic. The decline of democracy, ethics, and capacity seemed so precipitous under Trump that it called to mind what James Kurth (Kurth & Easterbook, 2008, p. 139) observed regarding abrupt dynamics in history:

> If one thinks organically, one can see that a slight change in the body politic or the body social can make a tremendous difference. It might be true, for example, that one's body is getting better and better all the time. But if only a small part of the body, the eyes, for example…should go bad, the entire body will suffer a catastrophe.

In this chapter, our framework suggests that the arc of administrative history was bending toward the Trumpian agenda. To control and shape the bureaucracy for his term and beyond, the Trump administration took a series of actions that may be grouped into two: (1) the deconstruction of the administrative state and (2) redefinition of administrative capacity through reorganization and personnel reform. Their immediate and long-lasting effects would test the resilience of the administrative state.

The first dynamic, deconstruction in the form of administrative disinvestment, bureaucratic delegitimization, and bifurcation, contributed to capacity's decay whose reckoning came when 2020 became the deadliest year in American history and life expectancy fell at a level not seen since the World War II (CNBC, 2021). As Chap. 2 described, the pandemic response was one of the biggest intelligence and public health failures in history. Yet Trump might have been the first president who actually strengthened his political base when his own government failed (Light, 2019). Partly due to that paradox, the system came close to the brink of collapse when voters soured on Trump. In January 2021, the Capitol transformed into a crime scene and a war zone when a mob attacked the lawmakers about to certify the results of the November polls. The whole world was stunned. Amid ongoing violence against the first branch of government, a president declared across the street, "Remember this day forever!" (O'Connell, 2021, para. 6).

The second dynamic, redefining capacity for the future through reorganization and the transformation of the merit-based civil service system, demonstrated the power of the unitary executive that had been quietly gathering strength under reforms to enhance the energetic executive. When the Brownlow Committee recommended actions to enhance the power of the president, some saw them as "a dagger into the very heart of democracy" (Morone, 1990, p. 137). That dynamic would reoccur somehow, each time adding to the presidential arsenal tools consisting of administrative reorganization, staffing, appointment, rulemaking, presidential bill signing statements, emergency directives, and executive agreements to advance executive objectives. Both political parties enabled the outsourcing of capacity yet left the march of the unitary executive unimpeded. It was only a matter of time for these simmering dynamics to intersect high technology and insurgency.

Trump's presidency revealed cracks in the founders' vision and the country's democratic illusions. George Packer wrote that people's sophistication failed them from seeing that institutional decay had set it in – the traditional mechanisms and democratic sentiments had broken down, exposing the real power of the presidency:

> Legal precedent could be deleted with a keystroke; law enforcement's independence from the White House was optional; the separation of powers turned out to be a gentleman's agreement; transparent lies were more potent than solid facts. None of this was clear to the political class until Trump became president. (Packer, 2020, para. 5)

7.2   The Deconstruction of the Administrative State

When presidential adviser Steve Bannon named deconstruction as one of the three pillars of Trump's governing strategy, the word did not show up on any directives, reorganization plans, or press releases. It was not immediately apparent if deconstruction merely involved shrinking regulatory agencies. Policy rollbacks were, after all, a staple of Republican platforms. This administration was no different as it quickly pushed the "one-in, two-out" *Executive Order 13771*, in which agencies had to identify two regulations to eliminate for every new one considered and a host of other proposals on Capitol Hill to limit agency advocacy. Nonetheless, the ideological right celebrated Bannon's strategy, hailing it as a long-term blueprint for reform. Wrote David French (2017):

> we should fully embrace the administration's expressed goal of dismantling the administrative state. Done correctly, it could be Trump's most lasting (and valuable) legacy...The administrative state exists in large part because Congress has intentionally *abdicated* authority... (An) administrative state built over generations won't be deconstructed in one term. (para. 2,8,12)

The transitive verb *deconstruct*, per Merriam-Webster (n.d.), could mean a number of things: (1) to *examine* (something, such as a work of literature) using the methods of deconstruction; (2) to *take apart* or examine (something) in order to reveal the basis or composition, often with the intention of exposing biases, flaws, or inconsistencies; (3) to *destroy*, demolish; and (4) to *adapt* or *separate* the elements of for use in an ironic or radically new way. Based on this definition and the evidence of the past 4 years with Trump, the third and fourth senses of the word – to destroy or demolish and to adapt or separate – described much of what transpired. They involved disinvestment strategies, political delegitimization, and a bifurcation (see Fig. 7.1) of administrative capacity (Joaquin, 2018). Delegitimization hurt the public service spirit while disinvestment attacked its body. Bifurcation and delegitimization cast bureaucracy in terms of political loyalty and split it between those parts that were politically expedient and those that were not, with adverse consequences for capacity. Instances of disinvestment, delegitimization, and bifurcation and their impact on capacity are discussed in further detail in the following sections.

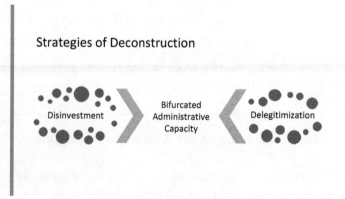

Fig. 7.1 Deconstruction as disinvestment, delegitimization, and bifurcation

7.2.1   Deconstruction as Disinvestment

Disinvestment occurs when an agency's capacity to act is severely weakened as a result of deliberate or unconscious actions. Carried out for the first time in the 1980s, disinvestment as a strategy weakens capacity through continuous resource cutbacks; subjecting agencies to constant manipulation of administrative structure through reorganization; failing to maintain key administrative processes such as budgeting, personnel, and policy-making; and sapping the strength of relationships among critical actors in administrative agencies (Terry, 2003; Lane & Wolf, 1990, p. 4). The following are the key instances of administrative disinvestment during the Trump presidency:

Decapitating the Federal Agencies   Major departments drifted without adequate leadership for years, exacerbating crises, citizen mistrust, and long-term national security risks. The administration was marked by the extensive use of acting officials in critical agencies and appointment of loyalists with questionable qualifications, even those whose nominations failed to advance in the Senate the first time. For example, more than a year after Trump's inauguration, no nominees had been sent up for Senate confirmation in 226 out of 636 key positions, and only 256 had been confirmed. Those positions included Cabinet secretaries, deputy and assistant secretaries, chief financial officers, general counsel, heads of agencies, ambassadors, and other critical leaderships, part of the roughly 1200 positions that required Senate confirmation (WashPostPR, 2016). And then, after almost 4 years, 39 positions in 15 different agencies were never filled, while 131 positions were vacant, all of them crucial. At the Justice department, 31% of Senate-confirmed positions were continuously vacant, and 55% were unfilled as of August 2020 (Tenpas, 2021, para. 2).

Ceaseless Attacks on Worker Benefits   Salaries and benefits were frozen or cut, and retirement systems were placed under tremendous uncertainty with proposals to revamp the Federal Employees Retirement System and the Civil Service Retirement System. The Senior Executives Association thought that the administration was "implicitly assuring applicants…that working for the federal government would mean enduring instability and ceaseless attacks surrounding even their most basic compensation" (SEA, 2019, para. 3).

Holding Capacity Hostage to Politics   Military and civilian agencies renounce government shutdowns as corrosive to agency mission, personnel morale, and national security. No less than three shutdowns occurred under Trump, with the longest occurring from December 22, 2018, to January 25, 2019, and the 21st since shutdowns began in 1976. The threat to capacity was amplified beyond dirty national parks, delayed permits, checks, and an economic hit of at least 0.2% of real Gross Domestic Product for the first quarter of 2019. Perhaps a prelude to greater bifurcation, OMB asked the agencies to submit a list of the highest-impact programs that would be jeopardized if the shutdown were to continue *for months*, forcing them to comprehend running their agencies without a budget for an extended period of time (Paletta & Eilperin, 2019). The CBO reported that the 2019 shutdown probably increased the risk of low-probability but high-cost events. It also reduced the credibility of the federal government as an employer and a contracting party (CBO, 2019). The president also delegitimized the furloughed workers by framing the shutdown as a punishment for leaning Democratic (Smith, 2018).

Hollowing-Out Capacity Agencies were hollowed out even as their workload increased and their strategic human capital management planning activities – an exercise fundamental to capacity – were set aside. Federal workers were cut in all but three Cabinet agencies, and at the 22 independent agencies with at least 1000 employees, all saw a workforce cut except for two – the Small Business Administration and the National Science Foundation (Katz, 2020c). These cuts, as the pandemic case study shows, would have enormous consequences for the expertise and surge capacities needed in times of crisis. Before the pandemic, some the agencies like the IRS, whose mission is crucial to governmental viability, even saw losses in their human resource management functions. The IRS had been meaning to conduct comprehensive workforce planning and assessment, but the GAO found it no longer possessed people with those skills. Its tax collection unit also saw disproportionate erosion under the Trump administration. GAO (2019a) also noted that the human capital planning exercise was pushed back and resources were allocated to accommodate the work entailed by Trump's tax cuts passed in 2017.

Yet contracting out increased across the agencies in this environment. "Trump opened the contract and grant spigots" with more than two million jobs added, particularly in DOD, DOT, and HHS. Large contracts are known to facilitate the influence of, and dependence on, large corporations on government, contribute to management complexity, and threaten accountability when inherently governmental functions are outsourced (Light, 2020).

Weakening Institutional Memory and Transparency The transparency movement that was revived by George W. Bush and strengthened in the digital age under Obama took backward steps under Trump, despite the passage of key laws on open data. "There's the maintenance of the facade of transparency in many cases. It looks like it's happening, but in fact what's happening is 'open-washing,'" according to advocates for more open government (Bublé, 2020a). Certain data on climate change, animal abuse, and violent crime went missing at the EPA, USDA, and DOJ. The lack of transparency became more pronounced with the disappearance of open data at the White House (Lynch, 2017).

Dismantling Labor Rights Trump abolished the labor management forums developed under the Clinton and Obama administrations. Then, with a series of executive orders in 2018, agencies were told to shorten the length of performance improvement plans to 30 days, exempt adverse personnel actions from grievance proceedings, streamline collective bargaining negotiations, and significantly reduce the number of work hours and activities union members could spend on official time. A

US district judge wrote that the orders "effectively eviscerated" workers' rights (Peters, 2019).

7.2.2   Deconstruction as Delegitimization

One of democracy's bulwarks against misinformation had been crumbling for a while. For almost two decades, the US local news industry was getting decimated by structural transformation wrought by technology and changing news consumption habits. The most consequential effects in civic and administrative capacities have been in community engagement and governmental accountability (Bolstad, 2020). But when a president tried to convince the people that the press was their "enemy" at the same time social media built him a megaphone like no other, it excacerbated the public's hunger for alternative sources of accurate information and their capacity to understand the complexities of public administration. Instead, deliberative capacities get overwhelmed when partisan perspectives acquire a monopoly over the means of communication.

During the deconstruction era, disinvestment was complemented by Trump's delegitimization of bureaucrats and government actions that did not support him. The dimension of *administrative conservatorship* was crushed by his rhetoric. In this aspect of controlling the bureaucracy, Trump evoked some comparisons with Nixon. Both men wielded the administrative presidency with impunity. Both men harbored intense distrust of the civil service. For Nixon, righting the machinery of government meant getting rid of the Democrats "infesting" the "convoluted and compartmentalized" bureaucracy so he could carry out "a new American Revolution" (Seidman, 1998, pp. 78–80). For the Trump administration, to whom the "spoils system" was an inspiration, antagonistic approaches went beyond DC and clashed with bureaucratic neutral competence at the state level. The following are some delegitimization tactics witnessed over the last 4 years:

Dishonoring Public Service Through Social Media In 1989, the National Commission on Military, National, and Public Service came out with a report about a "quiet crisis" in government. One of its recommendations was that "Presidents, their lieutenants, and Congress must articulate early and often the necessary and honorable role that public servants play in the democratic process" (Volcker, 1989, p. 6). At the height of the New Public Management movement, advocates explained they were only "ridiculing *bureaucracy*, not bureaucrats"; bureaucrats were "good people trapped in bad systems" (Fredrickson, 1996, p. 267). There was no such nuance under Trump.

Instead, the "deep state" that Trump conjured was at the receiving end of volcanic eruptions of derogatory comments that tainted the entire bureaucracy, even though the president might be targeting particular administrators only. According to former Republican House Speaker Newt Gingrich – architect of a minimalist government that ironically tilted the balance away from Congress and toward the

Executive – Trump's "deep state" referred to a sinister type of career employees conspiring against their elected principals (Lemire, 2017). Framing public servants in such rhetoric served to show how much the president wanted to oversimplify for his political ends an administrative state that was erected to professionally serve the public purpose: by vetting plans before they were implemented, anchoring policy on deliberative mechanisms, fostering stability and continuity, and ensuring accountability (Skowronek et al., 2021).

But the administrative state is far from being an unmitigated good. "Depth," from the perspective of leading political development scholars, may in fact be understood richly as the benefits and pitfalls of having an expanded administrative state. Against a unitary executive, depth is a counterpoint, and each has a case to make:

> The positive case for the unitary executive is that it maximizes the personal responsibility of presidents for the operations of the executive branch…The corresponding risks are that…Good government can become whatever the president says it is…Presidential administrations, singly and an in succession, then become an ironic perversion of original aspirations, a threat to the steady administration of the laws.

> Depth is, first and foremost, a function of public sector penetration into all aspects of national life. It is a reflection of the enormous resources now committed to social regulation and national security…The positive case for depth is that is steadies the state and maximizes the collective responsibility of the coordinate branches of government. When administrators respond to and mediate the interests of multiple principals, they extend the deliberative process and broaden protections for the public interest. The risk, however, is that all this administrative intermediation can blur the lines of control, thwart political direction, and devolve into subversion. (Skowronek et al., 2021, pp. 4, 61)

But like many things that Trump brought to the fore during his presidency, such a profound deliberation about these key complexities of American government was drowned out by his personalization of executive power and intense hostility against Obama and the Democrats.

Trump's stripped-down version of the deep state mired in rogue bureaucratic behavior - versus the capital "D" depth that Skowronek and his colleagues use to depict expansive bureaucracy - acquired such a strong following with technological power. Millions followed his keystrokes, right up to moment the Capitol was attacked. Social media's corrosive impact on civic health was scored not long after people celebrated their democratizing influence during the Occupy movement and the Arab Spring. Experts canvassed by the Pew Research Center on "Democracy in the Digital Age" noted that technology has amplified extremism and search engines have determined the outcomes of upward of 25 of the national elections in the world in 2015 (Anderson & Rainie, 2021). While technology offers pro-democracy forces the same tools, darker elements have more effectively used it for manipulation and surveillance. The confluence of social media with a political world of symbols and signal was severe. In *Twitter*, damaging tweets could be "weaponized" by high-tech processing capabilities and the platform's emotional channeling features, such as its:

- Conciseness – Where emotions are packed into a very small number of characters that then become easy to remember, repeat (retweet), and embed.
- Self-organizing feature – As *Twitter* lends itself to mastery in impact and reach the more one uses it.
- Exponential reach – Where tweets reach even those without *Twitter* accounts because of the interconnections among social media.
- Appearance of legitimacy – When social media easily create the appearance of legitimacy, legality, or popularity. For instance, *Twitter* "bots" accounted for a significant number of Trump's followers in 2018 (Axelrod, 2018).
- Long-lasting influence – Because the posts made by the head of a superpower, for example, are monitored and discussed more intensively, prolonging the lives of his tweets.
- Speed - Since *Twitter* is faster than conventional media and often escapes filtering, fact-checking, and impartiality in information processing.

Using social media as his bullhorn, Trump's countless aspersions on public servants put the entire government under a cloud. Public belief in the agencies' superior knowledge and competence in a particular field or realm was systematically dismantled. Two tweets encapsule the line of attack against career civil servants, Democrats, and fact-finding agencies investigating the Trump administration:

> FBI Deputy Director Andrew McCabe is racing the clock to retire with full benefits. 90 days to go?!!! – December 23, 2017 (Strohm, 2017, para. 2)

> Isn't the I.G. an Obama guy? Why not use Justice Department lawyers? DISGRACEFUL! – February 28, 2018 (Mangan & Breuninger, 2018, para. 3)

Cass Sunstein (2018, para. 10), a former OMB official, wrote that "words fuel attitudes, and attitudes fuel deeds." *Twitter* was slow to enforce its editorial oversight or policies; the tipping point was reached in 2021 when the platform banned Trump's account after the attack on Congress. Court documents described how the president's signals brought the mob to the Capitol on January 6, 2021, and led them to behave wildly because Trump's tweets made them believe it should be so on that particular day (Mangan, 2021).

Delegitimizing Science and Research   The administration attacked the distinctive competence or integrity of several agencies that collect, verify, and produce vital, peer-reviewed information for policy-making. Some were pressured to toe the political line, setting aside the science behind their work, tarnishing the agencies and confusing consumers of scientific data (Narea, 2020; Dmitrieva, 2019). "Climate change" was scrubbed in favor of terminologies like "future high-temperature extremes" and "future climate condition" in the US Geological Survey press releases (Waldman, 2019). The Census Bureau's director resigned amid congressional inquiry that he pressured statisticians to produce a "statistically indefensible" report due to the absence of complete and valid data (Gustafon, 2021). The Labor Statistics (BLS, 2020, para. 1) office, whose original mission is "the fearless publication of the facts," was among the first to receive Trump's "hoax" labels, when he called its statistics fictional, long *before* he became president. Thus, his attack made it harder for the agency to vouch for its integrity when he became the president, even when the numbers made him look good (Hains, 2016; Klesser, 2016). Under Obama, when the payroll jobs data for August 2011 came in at zero, Obama was quickly nicknamed "President Zero" by the Republican Party. Job numbers, however, are almost always revised, and that final tally became 107,000 jobs. Despite the seeming unfairness, Obama and his team did not attack the credibility of the BLS and other agencies that produced data on the economy (Sperling, 2017). When Trump's own numbers were subjected to a similar revision – misclassification – at the start of the coronavirus pandemic, the agency struggled, battling charges of conspiracy and ineptitude at the same time (Iacurci, 2020).

Scientists felt the brunt of Trump's ire as the president repeatedly failed to distinguish between those who set the policy and those who provide policy-makers and lawmakers with the underlying scientific data that inform those decisions (Katz, 2017b). Across 16 federal agencies, the Union of Concerned Scientists reported that the loss of critical staff capacities and political interference made it difficult to fulfill their missions (CSD, 2018). One of Trump's parting shots was a midnight directive subjecting FDA, CDC and other career scientists in the health sector critical of his pandemic response, to job reviews and 5-year term limits (Silver, 2021).

Incentivizing Instability Turnover Demoralizing attacks were not limited to bureaucrats; many times, they were directed even at Trump's own political advisers, with the president previously known for a management style that kept people on edge. The years saw "serial turnover" among the White House "A" team or the presidential senior advisers (Tenpas, 2021). Among the rank and file, morale plummeted with hiring freezes, early retirements, buyouts, and leadership chaos, corresponding with declining agency scores in the annual "Best Places to Work" (2018–2019) surveys. For some employees who felt forced out, seeking redress from adverse personnel actions was futile when the Merit Systems Protection Board (MSPB) lost its quorum in 2017, resulting in the largest ever backlog of cases before the board (Katz, 2018b). Almost 20% of the government's top managers, members of the senior executive service (SES), departed within the first 12 months of the Trump administration (Jahn et al., 2018, pp. 1–2). At the State department, where a tradition of sharing candid opinions was ended, foreign affairs specialists left in droves. The OPM's (2020) personnel data revealed that new claims for employee retirements kept shattering the previous year's records.

Looking back, a former general counsel at the Federal Bureau of Investigation (FBI) described how administrative conservators failed to anticipate these delegitimization strategies that would force them to leave the public service. He thought many joined the administration convinced that:

> they are either smarter than the president, or that they can hold their own against the president, or that they can protect the institution against the president because they understand the rules and regulations and how it's supposed to work, and that they will be able to defend

the institution that they love or served in previously against what they perceive to be, I will say neutrally, the inappropriate actions of the president. And I think they are fooling themselves. They're fooling themselves. He's light-years ahead of them. (Packer, 2020, para. 4)

Risking the Gains from Existing Innovations   Real reforms take time to gestate, and so the sunk costs from the previous reforms are always at risk of being neglected when turnover happens at the top. They can also become collateral damage of institutional hostility. Finally, deconstruction created a wariness about the politics spilling over to the capacities being nurtured at the meso-level. Administrators were attuned to the consequences of the political fights for their own, long-gestating initiatives under OMB's watch. The level of maturity that they were observing, for example, in some projects on government performance improvement was about to allow them to move up from the demonstration project phase to the institutionalization phase when Trump started personalizing government (Katz, 2020a). Such projects included systems for shared services in enterprise management and procurement. As the president kept the nation glued to his temper and his encroachments upon legislative prerogatives, a veteran (personal communications, March 10, 2019) expressed to us that:

> Below the waves, below the hurricane level, in the ocean, there's some really good stuff that's going on, and in a way, nobody wants to say anything out loud about it because they don't want to get into the political world.

Experience had taught veteran reformers to be wary of the pendulum swing as a congressional response to presidential excesses (e.g., reprogramming budgets for the border wall, against congressional wishes) could impede or create unanticipated consequences for continuing agency innovations.

Delegitimizing Election and Transition Processes   One of the final and most serious acts of delegitimization occurred in connection with Trump's loss in the November election. Trump's wrath against bureaucrats who dared to blow the whistle leading to his first impeachment spilled down to the state election administrators. In what has now become a subject of criminal investigation, Trump refused to accept as legitimate the work of state election bureaus and demanded that they "find" him enough votes to overturn the election. In a paradox of this era that evokes the "depth vs. the unitary executive" that Skowronek and his colleagues wrote about, Republican state bureaucrats defied Trump and helped preserve the legitimacy of his rival's victory (Gardner & Firozi, 2021). When his own attorney general and his Cybersecurity and Infrastructure Security Agency (CISA) chief found no evidence of election fraud in the states, both were forced to resign, but there was no way the president could sack a state bureaucrat.

At the national level, where the work of presidential transition occurs, GSA and OMB, which hold much administrative power, impaired the Biden administration's planning and budgeting capacities with their foot-dragging (Bublé, 2021). A total of 46 legal statutes govern presidential transitions. Formal transition procedures were set after the Commission that examined the September 2001 terrorist attacks linked the nation's vulnerability to the shortened transition period that occurred between the Bush and Clinton administrations. A presidential transition index (PTI) created by the Keough School of Global Affairs to analyze the Trump-Biden transition found that only 76% of the transition requirements were fulfilled, owing to the outgoing president's refusal to recognize Joseph Biden and Kamala Harris as the legitimate winners. The Keough report concluded on a note that has become a regular refrain in critical analyses of the Trump administration: current legal statutes are not enough to restrain an executive who seeks unchecked power; democratic norms have to be enforced to prevent future derailment of democracy (Rice, 2020).

The obstinacy of GSA and OMB's top leaders in the transition somehow reprised a similar dysfunction seen 4 years earlier. *The Fifth Risk* by Michael Lewis (2018) documented the willful devaluation of a proper transition by Trump's team when he won in 2016 – a troubling lack of regard for the important work happening inside nondescript government buildings. Demonstrating that control is often pursued at the expense of capacity, Trump's landing teams included inexperienced people who showed no appetite, nor, at times, courtesy, or the security clearance necessary for formal briefings. In one agency, the team reportedly sought a list of staffers who worked on climate change – evoking past episodes of political abuse engineered during the Nixon administration (Mufson & Eilperin, 2016). In highlighting these snubbed agencies, like Agriculture and Energy, Lewis chronicled the problem-solving and management capacities required for dealing with a potential nuclear weapon accident, wars with Iran or North Korea, and an attack on the electrical grid. However, equally threatening episodes could transpire from an incapacitated bureaucracy performing simple tasks. Without their vigilance and institutional knowledge, the nation could suffer from crises with very long fuses rooted in ordinary activities done wrong due to capacity neglect (Lewis, 2018). The lack of a proper briefing on such risks therefore started capacity in the Trump administration on the wrong foot. Four years later, resilient capacity was at risk, based on Biden's complaint against the transition hurdles:

> My team needs a clear picture of our force posture around the world and our operations to deter our enemies. We need full visibility to the budget planning under way at the Defense Department and other agencies in order to avoid any window of confusion or catch up that our adversaries may try to exploit. Right now, we just aren't getting all of the information that we need from the outgoing administration in key national security areas. It's nothing short, in my view, of irresponsibility. (Lewis & Spetalnick, 2020, para. 2–3)

History will judge how the chaos of the Trump-Biden transition impaired Biden's domestic and foreign policy initiatives, from securing global pandemic collaboration to domestic voting rights to withdrawal of forces from Afghanistan. Transition delayed is transition denied, in Brookings' view (Wheeler, 2020). The damage from the delay in 2021 was exacerbated by the slow, partisan pace of Senate confirmation of the incoming agency leaders, but it was partly ameliorated when more than 1000 administrative conservators were quickly sworn into appointed positions that did not need Senate confirmation (Katz, 2021a).

7.2.3   Deconstruction as a Bifurcation of Capacity

Dismantling administrative capacity would have meant weakening the presidency altogether. As Donald Kettl observed at that time, Steve Bannon's campaign would have been internally illogical if the administration wanted to achieve their national security and international trade goals:

> He can slash government's bureaucrats and use the resulting poor performance to make the case for more cuts. But, at some point, he'll have eliminated the capacity to do the things he—and we—*want* government to do. He can cut the bureaucracy with an ax, but he can't produce the other big items on his list—national security and better trade relationships with the rest of the world—without a competent government. (Kettl, 2017, para. 13)

As a result, disinvestment came with bifurcation. The other sense of the word deconstruction – a *separation of certain parts* (of the bureaucracy) *for use in a radically new way* – emerged as a management strategy. Through bifurcation, aspects of capacity lodged in the agencies that were not deemed relevant or expedient to the Executive's governing strategy were delegitimized, neglected, or disinvested, while those deemed relevant were shielded from cuts, repurposed, or redeployed in politically strategic ways. Within a big federal agency, dismantling and preservation could also occur and result in real bifurcation. The following examples show how bifurcation occurred and its ultimate impact.

Promoting Dualistic Administrative Capacity   Bifurcation showed up in budget and staffing levels, particularly as the massive 2017 tax cuts forced the administration to advance its goals at the expense of low-income support programs. Hard power was prioritized over diplomacy or soft power (Memoli & Bierman, 2017). Defense, Homeland Security, and law enforcement were favored over nondefense discretionary and fact-finding agencies. According to OPM data, the VA, DOD, and DHS saw growth in their workforce that surpassed the losses in the rest of the bureaucracy (Katz, 2020c). The cybersecurity budget for DOD expanded, while civilian agencies saw small cuts or relatively flat funding (Warminsky, 2019). Science, research, and environment saw consistent reductions in force and budget. The CDC and HHS were hollowed out amid a pandemic, while agencies that supplied critical data – a capacity-enhancing service – to government and other economic actors were undermined (Malakoff & Mervis, 2020).

A curious case of dualism must be mentioned here in the case of unions, the unitary executive, and political party dynamics. The capacity of the bureaucracy to solve problems, engage, manage, and be accountable at the border regularly hounds presidents but has recently taken a fierce turn. Republican presidencies have no love lost with federal worker unions; Trump's term saw them weakened widely, curbing workers' rights to speak with Congress, for instance, or allowing union members to opt out of paying dues. However, at the US Citizenship and Immigration Service (USCIS), the union was given power over changes in agency policy, hamstringing the incoming Biden administration effort to change policies at the border (Aleaziz, 2021; Dlouhy, 2021). This bifurcation within government worker unions, themselves, can be traced to the first- ever presidential endorsement (of Trump) made by the Immigration and Customs Enforcement (ICE) officers in 2016, after the Obama administration struggled to get its immigration policy accepted within the ranks.

How are we to reconcile the policy preferences of the immigration bureaucracy with the notion of administrative conservatorship (Terry, 2003)? The latter speaks to distinctive competence, guardianship of agency integrity, defense of agency mission against encroachment, cuts to capacity, and politicization. The former, instead, seemed to be characterized by ideology. Trump often spoke against the "deep state," and yet a group of employees who had behaved as a rogue unit under Obama became Trump's favorite union:

> Where immigration is concerned, Trump has installed a group of committed ideologues with a deep understanding of the extensive law-enforcement machinery they now control….In February, (agency chief) Cissna rewrote its mission statement, erasing a phrase that described the United States as a "nation of immigrants…" Then, in June, he announced the opening of an office that would review the files of naturalized citizens, reexamining fingerprints and hunting for hints of fraud that might enable the revocation of citizenship. (Foer, 2018, para. 54–55)

Are the ideologues at the ICE different from the scientists at government agencies who vow to fulfill their scientific mission as they see fit? Are the resisters at immigration now the "deep statists" under Biden? Reports have emerged that the border patrol union was teaming up with the Republican Party in attacking the current administration's policies and treating the immigrants in custody as if Trump was still the president (Fienberg, 2021). The Republican Party's alliance with the union led former Republican President George W. Bush, who lives in Texas and sees the crisis and politics up close, to call on lawmakers to tone down their harsh rhetoric on immigration. Regretting his failure to pass a comprehensive reform in his time, Bush expressed doubts whether his own party listens anymore to him (Robertson & Duster, 2021). The humanitarian crisis at the border grows as of this writing, requiring surge capacities unlike anything before. The long-term implications of deconstruction are just beginning to manifest. Instead of viewing any recalcitrance against the Biden immigration policies as a demonstration of administrative conservatorship, what we are seeing is a consequence to capacity of Trump's deconstruction: the politicization of agency mission against the neutral competence and responsiveness expected of the administrative state.

Weakening Checks and Balance   Bifurcation diminished the capacities that would have fostered checks and balance. Watchdogs, themselves a product of reform, were put in the doghouse. Established in 1978 in the wake of Watergate, inspectors general were systematically weakened upon opening investigations into Trump administration policies or appointees. This action risked rampant fraud, misappropriation, and other questionable activities. In 2019, GAO put a total of 35 areas on its list of programs and operations that were deemed "high risk" – vulnerable to fraud, waste, abuse, and mismanagement (GAO, n.d.). As oversight diminished, ethics concerns mounted. The Federal Employee Viewpoint Survey (FEVS) in 2019 showed that only two-thirds felt that they could disclose suspected violations in their agencies without fear of reprisal (OPM, 2019). Accountable capacity was swept up in an administration marked by more than 3700 conflicts of interest, according to the Citizens for Responsibility and Ethics in Washington (CREW, 2021).

Capturing Agencies and Reformulating Agency Missions   Top agency posts were captured by lobbyists and other groups that fought the agencies in court and even advocated for their abolition. The EPA, Education, HHS, and Labor Board, for example, were led by consistent critics of regulation and worker benefits. Offices were closed and consolidated in the delegitimized and bifurcated agencies like the HHS, DOE, EPA, USCIS, DOI, USDA, and Federal Labor Relations Authority (FLRA). The most profound reorganization push was for OPM, discussed later in this chapter.

Agencies also labored under reformulated mission statements (Emba, 2018). Organizations commonly rewrite their mission statement, but in government, care must be taken not to step on the statute creating the agency. The most controversial revision occurred at the USCIS, when "a nation of immigrants" was removed from its mission statement (Clark, 2018). Additionally, the head of Consumer Product Safety Commission (CPSC) was promptly fired when he claimed that the executive order to eliminate two regulations for every new one ran counter to the agency's mission. Speaking in the spirit of administrative conservatorship, he wrote:

> This Executive Order does not apply to independent agencies, including the Consumer Product Safety Commission…To voluntarily follow it would lead to poor public policy decisions…It would also be counter to our safety mission, as it would cruelly and unfairly have us pit vulnerable populations against each other when it comes to making safety decisions. (CPSC, 2017, para. 1)

Concerns around the executive's faithful execution of the laws were most prominent in the deconstruction of "Obamacare," where regulations the administration put in place undermined Medicaid and Medicare, the marketplaces, and FDA operations, required substantial agency staff time to implement, and diverted key resources from other priorities (CBPP, n.d.).

Hostile Takeovers   The 2020 summer confrontations seen between armed yet unmarked DHS agents and protesters revealed how an administrative state could be incapacitated in public health and cybersecurity, yet afford to carry out "performative authoritarianism" in aid of a president's reelection (Applebaum, 2020). In these confrontations, the secretary of Defense, not viewing response to protests as part of the military's mission, was sacked. For the DHS, which obediently carried out orders, experts thought that the breakdown of the relationship between the agency and local authorities could have potentially calamitous consequences for capacity in future disaster and emergency operations (Tucker, 2020).

Bifurcation also meant undermining some of the capacities built out of previous reforms, including sub-national ones. A trend, in which national politicians looked to the state and local governments for partisan wins, became even more pronounced

(Selin, 2020). "Punitive federalism" (Goelzhauser & Konisky, 2020) against Democrat-led states was ushered in by the Trump administration. Deconstruction as "hostile takeover" was seen in erasing through administrative action, Obama's legacy in the areas of climate, education, and health policies. The fact that the Trump administration shrunk the number of personnel in charge of key policies and agencies – for example, there were fewer than 40 people in the presidential personnel office compared to more than 100 for most presidential administration (Thompson et al., 2020) – and yet accomplish so much by way of deconstruction suggests that administrative control in the hands of the modern president has gotten powerful enough "that erasing a prior Administration requires little more than determination – and perhaps a dash of ruthlessness" (Mashaw & Berke, 2018, p. 607).

7.3   From *Energetic* to *Unitary* Executive in the Battle to Redefine Capacity

The theory of the unitary executive gears administrative capacity toward presidential priorities, not the lawmakers' whose constituencies are cast as parochial. Its alternative, republican theory, involves others in all aspects of administration and promotes a collective view of responsibility and accountability rather than resting them all on a single person selected in a nationwide referendum (Skowronek et al., 2021, pp. 120–121). Unitarism gained a staunch advocate with Richard Cheney, vice president to George W. Bush, who referred to the theory to comment and challenge provisions of the bills passed by Congress in over 700 instances of presidential signing statements (Library of Congress, n.d., para. 8). The unitary executive is an echo of FDR's *stewardship presidency* during the nascent period of administrative capacity building (Skowronek, 1982). Four decades after the New Deal, the "Malek Manual" of the Nixon years juxtaposed the unitary executive theory with popular control, arguing for the ability of the president "to insure a loyal chain of command" because "the executive is answerable to the electorate, every four years, for its management of the Government" (The Bureaucrat, 1976, p. 430). The muscular theory of the unitary executive also encompasses the notion of *administrative presidency* that Richard Nathan (1983) used to describe Reagan's effort to achieve political goals outside of thorny legislative bargaining and through centralized, administrative power. Through the use of presidential reorganization, budget reallocation, a centralized mechanism for clearing (or rejecting) administrative rules, executive orders, waivers, active federal litigation, agency rulemaking through guidance letters, Dear Colleague memos, questions and answers to frequently asked questions, and policy memos, a president could, the theory goes, enhance popular control rather than leave it with bureaucratic power centers (Thompson et al., 2020, p. 185).

In flexing the power of the unitary executive, Trump channeled Nixon more than any other president. Only the ejection of both men from power arrested a systemic bureaucratic transformation rivaling the Progressive era. At Nixon's impeachment, overshadowed by the Watergate scandal was the story of his last grand attempt at reorganization, calling for the abolition and merger of entire departments (Lee, 2012). Such radical moves had not been considered for quite some time, and the plan met intense opposition from cross-cutting coalitions and congressional committees fearing loss of jurisdictional power. Had the Watergate break-ins not been discovered, agencies would have lost their linkages with professional groups and congressional committees, and impeachment could have been left as the only means of holding the executive accountable (Seidman, 1998, p. 86).

For Trump, whose congressional majority afforded him even greater leeway, the unitary executive's agenda to redefine the contours of the federal bureaucracy and the shape of its future capacity was coursed through the three most powerful agencies of government. The three most important positions in government management are the deputy director for Management at OMB, the director of OPM, and the administrator of GSA (Miller, 2018). These are the capacity enhancers or what Max Stier of Partnership for Public Service called the "force multipliers," for better or for worse. Trump's executive directives to and through these agencies, including one that evoked the spoils systems, induced impacts that would last long after his presidency and whose dynamics should raise new questions for any rebuilding effort. In the following sections, we describe those directives.

7.3.1   Flexing the Unitary Executive Muscle Through OMB

Within the Executive Office, OMB houses a lot of the modern-day, transactionalist tools that could get a president's agenda accomplished. Its power over budget preparation and spending across government agencies informs the appropriations process. It sets government-wide policies on contracting, financial accounting, information technology, and other management functions. And its reviews of agency rulemaking through the Office of Information and Regulatory Affairs (OIRA) can have wide implications for the public, the economy, and the environment. OMB has gone through several transformations to help it cope with the evolving mandates on the budgeting side and later, as it learned how to gain more control of interagency efforts and personnel, on the management side of its mission. Advocates had envisioned OMB to command a high level of respect and authority with other governmental institutions to do its job well (Tomkin, 1998, p. 7). Over time, on the budgeting side, the complexities of negotiations in Washington since the fiscal crunch of the 1970s have developed OMB's institutional influence. OMB is the "scorekeeper, umpire, and judge" on federal spending (Shuman, 1984, p. 338). Its secretive apportionment process draws concerns across the ideological spectrum (Butler & Gianfortune, 2021).

It has also gotten more influential on the management side in pushing presidential priorities administratively. During the Clinton years, it was supposed to be the engine that kept the reinvention going (Tomkin, 1998, p. 301). During the George

W. Bush years, OMB was central to the President's Management Agenda (PMA) on linking agency budgets to performance, improving financial management, expanding e-government, and managing human capital. Besides the PMA, there was also the Program Assessment Rating Tool (PART), which, unlike its predecessor the Government Performance and Results Act (GPRA), let the executive control the agencies' plans and performance, shifting the locus of influence away from Congress and to OMB officials.

Congress has a similar, in-house equivalent to OMB, the Congressional Budget Office (CBO) that performs fiscal analysis at the request of lawmakers but without the policy-making role that makes OMB influential. The bigger clashes between the administrative "proxies" in the modern executive-legislative tussle have occurred not between OMB and CBO, however, but among OMB, GAO, OPM, and, to a certain extent, GSA, which played an active role in Trump's proposed abolition of OPM (House Committee, 2020).

Three dynamics represent the deconstruction of capacity *through* OMB and the deconstruction *of* OMB's own capacity: its leadership's role in the spending violations uncovered by GAO, the breakdown in political-appointee relationship within OMB that saw careerists being sidelined, and OMB's approach to controlling reorganization, including that of its rival, OPM.

With GAO, OMB's tussles were intense. Spending during the longest shutdown was one bone of contention. Shutdowns, as earlier discussed, harm capacity in insidious ways, and the country saw three under Trump. The congressional watchdog issued a legal opinion that agencies, with OMB direction, had violated the Antideficiency Act for political purposes. OMB allowed spending to occur at Interior and Agriculture programs that critics thought were favorable to the president's reelection chances. The move subverted the power of the purse when OMB's general counsel instructed the agencies to ignore GAO's decision as nonbinding (EOP, 2019; GAO, 2019c; Katz, 2019).

More proxy battles occurred when OMB figured in Trump's (first) impeachment. House Democrats moved against OMB's use of the apportionments and reserve law when it delayed $391 million in foreign aid to Ukraine without congressional knowledge or consent. The impoundment of the aid, according to GAO and the testimonies during the trial, turned out to have been for reasons that had nothing to do with budgeting or a budget audit that OMB was supposed to be conducting, but for policy – to pressure the Ukrainian officials to open an investigation on Joe Biden's son, which would have interfered with the upcoming election (Fogel, 2019). Trump was acquitted of impeachment by the Senators just weeks before the coronavirus pandemic began, but OMB was torn internally. Two career officials resigned from OMB to protest the agency's direction under Russell Vought and Michael Duffy, who defied congressional subpoenas. Vought and the leadership of GSA, Emily Murphy, came under fire for withholding or delaying transition resources requested by Biden's team. Vought was also known for issuing the controversial memorandum cancelling funding for racial sensitivity programs across government after the country was roiled by protests against police brutality and Trump denounced the Black Lives Matter movement (Milbank, 2020; Vought, 2020). Since Nixon,

OMB had not seen such politicization and internal division. A recent volume on OMB showed that while neutral competence was still valued and not perceived as declining among careerists, the political responsiveness demanded of the agency by presidents posed a real risk. OMB's own leadership had become more political, with an increasing number of political appointees (more than 50 in 2018 in an organization of 480). The agency had gotten more influential on overall administration policy, even as it struggled to impose rational budget decisions on a polarized Congress and presidency (Pfiffner, 2020; Dickinson, 2020).

Under Trump, OMB flexed its muscle early and strongly, and it saw the same leadership turbulence that visited a lot of agencies over the last 4 years. Beneath the storm, however, some careerists yearned for a time of organizational stability and integrity. Control was good, but they saw it within the original framework of the agency's mission, balancing supporting enactment of a president's agenda without becoming too politicized (Tomkin, 1998, p. 248). The days of the Bush-era PMA were recalled with pride for its demonstration of how OMB led in capacity building. While the Clinton-era National Performance Review operated out of Vice President Al Gore's office, employing private sector consultants for the ideas it incorporated in reinventing government, the PMA's substance and mechanics were OMB's own, a source of in-house pride but also a paradox in the one agency that had pushed initiatives in privatization and competitive sourcing. The PMA was cherished for the trust placed by the political appointees upon the career personnel and the integration of the budget and management roles, strengthening control over the bureaucracy. Clay Johnson, who led the Bush PMA effort as OMB's second in command or the politically appointed post of deputy director for Management (DDM), explained how such should be the blueprint for OMB's management of capacity in the future:

> The way [the PMA] was designed to be done made it successful, which I think is a huge lesson for DDMs of the future. It was not done as a separate deal. Some deal across the street from OMB where a bunch of smart people were trying to figure out how the government ought to work and then go in and do it to the agencies. It was done within OMB. Most intelligently and brilliantly, it was done with the resource management officers (RMOs) at OMB. One of the most important facts of fiscal life is everybody wants their budget officer to be really happy. *So, if the budget officer was involved in the management programs, they were going to be paying a lot of attention at the agencies on what the management folks wanted done because it almost certainly will impact what kind of budget they got.* (Italics ours) (Miller, 2018, para. 13)

The PMA was regarded internally as a superior initiative because of Johnson's empowerment of career personnel. An OMB veteran compared the Trump administration and shared with us how the Bush-era leadership did not undermine staff, but rather trusted them to do the job (Administration official, personal communication, March 9, 2019).

When the PMA lost its luster during Obama's first term, OMB's engagement scores in the "Best Places to Work" survey fell from a high level. But similar to previous reforms, some components of the PMA were revitalized during Obama's second term, particularly on procurement. OMB regained leadership of an agenda, and its employee engagement score rose, possibly reflecting the sentiment. During Trump's presidency, this force multiplier of an agency saw some of its biggest crises, and it did not adopt a similar agenda until a year after. Under Trump, they saw a lot of micromanagement, yet without the kind of trust, consultation, and policy direction that careerists were expecting to see. The "lost partnership" between the appointees and career workers in agencies like the VA, EPA, and DOJ (Levin, 2021) was also lamented at OMB. At OMB, there were suspicion and fear on top of it, hurting the agency's capacity:

> Whatever Administration comes in, they normally work with us, they find out we're professionals, trust us enough. People in several agencies feel like they are marginalized, they are not being recognized for their expertise. I haven't seen this in any previous administration. We're 500 people, tight and small, and we've always supported White House initiatives...Everybody's afraid of getting fired. They are careful not to overstep, what might be perceived as not in the right direction...So, it's kind of floundering. The management structure is definitely floundering in this Administration. (Administration official, personal communication, March 9, 2019)

Floundering captures well the effect on the agencies created by the third dynamic in which capacity was influenced through OMB: reorganization. OMB wanted to accelerate reorganization in 2017, which at that time was welcomed by many and called the most exciting opportunity in years by thrilled government managers (Clark, 2017). Like the PMA, the reality of what unfolded was far from the vision, as OMB's leaders like Mick Mulvaney advanced the agenda in a politicized way. For example, he portrayed the forced relocation of USDA's Economic Research Service (ERS) and National Institute of Food and Agriculture (NIFA) to Kansas City as "a wonderful way to streamline government" because it was "nearly impossible" to fire workers (CRS, 2018; Hanna & Knickmeyer, 2019, para. 2). In one stroke, bureaus, whose data-driven outputs could embarrass the administration's agenda in trade, lost their proximity and visibility to policymakers in Congress. The agencies came under fire when their reports on the impact of Trump's signature tax cut made the administration uncomfortable (Williamson & Bawa, 2018). Congress resisted their relocation, but the psychological effects of disinvestment and delegitimization on the workers took hold faster than the bureaucratic process could unfold. While the actual figure was hard to pin down, lawmakers said the vacancy rate reached up to 20% for ERS and 26.4% for NIFA (Carper, 2019), creating capacity damages whose consequences could be far-ranging.

7.3.2 Redefining Capacity Through OPM Reform

No reorganization under the aegis of OMB was more critical than the proposed shrinking of OPM. These agencies embody the two competing approaches for managing capacity: OPM is the late-stage version of the Civil Service Commission that represented the *traditional* approach, while *transactional approaches are often embraced by* OMB under direction from the president. OPM has resisted OMB advances to encroach upon its civil service guardianship but has been lacking in influence in recent decades. OMB has developed its control of performance management, while OPM struggles to evolve a human capital management strategy for the vast state.

Under Trump, OPM saw the departure of heads like Jeff Pon and Dale Cabaniss under circumstances that signaled their opposition to the president's plans for the agency. The proposed reorganization of OPM took off during the "dual-hatting" by OMB's DDM, at that time, Margaret Weichert, who became acting director for OPM when Pon was edged out for resisting at least part of the plans for OPM. Having an OMB official act as OPM chief made the two agencies look one and the same (Katz, 2018a). According to NAPA Fellow Peter Levine, the tension between OPM and OMB owed much to OMB's active role in personnel policy and performance management. "A mix of too many voices," he said, was undermining OPM's role in the human capital management (Wagner, 2021c, para. 7).

The long-recognized weaknesses of OPM as an independent agency in developing a government-wide vision and structure to ensure administrative capacity certainly invited that encroachment. Throughout its history, OPM has had to confront not only the human capital challenges of the nation; it did so while making itself a model of agency streamlining and privatization under various presidents. Dysfunctions afflicted what should have been a capacity enhancer in the administrative state. As discussed in the previous chapter, OPM came out of the Civil Service Commission, along with MSPB and FLRA under the Carter administration. Larry Lane's account of OPM's first decade of life saw that OPM was hobbled out of the gate as an offshoot of a declining entity. OPM had little that it could directly control in terms of management. It was unable to consistently and effectively intervene in agency activities in an informed way. The most widely accepted aspect of the original OPM – the agency relations function – was abolished. Failures marked OPM's first decade – in effectively monitoring the application by agencies of merit principles, in providing aggressive leadership, guidance, and oversight to agencies with their decentralized personnel authorities. It lost a lot of technical specialists, while Reagan nearly doubled its political appointees. The outflow of competent career staff, the politicization of the top ranks, and the turning away of the agency from its core mission marked the decline of OPM as an institution of human resource management (Lane, 1992, p. 108). By the second decade of OPM's life, the federal government's uniform merit system was "neither uniform, merit-based, nor a system" (Kettl et al., 1996, p. 1). OPM simply did not evolve from its regulatory beginnings into a genuine human resource management agency. Patricia Ingraham's observation of OPM's failures more than a decade after its reorganization might be worth repeating:

> Past efforts at reform, whatever their intent, have not changed the base, but have operated at the fringes of the system. Jimmy Carter's "comprehensive" effort did not significantly affect the base of unreformed classification, compensation, and procedural complexity. That base continued to perform as it had for a century; the various components of the reform were confounded by it. The base itself must be the target in the future. (Ingraham, 1995, p. 132)

Indeed, echoes can be heard from the 1940s when people from private enterprise joined bureaucracy. According to Paul Van Riper, public and private management began blending then, removing the almost watertight compartmentalization of the two. But the merger spawned debates about the merit system and doing government work using business philosophy. There were those who saw:

> the prime function of the merit system as control of the patronage and those who looked forward to the elimination of rigid controls in favor of the industrial concept of personnel work as a positive aid to line management. (Van Riper, 1958, p. 545)

It seems the same battles were being fought at OPM during the Trump administration. But some believed that OPM under Trump was being unfairly scapegoated for leadership problems found across the agencies. According to Max Stier:

> I think in many instances, with complaints about OPM, the folks in the agencies making them need to look in the mirror…The responsibility is not simply OPM's but theirs as well … OPM has been in the area of supporting agencies, but under-resourced…these issues don't get addressed just by moving the boxes around. It would be a mistake to believe that a structural reorganization could address these fundamental issues. (Wagner, 2018, para. 13)

Like OPM, the other two personnel policy entities that came out of the 1978 reorganization met Trump's deconstruction. The MSPB and FLRA faced charges of systemic bias against federal employees. The two agencies were spared reorganization but the MSPB was left to flounder without a quorum to hear employee appeals, while the FLRA, which oversees collective bargaining, overturned one precedent after another in labor management relations under Trump (Wagner, 2019a).

As a target of presidential reform, OPM had long been considered a weak entity, despite its independence, or perhaps because of it. In Rubin's account, OPM's nature as a "primarily housekeeping agency," with little or no interest group support, made it powerless to resist during the cutback era and instead became the president's model for agency streamlining. It was constantly criticized by Congress and GAO; federal employees simply did not rally around OPM as an advocate of their rights (Rubin, 1985, p. 163). Under the Democratic Clinton administration, which shed some of its background investigative functions, OPM still struggled to redefine its core mission (Kettl et al., 1996, p. 64). Some reformers were so dismayed with OPM and attempts to reform OPM that they only half-joked when they talked about blowing the whole thing up to see where things would land (Government expert, personal communication, March 10, 2019).

Reorganizing OPM: Executive Advance

Similar to many reforms in history, the OPM story showed the pattern of executive advance-congressional counter-reaction-confrontation-and-stalemate that Stephen Skowronek (1982) saw at the beginnings of the administrative state. Within that dynamic, the questions that Rubin asked of OPM's decline during the Reagan years still rang true under Trump:

The president tends to have more autonomy over personnel decisions than over program design or budget decisions; thus, if he controlled the agency that set personnel policy, he would have enormous control over the policy itself. How effective was the president's control in this area? How significant were the changes that were made? What were the constraints, if any on the president's autonomy? (Rubin, 1985, pp. 161–162)

Like Reagan, and Nixon before him, Trump eyed greater control of the federal apparatus through OPM. Initiated under the wing of OMB's Weichert, plans for OPM reform were announced in pieces. At first the White House directed all the agencies to submit reorganization plans within 180 days, to "consider redundancies in government, whether functions would be better left to states or the private sector and a cost-benefit analysis of the agency itself" (Katz, 2017a, para. 3). In 2018, it put together a document called "Delivering Government Solution in the 21st Century," containing some new and some old proposals from the Newt Gingrich-led House Republicans. Among them were a merger of Education and Labor departments, reorganization of safety net programs under the Department of Health and Public Welfare, privatization of the US Postal Service, revamping the Army Corps of Engineers, and relocating staff, such as those of Interior and the USDA, outside the National Capital Region. For OPM, the plan called for shrinking the agency to break free of what the White House viewed were archaic personnel policies that did not reflect the realities of the contemporary workforce (EOP, 2018a). Under the plan, key components of OPM's work would be cannibalized and sent to three different agencies: the GSA – an agency traditionally in charge of buildings and facilities and whose management practices before the Trump presidency had constantly landed it on GAO's list of high-risk agencies, the Pentagon, and the Executive Office, home of OMB.

Some of the components of OPM's reorganization would be administratively implemented. But modifying the pure policy and oversight aspects of its work and creating changes to the federal workers' trust funds, like the health benefit programs, required congressional approval. Since a lot of OPM's operational activities would move over to GSA, it was effectively merging OPM with it, with the new entity to be renamed *Government Services Agency*. GSA would assume the HR Solutions and IT services. Two new offices would absorb OPM's work with GSA called Employee Services and Health Care and Insurance Office. As for the work of ensuring that the merit systems principles are upheld in government, a Merit System Accountability and Compliance Office would be established in the new GSA. According to the (old) GSA's budget proposal for FY 2020, 3315 employees would go to the Pentagon, 152 to GSA, and 3 to EOP. With these proposals, GSA would assume the majority of OPM's function, effectively making OPM a human capital service alongside GSA's existing Public Buildings Service and Federal Acquisition Service (Wagner, 2019b). The Pentagon would assume the majority of OPM employees who worked on security clearance function in the National Background Investigations Bureau. It would formalize the process authorized in the 2018 National Defense Authorization Act, which ordered the transfer of DOD security clearance investigations away from OPM.

The more controversial parts were those of OPM going to the Executive Office focused on policy issues, in a new unit modeled after the OMB's Office of Federal Procurement Policy (OFPP), "a more streamlined personnel management unit that is less expensive to operate." To "transform and elevate" this new office, a change management and capacity-building process would be part of the process, led by the director of the OMB and the director of OPM (EOP, 2018a, p. 55). The administration defended its blueprint as arresting OPM's declining capacity. In its view, management of OPM's core function of setting personnel policy had been overrun by nonessential activities such as performing background checks for security personnel. OMB also saw reform as bringing federal compensation and benefits in line with the private sector and reforming federal workers' pension schemes. OPM was presiding over an outmoded personnel classification scheme (called the General Schedule). Indeed, the plan cited as evidence of OPM's decline the creation by Congress in recent years of a variety of alternative personnel pay systems – the workarounds and bypasses that NAPA's president Terry Gerton alluded to as gumming up the machinery – and the lack of a strategy to address the ongoing human capital management crisis. According to the White House, "This has postponed a broader overhaul of the core personnel system, and left a fragmented personnel structure – roughly a third of which now lies outside the purview of OPM" (EOP, 2018a, p. 52).

Altogether, the White House argued for a civil service system that was performance-based and incentive-based. The plan tied back to the political responsiveness model and executive leadership value that were promoted in the past when bureaucracy was expanding. Responsiveness to the president within the agencies would be easier to achieve were it to be modeled by OPM. Reliving history, the reform asked for centralization. Only OPM's governing statute and the presence of Democrats in Congress saved it from elimination. By 2019, the atmosphere at OPM was said to have reached a new low (Wagner, 2019c).

Congressional Counter-Reaction and Stalemate

Experts were skeptical of parts of the design, if not the overall goal. The transfer of the security clearance function found support from Robert Tobias, veteran manager and union leader, who thought nonetheless that the nonpartisan nature of OPM would suffer were its policy shop to move over to the White House. Donald Kettl, who led various studies on the civil service, thought that the OMB-led plan seemed more intent on dismantling OPM rather than designing an effective personnel management agency (Wagner, 2018). Lawmakers, Democrats in particular, wanted to make sure OPM's independence and the merit principle stayed intact and that any reorganization would come from Capitol Hill. The tension with OMB was the sticking point. The *Congressional Research Service* review of the reorganization plan noted that OMB left many pieces of the plan uncomfortably vague:

> It remains to be seen what venues OMB may use to promote its…agenda, how much influence OMB will attempt to exert on agencies, and the extent to which agencies consult with Congress and nonfederal stakeholders. (CRS, 2018, p. 96)

Many details were not immediately made available, such as whether a new OPM director would remain a Senate-confirmed presidential appointment. Lawmakers then blocked any budget that would go toward an administrative reform of OPM. Then, in July 2020, a Project on Government Oversight Report led lawmakers to investigate if the White House deliberately misled Congress on the OPM-GSA merger. The Justice Department Office of Legal Counsel (OLC) reportedly advised the administration that the plan would be illegal, yet that information was withheld during a hearing in 2019. OPM had denied the opinion; however, experts believed that oral, rather than written, guidance subject to Freedom of Information Act requests could have been provided by OLC. Between 1987 and 2017, OLC's written opinions had supported the expansion of presidential power (Bublé, 2020b; Kim, 2018).

None of these meant that OPM did not deserve a transformation, but between congressional inaction and executive assertion, turnover and demoralization in the ranks were the immediate results. OPM had a reputation as an agency in decline, a locus of uncertainty, where "people get tossed about one way or another" (Katz, 2018a, para. 10). NAPA's leaders noted that OPM's key failing stemmed from a lack of clarity and consensus on OPM's mission and role, together with constrained funding and staffing resources and leadership turnover (Gerton & Hale, 2021). The last director to serve a full term at the agency was John Berry during the Obama administration.

Lawmakers themselves knew that the system was eroding, since any agency "opt-outs" from OPM's rigid hiring system mandates had to be approved by Congress. Over the years, many agencies had successfully approached Congress and been delegated direct hiring authorities (DHAs) or wiggle room from OPM oversight and mandates. The DHAs' popularity rose among those wanting to gain more flexibility in their compensation and position classification schemes, if they faced critical needs or severe shortages. These agencies included the DOD, Securities and Exchange Commission, Federal Deposit Insurance Corporation, and other financial regulatory oversight agencies. DHA waived the requirement for those agencies to give preference to veterans and used the OPM-required formal rating of applicants. Paul Verkuil (2017, p. 119) observed that by permitting these opt-outs, Congress, without intending to do so, had set up intriguing possibilities for civil service reform.

As DHAs matured in some agencies, a recent study of DHAs by the Merit Systems Protection Board (MSPB) saw important trends that signify bifurcations within human capital management itself. They signified (1) a clear frustration with the competitive service hiring procedures, (2) increased number of new employees hired using DHAs, and (3) a divergence between OPM and the agencies in their understanding of the intent of the mechanism. In 2018, DHAs were used to onboard 30,000 employees or a 460% increase since 2008, proof that agencies preferred the quicker alternative. But the report noted a fundamental difference between the agencies and OPM in understanding the goal and role of direct hiring. Per OPM, selection had to be made based on the order in which the qualified applications were received, rather than based on who is the most qualified. However, agencies seemed to be going beyond that DHA intent by expanding recruitment, implementing additional assessments, and doing more to draw distinctions among applicants (MSPB, 2021, p. 23; Katz, 2021b). The flexibility was making agencies improve the quality of their hires, rather than just hiring more. Given that difference, OPM was tasked to look closely and ensure consistency in its messaging about the aim of direct hiring.

The evolution of DHAs represents some of the many challenges confronted by OPM in managing government personnel for the new century. Congress' own oversight arm, GAO, had prepared various ideas for OPM to address in conjunction with OMB – a sign of OPM's weakness as an independent body. The expansion of access to DHAs was one, and conducting a review similar to what MPSB suggested: establishing a baseline, tracking and evaluating the special pay authorities across the federal landscape, and identifying areas for improvement, including any necessary legislation to carry them out. Another significant challenge was how to reform the pay and position classification system. GAO asked OPM to work through the Chief Human Capital Officers Council – a body created by the Homeland Security Act of 2002 to advise agencies on modernizing HR systems – to learn from demonstration projects and alternative classification systems. Other reforms suggested for OPM included improving Enterprise Human Resource Integration (EHRI) payroll data, addressing employee misconduct and improving performance management, and strengthening controls over IT systems. Information going back to 1985, theft of fingerprint data, and clearance adjudication information for individuals who require access to classified information, including polygraph examination, were among those stolen in 2014. OPM was advised to implement an automated system for management of security controls and security plans, define and complete its planned corrective actions on training, and conduct reviews of completed security control assessments (GAO, 2019b).

The National Academy of Public Administration advocates for making OPM a Cabinet-level agency with the resources and power necessary for its mission: to lead in human capital management, rather than focus on compliance with "one size-fits-all" rules. OPM's relationship with OMB has undermined OPM's role in setting the direction for the management of the workforce, according to Fellow Peter Levine (Wagner, 2021c). In the Academy's view, the Trump administration proposal to merge OPM's policy function with OMB and the rest with GSA would not have resolved the problems or challenges identified in the administration's proposal. In its latest report, *Elevating Human Capital: Reframing the U.S. Office of Personnel Management's Leadership Imperative*, the Academy calls for reform to reaffirm OPM's independence and strengthen the agency, which means elevating it from the work of OMB's deputy director for management. OPM must redefine merit and empower the agencies to focus more on solutions and innovation (NAPA, 2021, pp. 2–3).

Congress eventually blocked the Trump administration's attempt to shrink OPM and move its key central personnel policy role under executive control. Stalemate from congressional blockades however, viewed from a long horizon, is just fodder for more transactional, executive approaches to create or seek capacities that advance presidential objectives. The Trump administration's failed reform of OPM might have been the impetus behind the proclamation of *Schedule F* – a work-around for the books discussed in the following section.

7.4   A Failed Reform as a Road Map for Capacity's Future

One of our findings from historical analysis is that reforms are not merely cyclical; they can come back with a vengeance. The boldness of Trump's *Schedule F* sought a first-mover advantage by a conservative movement that, even if reversed by succeeding presidents, already carried much symbolism, as James March and Johan Olsen observed of the rituals of governmental reform. What was Schedule F, and what would have made it one of those tectonic plate-shifting (Koppell, 2010), equilibrium-punctuating changes in American political development?

With the Trump administration, history will mark the potential start of a significant shift arising from *Executive Order 13957 on Creating Schedule F Within the Excepted Service* (EOP, 2020). Called by the American Federation of Government Employees (AFGE) as a declaration of war on the civil service, the EO fizzled out eventually in the chaos of the transition. Nonetheless, Schedule F made an impact by providing a road map for a future workforce policy.

Not many people have heard of Schedule F, as EO 13957 was called, amid the COVID-19 and election crises. Issued on October 21, 2020, just weeks before the presidential election, the directive was supposed to be a game changer for the hundred-year-old merit-based system. The order gave agencies the authority to identify and reclassify into new Schedule F positions that were not in the competitive service and contained certain "confidential, policy-making, policy-determining, or policy-advocating positions" within their organization. Critics saw the order bringing patronage back in place of merit. Merit means that recruitment and tenure of federal employees are based upon competitive entrance examinations, protection from politically motivated removal, and neutral competence in public office. Schedule F would have stretched even more the number of positions already outside this merit system. Called "excepted positions," they are those requiring Senate confirmation; positions filled by senior executive service (SES) or "the cream of the crop of professional managers in government;" positions for which it is not feasible to hold examinations or what are known as Schedules A, B, and C; and positions in agencies that Congress have given authority to govern their own personnel systems apart from OPM (Lewis, 2008, pp. 21–25). Agencies were given 90 days to determine and submit those positions that could be shifted into the new employment category or by January 19, 2021, which would happen to be Trump's last day in office.

Perhaps numbering in the thousands in a workforce of 2.1 million, positions submitted in pursuit of the Schedule F directive would have made them at-will employment, stripped of any protections against adverse personnel actions. The order asked agencies to establish rules to prohibit the same personnel practices prohibited under statutory law. The Project on Government Oversight (POGO) believed, however, that the overall aim was to streamline and speed up the firing of "poor performers," as the order itself did not give federal employees any right enforceable in the courts (Schwellenbach, 2020). The directive would prevent any reclassified Schedule F employee from seeking recourse for political retaliation with the Merit Systems Protection Board (MSPB) or the Office of Special Counsel (OSC), the two federal personnel bodies normally hearing such grievances.

The only two agencies that complied with Schedule F were volunteers. Pushing the irony under Trump, those agencies happened to be the so-called "force multipliers," OMB and OPM. Much of OPM's 3500 staff were reportedly identified as reclassifiable under the directive (Rein, 2021). Any alteration in the capacities of OPM and OMB would have had ripple effects on the federal landscape, so their eagerness for Schedule F was significant. Nonetheless, both have supported the tectonic shift in externalizing capacity since Reagan. Their compliant attitude to presidential objectives is chronicled well in the bureaucratic politics and budgeting literature. Irene Rubin's study (1985, p. 190) of OPM showed how the Reagan appointees reduced and politicized the independent body "with a sense of combat" in the 1980s. In Shelley Tomkin's (1998, p. 293) biography of OMB, on the other hand, the agency took its own "medicine" during the Clinton deficit-cutting years. Later, a study of the George W. Bush management directives found that contrary to the portrayal of bureaucrats in anti-government circles, agencies not only did not always resist threats to cut their organization, but they could even over-comply, potentially damaging their capacity to achieve their mission (Joaquin & Greitens, 2009).

To model compliance with the directive, nearly 90% of OMB's staff, or 425 workers, were deemed suitable for reclassification (Wegmann, 2020). Robert Shea, a former OMB associate director during the Bush years, was worried that the careerists at OMB tended to tell politicians the limits and complexities surrounding what they wished to do; Schedule F would now make those workers hesitate, to the detriment of sound policy-making. If even a portion of those 425 employees identified by OMB for Schedule F had been fired before Biden's inauguration, succeeding presidents from both parties would have reaped the negative results of even more pronounced incapacity from the politicized staffing:

> You'll see an acceleration in the proposal of policies likely to be ineffective. Policies will be proposed that are likely to be met with not only resistance among stakeholders in Congress, but also in the courts. They will be inconsistent with current law and therefore challenged in the courts, and that will put inordinate delays in the implementation of a president's policies. (Wagner, 2020b, para. 11)

What the critics may have missed with Schedule F and other "failed" Trump initiatives was that losses were a victory in an administration that learned fast how deconstruction could be achieved. The frayed capacities from sidelining careerists did not seem to be as important as the higher, symbolic battle to control the Fourth Branch (i.e., the federal bureaucracy). Such rebuffed policies serve as learning and focusing events – signals and symbols in the service of future reform movements.

Administrative reforms tend to create their own momentum, even if the political dynamics are often the same. Schedule F was preceded by one successful reform and succeeded by one that encountered legislative roadblocks. Before Schedule F came Schedule E, a successful strategy to solidify the president's power over staffing, with OMB and OPM naturally at the forefront of the battle. Two years before Schedule F was issued, the White House ordered the reclassification of the country's administrative law judges (ALJs) from the competitive service to the excepted service, a new Schedule E (EOP, 2018b). The ALJs bear the adjudicatory work in agencies such as the Social Security Administration (SSA) and 30 other agencies. The ALJs preside over appeals by citizens who are unsuccessful in their claims for SSA benefits, for example, or, in consumer finance areas, on matters such as fines for mortgage lenders who violate certain rules. These administrative judges are a big part of the administrative state that conservatives deride, their judicial power as unelected bureaucrats attracting criticisms of favoring their agencies heavily and failing to conduct rigorous examinations of the facts that come before them (Phillips & Raso, 2020).

ALJs were formerly vetted by OPM before the agencies selected them. But the capacity to do this always lagged. For example, OPM failed to certify enough ALJs to handle a backlog that in 2016 numbered 800,000 cases across the agencies. Government administration expert Paul Verkuil, who was part of a team facilitating meetings to help solve the issue at that time, described the problem and dissatisfactions with OPM that led to a transactional approach to get the work done:

> Congress, the President (through OMB), and the agency (SSA) all want to move forward to solve a crisis, but that didn't budge the bureaucrats in OPM. Preserving the status quo and protecting turf seemed a more important outcome than solving the problem.

> Since OPM wouldn't budge…the SSA was forced to turn to a more controversial solution – supplementing the ALJ disability corps with non-ALJs (called AAJs.) AAJ appointments do not fall within OPM jurisdiction, since they are in the excepted, not the competitive, service and can be hired by SSA directly. (Verkuil, 2017, pp. 105–106)

Moving the ALJs to Schedule E in 2018 gave the president and the agencies more latitude. Congress promptly introduced a bill to reverse the directive, accusing the administration of politicizing the administrative judiciary. Verkuil thought that creating the excepted positions of Schedule E was a giant work-around driven by the frustrating limitations of the formal civil service system and that more effective ways might be found after Schedule E was given a try (Verkuil, 2017, p. 113).

Indeed, a momentum had built for addressing human capital management in Washington, leading the White House OMB to push for OPM's reorganization. When OPM's reorganization stalled in Congress, OMB had a backup strategy – it released the Schedule F directive.

More radical than Schedule E, Schedule F came amid the conflagrations of the election. The deadline to submit the list of positions was only several days after a deadly assault was launched on the Capitol in a bid to keep Trump in power. Because getting the lists finalized by the agencies with OPM approval was right between the assault and the motion for a second Trump impeachment, it looked as if Schedule F could be a vengeful parting shot as well as a loyalty test on a scale never before seen in the history of civil service (Kettl, 2020). Given that most employees, except for those working in DOD and DHS, signified their preference for Democratic candidate Joe Biden (Katz, 2020b), experts thought the broadly worded, fuzzy Executive Order was setting up a mass layoff of federal administration. Illustrating how it could play out, Donald Kettl explained:

> Dr. [Anthony] Fauci...as well as individuals at the [Centers for Disease Control and Prevention] who are producing analysis about the spread of the coronavirus, social distancing and the importance of masks... people within the State Department raising questions about the administration's expansion of efforts to engage in crackdowns and change other policies... people counting the number of immigrant children who cannot be reunited with their parents...anyone who says anything that would be in opposition to the administration's policy could be viewed as in a policy-making position, put in Schedule F and fired. (Wagner, 2020b, para. 13)

Equally worse, the new government could be met with a logistical nightmare, and all kinds of security risks were key agencies to be relieved of responsible people. Sabotage was widely feared (Wagner, 2020b; Zitser, 2021). Even if Biden were to somehow reverse the purge to get any employee reinstated using the same EO, the time and effort it would have taken, not to mention the unknown landmines it could have opened up in a judicial system packed with Republican appointees, would surely have crashed whatever capacity was left of the new government. *The Hill* explains:

> To reverse the firings, Biden will still have to process the terminations and rehiring, offer severance or deal with retirements of frustrated workers. To reverse the burrowing in of political appointees hired into permanent Schedule F jobs, those fired can file complaints of political discrimination with the Office of Special Counsel (OSC). If they lose, it sets a precedent for future Republican presidents wishing to fire civil servants. (Silver, 2021, para. 6)

The president of the Partnership for Public Service saw the landmines and called for getting rid of the tool as quickly as possible. Its head noted that Schedule F "is a little bit like...the One Ring. There's a pull that makes you believe it can be used for good, but it just can't" (Wagner, 2021a, para. 14). Like Nixon's grand reorganization plan for super-Cabinets in the 1970s, Schedule F would have wrought a tremendous reordering of politics and administration that Congress could not ignore. An alliance of academics and good government community promptly protested the measure. The community acknowledged that the personnel system needed modernizing, but it should not happen by empowering the executive even more at the expense of Congress:

> Failing to act will set a dangerous precedent, signaling congressional indifference to a substantial expansion of executive power. The EO upends a longstanding legislative framework that ensures a nonpartisan civil service – a framework that assures the laws Congress passes will be implemented as written, and the funds they appropriate will be disbursed as directed. (PPS, 2020, para. 5)

Former intelligence community officials from both Republican and Democratic administrations, joining their academic counterparts penned an editorial that called Schedule F "an insider threat":

> far more subtle than an attack from a foreign adversary…to facilitate a wholesale "remove and replace" strategy in the upper reaches of the career civil service…with malice afore-thought. If it is not addressed, the peaceful transition of power—one of the most sacred and treasured tenets of the nation's government—could be threatened. (McConnell & Sanders, 2020, para 1)

Lawmakers moved to kill the measure by filing H.R. 302, "Preventing a Patronage System Act," and to block future administrations from reclassifying career civil service positions (Ogrysko, 2021). Advocates also turned to the courts and media. The chair of the Federal Salary Council, a Trump appointee himself, resigned in protest. The National Treasury Employees Union (NTEU) sued to have the EO declared unlawful and ultra-vires (Silver, 2021).

Once Biden was sworn into office, his most immediate orders were in the dimension of human capital management and administrative conservatorship, appointing people at the MSPB and FLRA, reversing Trump's workforce rules, reopening contracts negotiated under the 2018 EOs, and getting rid of Schedule F with the *Executive Order on Protecting the Federal Workforce*. Invoking the progressive reform movement, the memo stated that Schedule F undermined the Pendleton Civil Service Reform Act of 1883's repudiation of the spoils system (EOP, 2021).

With Trump out of office, deconstruction left the most powerful agencies, OPM and OMB, and perhaps GSA and GAO on an uneasy, if equal, footing, once again. But the administrative state still could not avoid going into a "holding pattern" post-Trump. Biden's nominees faced stiff resistance in the Senate. Even with Biden's executive reversals, things could not be restored so easily: internal and external agency contracts had been prepared, and directives had gone out, and some of those policies had gone through proper rulemaking procedures (Wagner, 2020a, 2021b). Reversing Trump's directives in collective bargaining, for example, would take a lot more than Biden's own executive orders. Stanford University's Immigration Policy Tracking Project described the legacy of Trump's administrative presidency as one of "bureaucratic archaeology" on the part of the Biden administration. To undo the previous directives would require "an assessment of what the replacement ought to be, what the legal requirements are for changing it, and what the operational and logistical challenges are for implementing a new policy" (Beitsch, 2021, para. 9). A stalemate in administrative reform right now may look like it has created space for new ideas about capacity. But the grand dismantling that tested administrative and democratic resilience over the last 4 years, and the cascade of reforms promoting the language of the energetic executive for the benefit the unitary executive, might have already set in motion forces impacting capacity long after the Trump presidency.

7.5   Reformism in the Aftermath of Deconstruction

It was not a coincidence that the decline of American administrative capacity occurred at the same time the government recognized that human capital management was failing. Decay set in as solutions were externalized and a patchwork of individual agency solutions left the national personnel body itself rigid and vulnerable to "hostile takeovers." That Trump's disinvestment, bifurcation, and delegitimization of bureaucracy and bureaucrats happened after decades of PMAs to improve performance and accountability were lamentable but not unforeseen. It has scarred public administration, while his election fraud campaign shook its democratic foundations. The test of resilience among the administrative conservators and reform advocates now is the extent to which they could resuscitate what was left of administrative capacity and move forward with new strategies in the aftermath of deconstruction.

Since the New Deal, the civil service has been viewed as an effective center of political power (Van Riper, 1958). The powers that countless reforms had accumulated in the president's office granted Trump an easier time to erase his predecessors' policy legacies and launch bold personnel reforms. What was ironic about deconstruction, Schedule F, and OPM's reorganization under the 45th president was that those reforms displayed once again how conservative reformers more fully grasp the symbolic and political grounding of reform *movements*, while liberal reformers and perhaps their allies in the good government community and academia struggle to locate capacity within the *realpolitik* of political control.

Conservatives in the good government community promote reforms that fail to arrest capacity's decline or to improve capacity for long durations perhaps because they put more weight on the *control* element of bureaucracy rather than its *capacity*. They have mastered the art of transactional reforms, but those reforms weaken some fundamental aspects of capacity. Breakdowns are too easily pinned on faceless bureaucrats, but centralized power in the presidency is not strongly questioned, when a conservative occupies the Oval Office. They, however, seem to recognize the long game and the role of symbols and signals in transforming a system. Their unitary executive theory (that benefits Democratic presidents, as well), combined with a small government philosophy, has a logical coherence and lands the message well in pushing for bureaucratic transformation. In their framework, capacity would flow to wherever their chosen unitary leader would wish it to be: the macro-political and the developmental aspects of reform and bureaucratic control are tied together in framing the government of tomorrow. Trump, in retrospect, was a gift to the deconstruction movement until his final year, because of his unmatched reframing skills in pushing an idea. But the narcissism in his reelection quest undermined the message at the end. This might be why so many conservatives stayed with him for as long as possible but bolted from his camp after the Capitol attack: he muddied the signals that accompany reform movements. Schedule E, reorganization, OPM reform, and Schedule F were all instructing the public a vision and belief. But Trump's self-serving dalliances with the extremists who stormed a hallowed ground took the fight out, for a brief moment, from among those trying to mold the administrative state.

Reformers on the left, on the other hand, have not perhaps been clothing their approach enough in the politics of reform or control – they promote capacity building in government in most of the dimensions we identified in this book, but their calls still come across as academic and lack the language of a *movement* that would inspire change with the public behind it. Their signals lag, their symbols too traditional and their recommendations too practical to a fault – meso-level changes that could happen incrementally, but do not yet inspire a vision massive enough to break through the political deadlock that has favored transactionalist presidents and transactionalist ideas. Advocating that OPM lead in shifting "mindsets and behaviors," as NAPA (2021) is calling for in its most recent report to Congress, for example, is a step in this direction, but the shift in the mindset may have to occur first in academia, from which a lot of academy members emerge, unlike conservative reformers that draw from the business sector.

If political development theory must inform public administration in the post-Trump era, good government reformers would need to ground their ideas in macro-political trends and strategies, connect capacity more closely to its drivers in executive and legislative politics, and address capacity's core dimensions for the long term. We tie these elements together in the concluding chapter.

References

Adams, M. (2016, March 11). *Why the OPM hack is far worse than you imagine*. Law Fare. https://www.lawfareblog.com/why-opm-hack-far-worse-you-imagine. Accessed 21 Oct 2020.

Aleaziz, H. (2021, February 1). *A whistleblower alleges a top Trump official signed a last-minute agreement with ICE's union that could hamstring Biden's immigration policies*. Buzzfeed. https://www.buzzfeednews.com/article/hamedaleaziz/ice-union-agreements-biden-policies. Accessed 21 Feb 2020.

American Federation for Government Employees (AFGE). (2014, December 11). *House budget committee ranking member shines spotlight on expensive contracted workforce*. [Press Release]. https://www.afge.org/article/house-budget-committee-ranking-member-shines-spotlight-on-expensive-contracted-workforce. Accessed 20 Oct 2020.

Anderson, J., & Rainie, L. (2021, February 21). *3. Concerns about democracy in the digital age*. Pew Research. https://www.pewresearch.org/internet/2020/02/21/concerns-about-democracy-in-the-digital-age/. Accessed 1 Mar 2021.

Applebaum, A. (2020, May 3). The rest of the world is laughing at Trump. *The Atlantic*. https://www.theatlantic.com/ideas/archive/2020/05/time-americans-are-doing-nothing/611056/. Accessed 5 May 2020.

Axelrod, T. (2018, October 26). *Twitter defends removal of fake accounts after Trump criticism*. The Hill. https://thehill.com/policy/technology/technology/413318-twitter-defends-removal-of-fake-accounts-after-trump-criticism. Accessed 17 Sept 2020.

Beitsch, R. (2021, March 14). *Biden struggles to unravel web of Trump immigration rules*. The Hill. https://thehill.com/homenews/administration/543041-biden-officials-struggle-to-unravel-web-of-trump-immigration-rules. Accessed 19 Mar 2021.

Best Places to Work in the Federal Government. (2018–2019). *Best places to work agency rankings*. https://bestplacestowork.org/rankings/overall/large. Accessed 1 Aug 2020.

Bolstad, E. (2020, September 8). COVID-19 is crushing newspapers, worsening hunger for accurate information. *Stateline.* https://www.pewtrusts.org/en/research-and-analysis/blogs/stateline/2020/09/08/covid-19-is-crushing-newspapers-worsening-hunger-for-accurate-information. Accessed 11 Mar 2021.

Bublé, C. (2020a, March 10). Transparency in the Trump era. *Government Executive.* https://www.govexec.com/management/2020/03/transparency-trump-era/163574/. Accessed 11 Mar 2020.

Bublé, C. (2020b, June 24). White house concealed finding that OPM merger was illegal, report says. *Government Executive.* https://www.govexec.com/oversight/2020/06/white-house-concealed-finding-opm-merger-was-illegal-report-says/166411/. Accessed 26 June 2020.

Bublé, C. (2021, April 5). White House blames transition in part for delay in releasing budget preview. *Government Executive.* https://www.govexec.com/management/2021/04/white-house-blames-transition-part-delay-releasing-budget-preview/173148/. Accessed 6 Apr 2021.

Butler, A., & Gianfortune, R. (2021, February 9). OMB's secret spending decisions [Audio Podcast]. *Government Executive.* https://www.govexec.com/oversight/2021/02/govexec-daily-ombs-secret-spending-decisions/171926/. Accessed 10 Feb 2021.

Carper, T. (2019, June 5). Ranking members Carper, Stabenow, Peters Demand answers on Trump administration's abrupt plans to relocate critical agencies.Washington, DC. [Press Release]. https://www.carper.senate.gov/public/index.cfm/2019/6/ranking-members-carper-stabenow-peters-demand-answers-ontrump-administration-s-abrupt-plans-to-relocate-critical-agencies. Accessed 21 June 2020.

Center for Science and Democracy (CSD). (2018). *Science under President Trump.* Union of Concerned Scientists. https://www.ucsusa.org/sites/default/files/attach/2018/08/science-under-trump-report.pdf. Accessed 19 Apr 2020

Center on Budget and Policy Priorities (CBPP). (n.d.). *Sabotage watch: Tracking efforts to undermine the ACA.* https://www.cbpp.org/sabotage-watch-tracking-efforts-to-undermine-the-aca. Accessed 21 Jan 2021.

Citizens for Responsibility and Ethics in Washington (CREW). (2021, January 15). *President Trump's legacy of corruption, four years and 3,700 conflicts of interest later.* https://www.citizensforethics.org/reports-investigations/crew-reports/president-trump-legacy-corruption-3700-conflicts-interest/. Accessed 21 Feb 2020.

Clark, C. S. (2017, August 9). Trump agency reforms are called the most exciting opportunity in years. *Government Executive.* https://www.govexec.com/management/2017/08/trump-agency-reforms-are-called-most-exciting-opportunity-years/140142/. Accessed 21 June 2019.

Clark, C. S. (2018, March 9). Reading between the lines on agency mission statements. *Government Executive.* https://www.govexec.com/management/2018/03/reading-between-lines-agency-mission-statements/146530/. Accessed 23 May 2020.

CNBC. (2021, February 18). *U.S. life expectancy drops a year due to pandemic, most since WWII.* https://www.cnbc.com/2021/02/18/us-life-expectancy-drops-a-year-due-to-pandemic-most-since-wwii.html. Accessed 21 Feb 2021.

Daniels, S. (2017, January 18). Government executive 2016 presidential poll: Post-election. *Government Executive.* https://www.govexec.com/insights/reports/government-executive-2016-presidential-poll-post-election/134667/. Accessed 16 May 2019.

Dickinson, M. J. (2020). Guarding the emperor's new clothes: OMB, the presidency, and the problem of neutral competence in the era of Trump. In M. Bose & A. Rudalevige (Eds.), *Executive policymaking: The role of OMB in the presidency* (pp. 233–264). Brookings Institution Press.

Dlouhy, J. (2021, January 12). *Trump rulemaking blitz cuts waiting period to restrict Biden.* Bloomberg. https://www.bloomberg.com/news/articles/2021-01-13/trump-rulemaking-flurry-skips-waiting-period-to-hamstring-biden. Accessed 14 Jan 2021.

Dmitrieva, K. (2019, October 23). *Trump irks agency behind the jobs report. Now researchers are ready to walk.* Bloomberg. https://www.bloomberg.com/news/articles/2019-10-23/trump-move-could-spark-another-exodus-of-u-s-jobs-researchers. Accessed 30 Oct 2020.

Emba, C. (2018, March 15). Opinion: The rewritten mission statements of Trump's federal agencies, annotated. *The Washington Post.* https://www.washingtonpost.com/blogs/post-partisan/wp/2018/03/16/trumps-edits-to-democracy-annotated/. Accessed 21 Mar 2020.

Fienberg, A. (2021, March 16). Border Patrol agents are 'working to sabotage the Biden administration', according to insiders. *Independent.* https://www.independent.co.uk/voices/border-patrol-biden-crisis-dhs-kevin-mccarthy-republicans-insiders-b1818116.html. Accessed 20 Apr 2021.

Foer, F. (2018, September). How Trump radicalized ICE. *The Atlantic.* https://www.theatlantic.com/magazine/archive/2018/09/trump-ice/565772/. Accessed 22 Mar 2019.

Fogel, M. (2019, October 22). *Amb. William Taylor testifies before impeachment inquiry.* Lawfare. https://www.lawfareblog.com/amb-william-taylor-testifies-impeachment-inquiry. Accessed 11 Dec 2020. Accessed 22 Mar 2019.

Fredrickson, H. G. (1996, May–June). Comparing the reinventing of government with the new public administration. *Public Administration Review, 56*(3), 263–270.

French, D. (2017, February 24). Trump wants to deconstruct the regulatory state? Good. Here's how you start. *National Review.* https://www.nationalreview.com/2017/02/administrative-state-deconstruction-trump-steve-bannon-cpac/. Accessed 21 May 2019.

Gardner, A., & Firozi, P. (2021, January 5). Here's the full transcript and audio of the call between Trump and Raffensperger. *The Washington Post.* https://www.washingtonpost.com/politics/trump-raffensperger-call-transcript-georgia-vote/2021/01/03/2768e0cc-4ddd-11eb-83e3-322644d82356_story.html. Accessed 21 Feb 2021.

Gerton, T., & Hale, J. (2021, March 18). OPM modernization is critical to building the federal workforce the nation needs. *Government Executive.* https://www.govexec.com/workforce/2021/03/opm-modernization-critical-building-federal-workforce-nation-needs/172748/. Accessed 25 Mar 2021.

Goelzhauser, G., & Konisky, D. M. (2020). The state of American federalism 2019–2020: Polarized and punitive intergovernmental relations. *Publius: The Journal of Federalism, 50*(3), 311–343.

Gustafon, P. E. (2021, January 12). *Request for information pursuant to the Inspector General Act of 1978, as amended [Memorandum].* U.S. Department of Commerce. https://www.oig.doc.gov/OIGPublications/OIG-21-019-M.pdf. Accessed 22 Mar 2021.

Hains, T. (2016, August 8). Trump: The 5% unemployment figure is one of the biggest hoaxes in modern politics. *Real Clear Politics.* http://www.realclearpolitics.com/video/2016/08/08/trump_the_5_unemployment_figure_is_one_of_biggest_hoaxes_in_modern_politics.html. Accessed 11 Apr 2019.

Hanna, J., & Knickmeyer, E. (2019, August 6). Union: Mulvaney comments confirm agency moves meant to cut. *AP News.* https://perma.cc/A7DD-KNZ7. Accessed 10 May 2020.

Iacurci, G. (2020, June 9). There's a conspiracy theory about the unemployment numbers. Labor experts call it baseless. CNBC. https://www.cnbc.com/2020/06/09/unemployment-rate-conspiracy-theory-called-baseless-by-economists.html. Accessed 18 July 2020.

Ingraham, P. (1995). *The foundation of merit: Public service in American democracy.* The Johns Hopkins University Press.

Jahn, M. M., Treverton, G. F., Bray, D. A., Jayamaha, B., Valdez, B., Carnes, B., Hutchison, L., & Will, M. (2018). Are declines in U.S. federal workforce capabilities putting our government at risk of failing? Senior Executives Association. Washington, DC. https://cdn.ymaws.com/seniorexecs.org/resource/resmgr/government_at_the_risk_of_fa.pdf Accessed 15 May 2019.

Jahn, M. M., Treverton, G. F., Bray, D. A., Jayamaha, B., Valdez, B., Carnes, B., Hutchison, L., & Will, M. (2019). Are declines in U.S. federal workforce capabilities putting our government at risk of failing? *Senior Executives Association.* https://cdn.ymaws.com/seniorexecs.org/resource/resmgr/government_at_the_risk_of_fa.pdf. Accessed 15 May 2019.

Joaquin, M. E. (2018, April 23). Questions in the aftermath of deconstruction: Public administration in a transforming world. *The PA Times.* https://patimes.org/questions-in-the-aftermath-of-deconstruction-public-administration-in-a-transforming-world/. Accessed 21 Oct 2019.

Joaquin, M. E., & Greitens, T. J. (2009). Presidential policy initiatives and agency compliance: Organizational adaptation to A-76. *Administration & Society, 41*(7), 815–849.

Katz, E. (2017a, March 13). Trump orders agencies to eliminate waste, workforce redundancies. *Government Executive.* https://www.govexec.com/management/2017/03/new-trump-order-ask-agencies-eliminate-waste-workforce-redundancies/136118/. Accessed 24 May 2020.

Katz, E. (2017b, May 3). Federal scientists march for their work, and against Trump. *Government Executive.* https://www.govexec.com/management/2017/05/federal-scientists-march-their-work-and-against-trump/137513/. Accessed 15 May 2019.

Katz, E. (2018a, October 9). Behind the Trump administration's 'brutal' decision to remove its federal personnel chief. *Government Executive.* https://www.govexec.com/management/2018/10/behind-trump-administrations-brutal-decision-remove-its-federal-personnel-chief/151893/. Accessed 11 May 2019.

Katz, E. (2018b, November 18). MSPB likely to remain powerless as Senate panel fails to advance Trump's nominees. *Government Executive.* https://www.govexec.com/pay-benefits/2018/11/mspb-likely-remain-powerless-senate-panel-fails-advance-trumps-nominees/153100/. Accessed 1 May 2019.

Katz, E. (2019, September 6). Trump officials threatened with fines, jail time over illegal spending during shutdown. *Government Executive.*

Katz, E. (2020a, July 7). Updated Trump administration goals reveal plans for the federal workforce. *Government Executive.* https://www.govexec.com/workforce/2020/07/updated-trump-administration-goals-reveal-plans-federal-workforce/166703/. Accessed 23 July 2020.

Katz, E. (2020b, October 27). Federal employees donate $1.8M in presidential race, mostly to Biden. *Government Executive.* https://www.govexec.com/workforce/2020/10/federal-employees-donate-18m-presidential-race-mostly-biden/169604/. Accessed 2 Nov 2020.

Katz, E. (2020c, November 19). Trump has slashed jobs at nearly every federal agency; Biden promises a reversal. *Government Executive.* https://www.govexec.com/workforce/2020/11/trump-has-slashed-jobs-nearly-every-federal-agency-biden-promises-reversal/170203/. Accessed 24 Nov 2020.

Katz, E. (2021a, January 21). Here's who is leading federal agencies as Biden nominees await confirmation. *Government Executive.* https://www.govexec.com/management/2021/01/heres-who-leading-federal-agencies-biden-nominees-await-confirmation/171512/. Accessed 28 Jan 2020.

Katz, E. (2021b, February 8). Federal agencies are increasingly avoiding normal hiring procedures to bring on new staff quickly. *Government Executive.* https://www.govexec.com/workforce/2021/02/federal-agencies-are-increasingly-avoiding-normal-hiring-procedures-bring-new-staff-quickly/171922/. Accessed 11 Feb 2021.

Kettl, D. F. (2017, February 28). The clumsy war against the administrative state. *Government Executive.* https://www.govexec.com/management/2017/02/clumsy-war-against-administrative-state/135733/. Accessed 22 May 2019.

Kettl, D. (2020, October 22). Trump's order sets the stage for loyalty tests for thousands of feds. *Government Executive.* https://www.govexec.com/management/2020/10/trumps-order-sets-stage-loyalty-tests-thousands-feds/169492/. Accessed 25 Oct 2020.

Kettl, D. F., Ingraham, P. W., Sanders, R. P., & Horner, C. (1996, July 1). *Civil service reform: Building a government that works.* Brookings Institution Press.

Kim, A. (2018, April 18). The partiality norm: Systematic deference in the office of legal counsel. *Cornell Law Review, 103*(3), 757–816.

Klesser, G. (2016, December 12). Donald Trump still does not understand the unemployment rate. *The Washington Post.* https://www.washingtonpost.com/news/fact-checker/wp/2016/12/12/donald-trump-still-does-not-understand-the-unemployment-rate/. Accessed 30 May 2020.

Koppell, J. G. S. (2010). Metaphors and the development of American bureaucracy. In R. F. Durant (Ed.), *The Oxford handbook of American bureaucracy* (pp. 128–150). Oxford University Press.

Kurth, J., & Easterbook, G. (2008, September 3). Cassandra versus Pollyanna. In F. Fukuyama (Ed.), *Blindside: How to anticipate forcing events and wild cards in global politics* (pp. 129–142). Brookings Institution Press.

Lane, L. M. (1992). The office of personnel management: Values, policies, and consequences. In P. W. Ingraham & D. H. Rosenbloom (Eds.), *The promise and paradox of civil service reform* (pp. 97–120). University of Pittsburgh.

Lane, L. M., & Wolf, J. E. (1990). *The human resource crisis in the public sector: Rebuilding the capacity to govern*. Quo-rum Books.

Lee, M. (2012). Nixon's super-secretaries: The last grand reorganization effort. Texas A&M University Press.

Lemire, J. (2017, March 14). *Trump white house sees "deep state" behind leaks, opposition*. Associated Press. https://apnews.com/363ccdba946548bfa4b855ae38d1797a. Accessed 22 Aug 2019.

Levin, B. (2021, January 21). Biden unveils no-assholes policy at the White House. *Vanity Fair*. https://www.vanityfair.com/news/2021/01/joe-biden-will-fire. Accessed 2 Apr 2021.

Lewis, D. E. (2008). *The politics of presidential appointments: Political control and bureaucratic performance*. Princeton University Press.

Lewis, M. (2018). *The fifth risk*. W.W. Norton & Co.

Lewis, S., & Spetalnick, M. (2020, December 28). Biden: Trump aides setting 'roadblocks' for his transition team. *Reuters*. https://www.reuters.com/article/us-usa-biden-nationalsecurity-idUSKBN2921U4. Accessed 21 Jan 2021.

Light, P. C. (2019, April 18). *The coming shutdown over government reform*. The Brookings Institution. https://www.brookings.edu/research/the-coming-showdown-over-government-reform/. Accessed 4 Sept 2020.

Light, P. C. (2020, October 7). T*he true size of government is nearing a record high*. The Brookings Institution. https://www.brookings.edu/blog/fixgov/2020/10/07/the-true-size-of-government-is-nearing-a-record-high/. Accessed 30 Oct 2020.

Lynch, M. (2017, February 16). White House open data disappears, raising transparency questions. *MeriTalk*. https://www.meritalk.com/articles/white-house-open-data-disappears-transparency-donald-trump-sunlight-foundation/. Accessed 21 July 2020.

Malakoff, D., & Mervis, J. (2020, February 10). Trump's 2021 budget drowns science agencies in red ink, again. *Science Magazine*. https://www.sciencemag.org/news/2020/02/trump-s-2021-budget-drowns-science-agencies-red-ink-again. Accessed 12 July 2020.

Mangan, D. (2021, February 21). Oath keepers boss told followers before Capitol riot that Trump 'wants us to make it WILD,' court document says. *CNBC*. https://www.cnbc.com/2021/02/19/oath-keepers-boss-quoted-trump-before-capitol-riot.html. Accessed 2 Mar 2021.

Mangan, D., & Breuninger, K (2018, February 28). Trump tweets: 'Disgraceful' that Sessions kicked surveillance probe to Obama appointee. *CNBC*. https://www.cnbc.com/2018/02/28/trump-criticizes-attorney-general-jeff-sessions-over-fisa-probe.html. Accessed 3 Mar 2021.

Mashaw, J. L., & Berke, D. (2018). Presidential administration in a regime of separated powers: An analysis of recent American experience. *Yale Journal on Regulation, 35*(2).

McConnell, M., & Sanders, R. (2020, December 4). Viewpoint: Move to politicize the career civil service is an insider threat to the country. *Government Executive*. https://www.govexec.com/management/2020/12/viewpoint-move-politicize-career-civil-service-insider-threat-country/170504/. Accessed 16 Dec 2020.

Memoli, M. A., & Bierman, N. (2017, March 15). Trump's 'hard power' budget makes sweeping cuts to EPA and State Department, boosts defense spending. *The Los Angeles Times*. https://www.latimes.com/nation/la-na-pol-trump-budget-20170316-story.html. Accessed 15 May 2020.

Merriam-Webster. (n.d.). "deconstruct". https://www.merriam-webster.com/dictionary/deconstruct. Accessed 1 July 2019.

Milbank, D. (2020, March 30). What kind of person calls 100,000-plus dead a 'very good job'? *The Washington Post*. https://www.washingtonpost.com/opinions/2020/03/30/what-kind-person-calls-100000-plus-dead-very-good-job/. Accessed 1 Apr 2020.

Miller, J. (2018, October 15). Having a consistent OMB DDM can impact federal management more than any specific agenda. *Federal News Network*. https://federalnewsnetwork.com/reporters-notebook-jason-miller/2018/10/having-a-consistent-omb-ddm-can-impact-federal-management-more-than-any-specific-agenda/. Accessed 13 Mar 2020.

Morone, J. A. (1990). *The democratic wish: Popular participation and the limits of American government*. Basic Books.

Mufson, S., & Eilperin, J. (2016, December 9). Trump transition team for energy department seeks names of employees involved in climate meetings. *The Washington Post*. https://www. washingtonpost.com/news/energy-environment/wp/2016/12/09/trump-transition-team-for-energy-department-seeks-names-of-employees-involved-in-climate-meetings/. Accessed 14 July 2020.

Narea, N. (2020, October 9). Trump's obstruction of the 2020 Census, explained. The Center for Public Integrity. https://publicintegrity.org/politics/systemfailure/trump-obstruction-of-2020-census/. Accessed 10 October 2020.

Nathan, R. P. (1983). *The administrative presidency*. Wiley.

National Academy of Public Administration (NAPA). (2017, July). No time to wait: Building a public service for the 21st century. .

National Academy of Public Administration (NAPA). (2019). *Perspectives on the President's management agenda*. Washington, DC https://napawash.org/academy-studies/perspectives-on-the-presidents-management-agenda-march-2019. Accessed 17 Dec 2020.

National Academy of Public Administration (NAPA). (2021, March). *Elevating human capital: Reframing the U.S. Office of Personnel Management's leadership imperative*. [PDF File]. https://s3.us-west-2.amazonaws.com/napa-2021/studies/united-states-office-of-personnel-management-independent-assessment/OPM-Final-Report-National-Academy-of-Public-Administration-March-2021.pdf. Accessed 31 Mar 2021.

O'Connell, O. (2021, January 7). 'Remember this day forever': Trump posts second tweet to rioters before Twitter deletes it. *Independent*. https://www.independent.co.uk/news/world/americas/us-politics/trump-twitter-rioters-capitol-congress-b1783589.html. Accessed 8 Jan 2021.

Ogrysko, N. (2021, January 14). New House bill would block future administrations from using Schedule F, or anything else like it. *Federal News Network*. https://federalnewsnetwork.com/workforce/2021/01/new-house-bill-would-block-future-administrations-from-using-schedule-f-or-anything-else-like-it/. Accessed 20 Jan 2021.

Packer, G. (2020, April). The president is winning his war on American institutions. *The Atlantic*.   https://www.theatlantic.com/magazine/archive/2020/04/how-to-destroy-a-government/606793/. Accessed 10 May 2020.

Paletta, D., & Eilperin, J. (2019, January 23). White House seeks list of programs that would be hurt if shutdown lasts into March. *The Washington Post*. https://www.washingtonpost.com/powerpost/house-democrats-to-offer-new-border-security-proposals%2D%2Dbut-no-wall/2019/01/23/6e39e0b0-1f21-11e9-9145-3f74070bbdb9_story.html. Accessed 30 Sept 2019.

Partnership for Public Service (PPS). (2020, November 20). *Coalition letter on Schedule F*. https://cdn.govexec.com/media/gbc/docs/pdfs_edit/112320ew1.pdf. Accessed 7 Dec 2020.

Peters, K. M. (2019, October 2). Agencies may now enforce Trump's controversial workforce orders. *Government Executive*. https://www.govexec.com/management/2019/10/agencies-may-now-enforce-trumps-controversial-workforce-orders/160320/. Accessed 4 Dec 2019.

Pfiffner, J. P. (2020). OMB, the presidency, and the federal budget. In M. Bose & A. Rudalevige (Eds.), Executive policymaking: The role of OMB in the presidency (pp. 11-40). Washington, DC. Brookings Institution Press.

Phillips, T., & Raso, C. (2020, November 17). *Debates over agency judges should focus on functions, not job titles*. The Brookings Institution. https://www.brookings.edu/research/debates-over-agency-judges-should-focus-on-functions-not-job-titles/. Accessed 29 Nov 2020.

Rampell, C. (2020, November 30). Trump lays the groundwork for a massive government purge on his way out the door. *The Washington Post*. https://www.washingtonpost.com/opinions/trump-lays-the-groundwork-for-a-massive-government-purge-on-his-way-out-the-door/2020/11/30/280519ac-333d-11eb-a997-1f4c53d2a747_story.html. Accessed 1 Dec 2020.

Rein, L. (2021, January 18). *Trump's 11th-hour assault on the civil service by stripping job protections runs out of time*. https://www.washingtonpost.com/politics/trump-civil-service-biden/2021/01/18/5daf34c4-59b3-11eb-b8bd-ee36b1cd18bf_story.html. Accessed 23 Jan 2021.

Rice, S. (2020, September 1). Opinion: Trump isn't here to serve the people. *The New York Times.* https://www.nytimes.com/2020/09/01/opinion/trump-corruption-democracy.html. Accessed 7 Jan 2021.

Robertson, N., & Duster, C. (2021, April 19). Bush calls on Congress to tone down 'harsh rhetoric' on immigration. *CNN.* https://www.cnn.com/2021/04/18/politics/george-w-bush-immigration-congress/index.html. Accessed 20 Apr 2021.

Rubin, I. S. (1985). *Shrinking the federal government: The effect of cutbacks on five federal agencies.* Longman.

Schwartz, P., & Randall, D. (2007). Ahead of the curve: Anticipating strategic surprise. In F. Fukuyama (Ed.), *Blindside: How to anticipate forcing events and wild cards in global politics* (pp. 93–108). Brookings Institution Press.

Schwellenbach, N. (2020, December 2). Schedule effed. *Project on Government Oversight.* https://www.pogo.org/analysis/2020/12/schedule-effed/. Accessed 15 Dec 2020.

Seidman, H. (1998). *Politics, position, and power: They dynamics of federal organization* (5th ed.). Oxford University Press.

Selin, J. (2020, June 8). How the Constitution's federalist framework is being tested by COVID-19. *The Brookings Institution.* https://www.brookings.edu/blog/fixgov/2020/06/08/how-the-constitutions-federalist-framework-is-being-tested-by-covid-19/. Accessed 16 June 2020.

Senior Executives Association (SEA). (2019, March 11). *The voice of career federal executives since 1980.* https://seniorexecs.org/page/StatementOnAdministrationsFY2020BudgeProposal https://www.brookings.edu/blog/fixgov/2020/06/08/how-the-constitutions-federalist-framework-is-being-tested-by-covid-19/. Accessed 16 Aug 2020.

Shuman, H. E. (1984). Politics and the budget: The struggle between the President and the Congress. Hoboken, NJ: Prentice-Hall.

Silver, H. (2021, January 19). Opinion: Trump's assault on the federal government isn't over. *The Hill.* https://thehill.com/opinion/white-house/534795-trumps-assault-on-the-federal-government-isnt-over?rl=1. Accessed 1 Feb 2021.

Skowronek, S. (1982). *Building a new American state: The expansion of national administrative capacities, 1877–1920.* Cambridge University Press.

Skowronek, S., Dearborn, J. A., & King, D. (2021). *Phantoms of a beleaguered republic. The deep state and the unitary executive.* Oxford University Press.

Smith, A. (2018, December 27). Trump now claims most furloughed workers 'are Democrats'. *NBC News.* https://www.nbcnews.com/politics/donald-trump/trump-now-claims-most-furloughed-workers-are-democrats-n952236. Accessed 11 Mar 2020.

Sperling, G. B. (2017, February 2). Government economists are going to produce statistics Trump doesn't like. *The Atlantic.*

Stivers, C. (2008). *Governance in dark times: Practical philosophy for public service.* Georgetown University Press.

Strohm, C. (2017, December 23). Trump pounces on report FBI's deputy director plans to retire. *Bloomberg.* https://www.bloomberg.com/news/articles/2017-12-23/fbi-deputy-director-mccabe-plans-to-retire-soon-wapost-reports. Accessed 30 May 2020.

Sunstein, C. R. (2018, March 7). What should worry Americans most about Trump. *Bloomberg.* https://www.bloomberg.com/opinion/articles/2018-03-07/what-should-worry-americans-most-about-trump. Accessed 26 Aug 2020.

Tenpas, K. D. (2021, January). *Tracking turnover in the Trump administration.* The Brookings Institution. https://www.brookings.edu/research/tracking-turnover-in-the-trump-administration/. Accessed 2 Mar 2021.

Terry, L. D. (2003). *Leadership of public bureaucracies: The administrator as conservator.* M.E. Sharpe.

The Bureaucrat. (1976, January). Federal political personnel manual: The "Malek manual". *The Bureaucrat, 4*(4), 429–508.

Thompson, F. J., Wong, K. K., & Rabe, V. G. (2020). *Trump, the administrative presidency, and federalism.* Brookings Institution Press.

Tomkin, S. L. (1998). *Inside OMB: Politics and process in the president's budget office.* M. E. Sharpe.

Tucker, P. (2020, July 20). DHS's Portland stunt could undermine the agency for years, former officials warn. *DefenseOne.* https://www.defenseone.com/policy/2020/07/dhss-portland-stunt-could-undermine-agency-years-former-officials-warn/167048. Accessed 25 July 2020.

U.S. Bureau of Labor Statistics (BLS). (2020, June 1). *About the U.S. Bureau of Labor Statistics.* https://www.bls.gov/bls/infohome.htm. Accessed 4 July 2020.

U.S. Congressional Budget Office (CBO). (2019, January). *The effects of the partial shutdown ending in January 2019.* Accessed 13 Dec 2019.

U.S. Congressional Research Service (CRS). (2018, July 25). *Trump administration reform and reorganization plan: Discussion of 35 "government-wide" proposals.* https://fas.org/sgp/crs/misc/reform.pdf. Accessed 19 May 2020.

U.S. Consumer Product Safety Commission (CPSC). (2017, February 2). *Statement of Chairman Elliot F. Kaye on CPSC's promulgation of federal safety rules.* https://www.cpsc.gov/about-cpsc/chairman/elliot-f-kaye/statements/statement-of-chairman-elliot-f-kaye-on-cpsc's. Accessed 19 March 2019.

U.S. Executive Office of the President (EOP). (2018a, June). *Delivering government solutions in the 21st century: Reform plan and reorganization recommendations.* Accessed 16 Dec 2019.

U.S. Executive Office of the President (EOP). (2018b, July 10). *Executive order excepting administrative law judges from the competitive service.* Accessed 8 Feb 2021.

U.S. Executive Office of the President (EOP). (2019, November 5). *Reminder regarding non-binding nature of GAO opinions.* Office of Management and Budget. Accessed 4 Dec 2019.

U.S. Executive Office of the President (EOP). (2020, October 21). *Executive order: Executive order on creating schedule F in the excepted service.* https://www.whitehouse.gov/presidential-actions/executive-order-creating-schedule-f-excepted-service/. Accessed 30 Oct 2020.

U.S. Executive Office of the President (EOP). (2021, January 21). *Executive order on protecting the federal workforce.* The White House Briefing Room. https://www.whitehouse.gov/briefing-room/presidential-actions/2021/01/22/executive-order-protecting-the-federal-workforce/. Accessed 30 Jan 2021.

U.S. Government Accountability Office (GAO). (2019a, March). *Internal Revenue Service: Strategic human capital management is needed to address serious risks to IRS's mission. GAO-19-176.* https://www.gao.gov/assets/gao-19-176.pdf. Accessed 14 Mar 2021.

U.S. Government Accountability Office (GAO). (2019b, April 3). *Priority open recommendations: Office of personnel management.* https://www.gao.gov/products/gao-20-543pr. Accessed 18 Nov 2020.

U.S. Government Accountability Office (GAO). (2019c, September 5). *Department of the Interior: Activities at national parks during the fiscal year 2019 lapse in appropriations. [Memorandum].* https://www.gao.gov/assets/710/701165.pdf. Accessed 21 Oct 2020.

U.S. Government Accountability Office (GAO). (n.d.). *High risk list.* https://www.gao.gov/highrisk/overview. Accessed 6 Jan 2020.

U.S. House Committee on Oversight and Reform Chairwoman Carolyn B. Maloney. (2020, April 1). *New emails show GSA involvement in the Trump Administration's plan to abolish OPM.* [Press release]. https://oversight.house.gov/news/press-releases/new-emails-show-gsa-involvement-in-the-trump-administration-s-plan-to-abolish. Accessed 10 Jan 2021.

U.S. Library of Congress: Research Guides. (n.d.). *Presidential signing statements.* https://guides.loc.gov/legislative-history/presidential-communications/signing-statements. Accessed 21 Mar 2021.

U.S. Merit Systems Protection Board (MSPB). (2021, February). *Direct-hire authority under 5 U.S.C. § 3304: Usage and outcomes.*

U.S. Office of Personnel Management (OPM). (2019). *Federal Employee Viewpoint Survey: Governmentwide management report.* https://www.opm.gov/fevs/reports/governmentwide-reports/governmentwide-management-report/governmentwide-report/2019/2019-governmentwide-management-report.pdf. Accessed 11 Aug 2020.

U.S. Office of Personnel Management (OPM). (2020, February 10). *CSRS/FERS new claims.* https://www.opm.gov/about-us/budget-performance/strategic-plans/retirement-processing-status.pdf. Accessed 11 Apr 2020.

Van Riper, P. (1958). *History of the United States civil service.* Row, Peterson and Company.

Verkuil, P. R. (2017). *Valuing bureaucracy: The case for professional government.* Cambridge University Press.

Volcker, P. A. (1989). *Leadership for America: Rebuilding the public service.* The report of the National Commission on the Public Service. [PDF File]. https://www.washingtonpost.com/wp-srv/opinions/documents/Leadership_for_America_Rebuilding_the_Public_Service.pdf. Accessed 14 Feb 2021.

Vought, R. (2020, September 4). *Training in the federal government.* [Memorandum]. Executive Office of the President. https://www.whitehouse.gov/wp-content/uploads/2020/09/M-20-34.pdf. Accessed 8 Oct 2020.

Wagner, E. (2018, June 21). OPM would lose its independence, service functions under reorganization plan. *Government Executive.* https://www.govexec.com/management/2018/06/under-reorganization-plan-opm-would-lose-its-independence-service-functions/149190/. Accessed 1 July 2019.

Wagner, E. (2019a, February 12). Labor relations authority chairwoman decertifies agency's own union. *Government Executive.* https://www.govexec.com/management/2019/02/flra-chairwoman-decertifies-agencys-own-union/154835/. Accessed 21 Jan 2021.

Wagner, E. (2019b, March 21). Trump administration outlines how the OPM-GSA merger would work. *Government Executive.* https://www.govexec.com/management/2019/03/trump-administration-outlines-how-opm-gsa-merger-would-work/155710/. Accessed 1 Apr 2019.

Wagner, E. (2019c, June 25). People are crying when they come into work: Unions protest OPM-GSA merger. *Government Executive.* https://www.govexec.com/management/2019/06/people-are-crying-when-they-come-work-unions-protest-opm-gsa-merger/158000/. Accessed 25 July 2020.

Wagner, E. (2020a, November 9). Rolling back Trump workforce policies won't be as simple as rescinding executive orders. *Government Executive.* https://www.govexec.com/management/2020/11/rolling-back-trump-workforce-policies-wont-be-simple-rescinding-executive-orders/169911/. Accessed 11 Dec 2020.

Wagner, E. (2020b, November 23). OMB reportedly designates 88% of its employees for schedule F. *Government Executive.* https://www.govexec.com/management/2020/11/omb-reportedly-designates-88-its-employees-schedule-f/170275/. Accessed 21 Oct 2020.

Wagner, E. (2021a, January 19). Don't expect Trump's workforce policies to be reversed overnight. *Government Executive.* https://www.govexec.com/management/2021/01/dont-expect-trumps-workforce-policies-be-reversed-overnight/171488/. Accessed 10 Feb 2021.

Wagner, E. (2021b, February 5). Union: VA continues stonewalling contract negotiations despite Biden order. *Government Executive.* https://www.govexec.com/management/2021/02/union-va-continues-stonewalling-contract-negotiations-despite-biden-order/171899/. Accessed 11 Feb 2021.

Wagner, E. (2021c, March 17). Study: OPM-GSA merger proposal would not have solved problems it aimed to fix. *Government Executive.* https://www.govexec.com/management/2021/03/study-opm-gsa-merger-proposal-would-not-have-solved-problems-it-aimed-fix/172735/. Accessed 30 Mar 2021.

Waldman, S. (2019, July 8). Trump officials deleting mentions of 'climate change' from U.S. Geological Survey press releases. *Science Magazine.* https://www.sciencemag.org/news/2019/07/trump-officials-deleting-mentions-climate-change-us-geological-survey-press-releases. Accessed 8 Jan 2020.

Warminsky, J. (2019, March 18). *Trump's cybersecurity budget emphasizes DOD while spreading cuts elsewhere.* FedScoop. https://www.fedscoop.com/cybersecurity-budget-2020-trump-white-house/. Accessed 14 Jan 2021.

WashPostPR. (2016, December 5). The Washington Post & Partnership for public service launch political appointee tracker. *The Washington Post.* https://www.washingtonpost.com/pr/wp/2016/12/05/the-washington-post-and-partnership-for-public-service-launch-political-appointee-tracker/. Accessed 17 July 2020.

Wegmann, P. (2020, November 21). OMB lists positions stripped of job protection under Trump order. *Real Clear Politics.* https://www.realclearpolitics.com/articles/2020/11/21/omb_lists_workers_stripped_of_job_protection_under_trump_order_144708.html. Accessed 8 Dec 2020.

Wheeler, T. (2020, November 18). *With only 11 weeks, a transition delayed is a transition denied.* The Brookings Institution. https://www.brookings.edu/blog/techtank/2020/11/18/with-only-11-weeks-a-transition-delayed-is-a-transition-denied/. Accessed 11 Jan 2021.

Williamson, J. M., & Bawa, S. G. (2018, June). *Estimated effects of the tax cuts and jobs act on farms and farm households.* U.S. Department of Agriculture. https://www.ers.usda.gov/webdocs/publications/89356/err-252.pdf?v=0. Accessed 19 Mar 2020.

Zitser, J. (2021, January 6). Biden official accuses Trump administration of 'sabotage,' following a string of controversial foreign policy decisions in the final days of the presidency. *Business Insider.* https://www.businessinsider.com/biden-official-accuses-trump-administration-of-sabotage-pbs-2021-1. Accessed 13 Jan 2021.

Chapter 8
Resilience: Reconstituting Capacity

> *The Deep State is a political allegation. The unitary executive is constitutional inference…Congress could accept its relegation to the sidelines, or it could try to double down on its prerogatives.*
>
> Stephen Skowronek, John Dearborn, and Desmond King (2021, pp. 9, 199)

8.1 Summing Up

In this condensed history of the monumental changes in federal administration, we have defined administrative capacity, explored it as an academic and a political development concept, and examined its evolution to understand how it decayed to the point that a number of significant failures recently occurred. To define administrative capacity, we identified its various meanings in the literature, including conceptions that went beyond staffing and budgeting. We then synthesized those meanings and grounded them in the political development literature to arrive at a new *definition*, a set of core *dimensions*, and a *framework* of capacity that would let us understand its swift deconstruction and imagine its path, moving forward.

We advocate moving past perceptions of administrative capacity that commonly referenced personnel and budget appropriations. Administrative capacity is more complex than that. The *definition* we arrived at reflects the difficult reconciliation of politics and administration. Today's extraordinary demands upon local and national public service compel a higher level of appreciation for how capacity is built and preserved. The *dimensions* we identified consist of management, problem-solving, administrative conservatorship, accountability, and engagement and communication. While problem-solving and management capture the functions of administration, administrative leadership, engagement, and accountability reflect those fundamental capacities required of bureaucracy in a democracy.

The *framework* we developed locates administrative capacity on two "planes" of understanding. One conceptualizes how, in history, capacity was treated by

© Springer Nature Switzerland AG 2021
M. E. Joaquin, T. J. Greitens, *American Administrative Capacity*,
https://doi.org/10.1007/978-3-030-80564-7_8

presidents and lawmakers when they tweaked those different dimensions to promote the *energetic executive*. The foundational balance of the energetic executive
led us to these five core dimensions. Some of the dimensions were emphasized at
different periods in history, as reformers used traditional approaches and transactional approaches to controlling capacity in federal personnel, budgeting, and other
processes. From the pre-administrative state era to professionalization away from
patronage, to managerialism, and to the use of entrepreneurial approaches that leveraged capacities outside of government, an understanding of how past administrative reforms failed to achieve resilient capacity and ultimately drove decline and
decay becomes evident. Most of the reforms implemented at the federal level since
the 1790s have emphasized a variety of dimensions over time, ranging from accountability enhancements to the latest management fad that could help increase efficiency and effectiveness. But it is also interesting to know what those reforms
generally minimized in their approach, such as considerations of problem-solving,
administrative conservatorship, and engagement, even as more administrative control was ceded by Congress to the president. Solutions in some dimensions bred
problems in other dimensions. Neglecting that balance over time contributed to the
breakdowns, shutdowns, and failures seen in the modern era. This then intersects
with that other "plane" of understanding capacity, the *unitary executive* theory bub-
bling underneath the experiments of the energetic executive. National commissions
looking into federal administrative efficiency over time addressed the performance
and scope of the administrative state to varying results, but they mostly
expanded the power of the president, even if incrementally. Whether controlling
the bureaucracy through performance or accountability measures, seeking capacity
in house or sourcing it from the private sector, invariably it's the presidency that
gained. Together, those two planes of analysis allow us to zoom in and regard more
wholly, at the same time, the changing character of federal administration. This
framework alerts us, amid the arriving and receding tides of administrative reforms,
to the macro drivers of capacity buildup and decline. With the dimensions of capacity oscillating during different eras, the framework tracks a second dynamic that was
operating almost imperceptibly, gradually pushing overall capacity away from the
direction of resilience and toward decay.

8.2   Reconstitution, Not Repair

Today's crises drive the hope of a greater appreciation from the American public
of the need for a capacitated government. That challenge had been met before, when
professional government emerged from decade-long efforts by reformers to negoti-
ate what an administrative system should look like within a democratic system. By
World War II, America possessed a bureaucracy that garnered widespread faith in its
competence despite a "hole" in the Constitution where public administration might
have been (Mashaw, 2009, p. 1). Yet, no sooner than it was dubbed the "fourth
branch of government," powerful and relevant, the administrative state was set on a

gradual path of decline and decay. This period of *capacity decay* reveals the fragility of American political and administrative institutions. We are reaping what the National Commission on the Public Service proclaimed as "a quiet crisis" in government in 1987. In fact, as recently as 3 years before the tumultuous winter of 2020, NAPA released *No Time To Wait: Building a Public Service for the 21st Century*. Pressing the urgency, the Academy pushed for transforming the government's human capital backbone and the development of systems that would let agencies adapt to wicked problems, demographic changes, and evolutions in the world of work. They called for recommitting to merit system principles, focusing agencies on results, and ensuring that accountability would accompany any grant of flexible management authorities.

In hindsight, the time between the Academy's report and the change in Washington in 2021 was eaten up not by a stagnancy in picking up those proposals but by the enactment of the very failures the Academy had feared. Administration crumbled in the face of a public health crisis. With a wobbly state unable to shield its polarized citizens from high-tech manipulation, democracy proved equally brittle. Stunning the world, a superpower displayed a decayed *capacity to marshal the authority, expertise, resources, and relationships needed to respond in an accountable way to people's needs.* But *repairing* capacity may not be sufficient to describe today's challenge, as some things cannot be walked back, nor should be restored to their pre-Trump era condition. To undo some of the damages his agenda has wrought to administrative capacity requires "bureaucratic archaeology" (Beitsch, 2021), but national problems keep mutating. New conflagrations in the nation's chronic flashpoints – immigration, inequality, national security, and climate change – require government to deploy its capacities, with no room for pause. For instance, a national move by the Republican Party to politicize state election infrastructure is afoot, endangering democracy – the very foundation of an *accountable* administrative capacity. Hate groups have become existential threats to the national legislature. Several months after mammoth wildfires turned the sky orange over California, Texas turned into a frigid tundra amid widespread power grid failure, raising fresh questions about the externalization of capacity. The silent, second-order, and unequal effects of the coronavirus pandemic have yet to capture the nation's attention. Amid vaccine hesitancy in a wide swath of the population, a fourth wave of coronavirus infections is at hand, reminding us of the significant failures to contain the initial threat and foster unity across the country.

Given the limited capacities at the state and local levels, surge capacity is again being demanded of the national bureaucracy, even as central budgeting and planning processes reel from the effects of the delayed presidential transition and the slow confirmation process for political appointees. Asylum seekers from hotspots across the globe where the American military is expected to withdraw are set to overwhelm the Biden immigration and intelligence bureaus. Government has, in this post-deconstruction era, become a composite of one surge capacity deployment after another: the National Guard travelling from the states to protect the Capitol from domestic enemies, FEMA and the military speeding up vaccination efforts in the lagging states and tapping an emergency law to create a Surge Capacity Force, and agencies rushing to disburse economic relief to distressed households. Clearly no single agency has the capacity to do the job alone, suggesting administrative depletion, perhaps even outmoded administrative structures. Despite the obvious flaws of the Trump reorganization attempts, there are more reasons now (for Congress) to rethink the public service apparatus.

At the same time, pandemic fatigue has dwindled the ranks of administrators and leaders, in local health offices, school districts, federal agencies, and the halls of Congress, itself. The extraordinary pressures upon leadership and administration as polarization and pandemic rage on make the crises even more dangerous than most people realize. With surge capacities not being replenished within the agencies, baseline capacities pushed to the limits at all government levels, and officials and bureaucrats scarred from harsh public attacks, mobilizing toward strategic goals has never been more tenuous. As Max Stier surmised of the wreckage of capacities post-Trump, it is mighty difficult to run a broken car while trying to fix it.

Indeed, the car may never again drive the same. This, despite the massive powers in the presidency over the administrative state, which, as this book has attempted to show, contributed to the solution, first, and then to the problem, of creating and maintaining a capacitated government. It is no paradox that capacity's coevolutionary dynamic has been the untrammeled rise of presidential power.

At the beginning of this project, we asked whether things could be walked back and where zones of resilience might lie in capacity rebuilding. Capacity has not merely declined; it has decayed and bears the scars of deliberate dismantling. So, if running the car while fixing it is arduous, could the answer be a different way of driving the car? And by whom? Perhaps, the challenge for the new government, the nation, and future reformers is not picking up the pieces and putting them back again, but *forging* a new, resilient administrative capacity after seeing how system failure and the emergence of tyranny became real possibilities. Over 200 years ago, these were the same concerns of the founders and especially Alexander Hamilton. With his idea of the *energetic executive*, he at least theoretically devised a way to solve such concerns in ways that protect democracy. The question left for us is whether such ideas – after being put to the test by the modern *unitary executives*, from Nixon to Trump – can survive into the future. To reconstitute capacity, Hamilton's ideals of the accountable, energetic executive must be brought forward to the twenty-first century, tempered by the *realpolitik* that attends the theory of the unitary executive, and layered with the post-pandemic imperative of *resilience*.

8.3 Reform Implications of the Coevolutionary Dynamics

The sight of newly elected presidents with a stack of executive orders to sign on their first day to "erase" or "reverse" the executive actions of their predecessors, and put their own stamp on the bureaucracy as well as various national policies, speaks to so much of the drivers of capacity that we identified in this book. This book has tried to show that the constant tinkering with bureaucracy has failed to incorporate capacity's multidimensional and political nature, with reformers prioritizing instead objectives that had to do more with presidential control. In the process of reform, the enhancement of executive power degraded overall administrative capacity.

The previous chapters showed how the presidency as an institution changed dramatically in the twentieth century. With the passage of the Budget and Accounting Act of 1921 and the implementation of reforms associated with the Brownlow Committee of the late 1930s, the presidency became more powerful as an administrative force. It now had the power of crafting a budget proposal for the entirety of federal administration and also possessed an Executive Office of the President to help implement more direct control over federal administration. Such powers only increased as the Bureau of the Budget, enabled as a Department of Treasury entity in the Budget and Accounting Act, eventually transformed itself into what is now OMB. This allowed the president an even greater way to imprint presidential priorities onto the entirety of federal administration. Additional administrative powers came from the ability to implement administrative reorganizations without congressional debate (albeit only temporarily as the power lapsed by the 1980s), the ability to contract out more and more administrative services, the end of the Civil Service Commission in the late 1970s as a counterbalance to presidential power, and the relative failure of its successor agencies, OPM, and even the MSPB, to act as a counterweight to presidential influence over federal administration. The outcome was executive dominance from an amalgamation of forces that accelerated beginning in the 1980s: transactionalism, congressional abdication of its role in a vibrant bureaucracy, and the public's disillusion with government and detachment from those bureaucratic routines that Lewis (2018) featured as so vital to guarding the country from low-probability but high-risk events.

Our close look at reforms tells us we need a greater awareness of the unintended consequences of reform ideas. Reforms can take a life of their own when neglected by Congress and result in administrative decline. The Brownlow Committee of the late 1930s, which embraced reforms then in favor within the discipline, directly led to the formation of the managerial presidency of the twentieth century. As administrative powers expanded, presidents were able to leverage more aspects of politics into their management of administration. While all presidents exercised such political tools to a degree, the Nixon administration's use of the tools reached a zenith with several massive reorganization efforts shrouding politicized presidential priorities. In just a few decades, *the energetic executive morphed into the unitary executive* that could do more harm than good for capacity.

The constellation of political actors and the changes they induced to American political development hopefully are clarified in this book. Congress has not been the same since the speakership of Newt Gingrich, when it unintentionally transferred powers to the executive and accelerated the privatization that started under Reagan. Business interests had always been influential in administrative development, but the shift from the Constitutional era of power separation to the Administrative era of expert administration to the Privatized era of running government like a *politicized* business was so profound that the contracting industry effectively mounted a "Constitutional coup" (Michaels, 2017). With party politics overriding their obligations, lawmakers allowed presidents to promote the narrative of a government that worked "cheaper, faster, smarter" through schemes that stripped the agencies of many of their inherently governmental functions. When the "shadow bureaucracy" expanded, it slipped gradually from public scrutiny, legal constraints, and congressional control and paradoxically demanded complex contract management capacities that agencies no longer possessed due to the very nature of privatization. This hybridized state became more amenable to the administrative presidency with its array of budget, personnel, and regulatory powers lodged within OMB. Congress' oversight of a thinned out civil service waned, while OPM, bereft of congressional and widespread employee support, became moribund, unable to lead in modernizing the fragmenting workforce. For its part, the public, not comprehending the magnitude of the governmental transformation and disillusioned by failed political promises, increasingly retreated from meaningful engagement. Yet they became more susceptible to market-favoring narratives and superficial digital participation that pushed them away from a place where they could compel Congress to fix bureaucracy's decline (Durant, 2010).

Examined longitudinally within the history of reform, therefore, we see how capacity rose alongside FDR's stewardship presidency, declined under Nixon and Reagan's administrative presidencies, and then accelerated to decay under Bush and Trump's unitary presidencies, with congressional consent. That disturbance of Constitutional design allowed capacity issues to get camouflaged by the rhetoric and "mirage of cost savings" (Chenok & Kamensky, 2021, p. 25) during the period of concealed decline. When the real state of capacity was uncovered by an insurgent executive, it came with a heavy price. With Trump, the unimpeded march of power centralization had left the apparatus exposed to what Constitutional historian Bruce Ackerman (2016) feared, the "unapologetic ideologue":

> (who) wins the White House and from day one exploits and creates "emergencies" as he vindicates his "mandate from the people" with sweeping unilateral initiatives. With Congress at an impasse, and the Court on the sidelines, the civilian and military bureaucracies impose the president's vision of a brave new world on a confused citizenry. This isn't quite what Woodrow Wilson had in mind. (p. 486)

This unitary thesis led to the recent years' efforts to shrink the scope of the merit system and solidify OMB's control over OPM. While those plans fizzled out with Trump's exit, their boldness has already moved the trajectory of political development – the tectonic plates under the swirling dimensions of capacities – through belief making and offering future Republicans a road map for dealing with the civil service that they regard as obstinate. Even failed reforms are celebrated among movement adherents intent on signaling their brand in the long game of shaping the administrative state. However, when reform is more ritual than reality and ignores the pressing challenges of the day, then we should expect breakdowns and failures to persist. Capacity is traded off for the chance to leave behind durable political movements or solidify partisan majorities: this political element is something we should keep sight of, as reform advocates.

In sum, these drivers of capacity's decline – congressional brokenness, executive dominance, politicization of the civil service, the severance of public identification with a capacitated government, and a reformism that focuses on political expediencies rather than the long-term complexities involved in a democratic public administration – serve as the markers for our ideas in forging a more resilient administrative capacity.

8.4   A Capacity-Centered Approach to Reform

Amid the pandemic, we came across several instances of resilience despite the disinvestments, delegitimization, and polarization in the public sphere. We saw *bureaucratic resilience* among federal and state administrators as they protected the 2020 election infrastructure and the integrity of the COVID-19 vaccine approval; *civic or societal resilience* among the front liners and their community supporters in healthcare, education, food, sanitation, and other essential services; *economic resilience* among companies that swiftly repurposed their base competencies toward producing those pandemic necessities; and *democratic resilience* among those who tirelessly campaigned on behalf of social justice, those who voted, and those who volunteered in the polls amid intimidation and a virus scare. Women activists and candidates, in particular, persisted and triumphed at the 2020 polls. Some experts doubted if that kind of resilience could have withstood another 4 years of Trump's unitary presidency (Frum, 2020).

More frequent and newer crises may be anticipated to occur in this hyper-connected but hyper-uncertain milieu. There is a window of opportunity around resilience that we must therefore quickly grab. Three hundred federal leaders revealed in a recent survey that "America's resilience depends on the resilience of its government" and it is time to act decisively (Partnership for Public Service et al., 2021, p. 1). Resilience is the capacity to adapt and recover from shocks or disturbances that are not normal or expected (Comfort et al., 2010, p. 273). In some ways, the unprecedented violation of government norms over the last 4 years could themselves be considered a type of shock and the change in national leadership a measure of recovery. The harder part is the adaptation after the disturbance.

The next reforms will need to consider the extent to which resilience is built within capacity, recognizing that delegitimating forces would never disappear, disinvestment is possible with greater economic uncertainties and the broken public budgeting system, and a bifurcation of capacity increases with each pendulum swing between one unitary president and the next.

In these concluding pages, we aim not to repeat the various ideas out there from the likes of NAPA that offer comprehensive and smart strategies to fix what ails the federal government. Instead, we offer some thoughts from a capacity-centered approach to reform that involves revitalizing Congress, promoting administrative engagement, rethinking the reform community's advocacy strategies, and renewing trust, the democratic bargain and citizens' sense of a shared fate.

8.4.1   Putting Congress in Charge of Resilient Capacity Building

The American government system was designed to be self-correcting in terms of Constitutional and political balance, but recent national crises put this notion in doubt (Kettl, 2020, pp. 187–188). The most restorative step forward involves addressing the political root of the current administrative imbalance: the dissipation of congressional capacity to oversee the administrative state. We can renew "the broken branch" by giving it the responsibility of spearheading this task of resilient capacity building.

The reasons for this are political and practical. In the past, many of the more successful reforms that helped to increase federal administrative capacity had direct linkages back to Congress. For example, in the late 1860s, Congress' Joint Select Committee on Retrenchment helped to publicize the abuses of the spoils system while also showcasing reforms in Great Britain that implemented a nonpartisan civil service (US House, 1868). That work eventually helped lead to the creation of the Civil Service Commission and the gradual fading of the spoils system within federal administration. Additionally, in the 1880s and 1890s, the work of the congressional Cockrell Committee and the Dockery-Cockrell Commission helped routinize the systematic analysis of federal administration within Congress. Arguably, such work influenced later administrative reform efforts throughout the early 1900s. However, in the modern administrative state, Congress often acted as a secondary force in administration. It delegated authorities to executive branch agencies and gave the president more administrative power under the assumption that leadership power concentrated in one executive was better than leadership power dispersed between an executive and legislature. By the time of Trump administration, partisan dynamics mixed with congressional acquiescence or inaction ensured the presidentialization of federal administration.

To regain its institutional bearings, Congress would have to do something it has not been increasingly able to do: rise above partisan politics. The recent attempts to overhaul the civil service by executive means have probably stirred congressional interest in grand administrative reforms again. Giving the body, this charge might be the best medicine for its own ailment. Congress already has a committee studying its own modernization; this should build on top of that committee's effort in defining Congress' vision for, and relationship with, bureaucracy in the next century. In the same way that its institutional erosion is associated with bureaucracy's gradual move out of its shadow, focusing Congress' energy on reversing that trend might revive it at the same time. But rather than fragmenting this task among its several committees that create their own task forces or commission their own studies, Congress should elevate this concern by creating a bipartisan group from the two chambers, with an explicit mandate to arrive at a series of reform measures tying administration to economic, democratic, and civic resilience.

Congress as the leader of a *resilience movement* would involve harvesting and distilling every floating package of proposals out there and facilitating a courageous conversation about capacity failures and capacitated futures. Ideas for public sector renewal and transformation are literally bursting from every corner right now, at all levels, from the Government Accountability Office to California's Little Hoover Commission, and in different learning communities, from NAPA to the IBM Center for the Business of Government. A new bipartisan commission would not lack for insightful data right now from the recent crises that have served as natural-type experiments on the country's political development and the behaviors of governments and groups under conditions of extreme stress.

Because it holds the power of the purse, investing in capacity in and out of the bureaucracy is Congress' natural responsibility; how it does so to build resilient capacity able to withstand the next unitary executive is a higher calling worthy of the first branch. It must not merely allocate resources for current public needs; it has to find that balance that would prepare the administrative state for "black swan" events. To build administrative resilience, decoupling or sacrificing certain administrative integrations or efficiencies might be needed to minimize catastrophic domino effects from the shocks that are surely coming (Friedman, 2020). Our grasp of costs and vulnerabilities must be adjusted. Resilience means understanding the trade-offs in the present – be they in fiscal policy, in human capital management, or in the regulation of vital infrastructure – to prevent a more calamitous future. Before any citizen could be expected to do it, lawmakers themselves must acquire a full grasp of the problems of bureaucratic fragmentation, including the mismanagement of federal contractors that can affect our ability to respond to disasters, natural and otherwise (Perrow, 2011).

In addition, Congress must find a way to prevent toxic national politics from inviting disasters from within and abroad. "We no longer have to fear the tweet," the president of the Truman National Security Project and a former State department official declared, conveying what millions had felt were severely destabilizing erraticism under the 45th president (Borger, 2021, para. 5). Only a national body like Congress, with bureaucracy at its side, could forge a sense of national unity that would not come on its own. They would need to take this movement out of the capital when ready and develop reform communities at the local levels.

8.4.2 Empowering Administrative Conservators in Engagement and Problem-Solving

Reform as an exercise does not always lead to capacity enhancement, nor is capacity simply about the levels of budget and staffing allocated in a fiscal year. The complexity involved in public administration must be understood as political dynamics evolve over time, social and economic challenges change, and public demands for policy and services increase without a commensurate understanding of how everything ties together. We need to reconceptualize administrative capacity in those five core dimensions that we identified. Belittling the work of public administration, as grandstanding politicians like to do, and the capacity it requires invites citizen indifference, at best, and demagoguery of bureaucracy, at worst. When the capacity dimensions are ignored or become unbalanced, decay and decline occur. Throughout history, the dimension of *management* often received extensive attention. For balance, we recommend additional capacity enhancements in the rest of the areas of administrative conservatorship, problem-solving, accountability, and engagement.

First, *administrative conservatorship* needs to recover from years of "deep state" accusations. Reforms never seem to value the administrative conservators, repository of institutional memory and guardians of agencies' distinctive competence at the top and middle levels of the hierarchy. Often conflated with the worst tendencies of bureaucratic politics and the failure to quickly follow a presidential directive, administrative conservators preserve programmatic integrity and a wealth of expertise to help programs increase efficiencies and effectiveness. We could, instead, "unleash" those phantoms conjured by Trump and let them demonstrate their administrative "depth" in knowledge, in promotion of democratic norms, and in seeing to it that ethics and public service values are preserved and observed (see Skowronek et al., 2021).

Structuring the work of conservators enables resilience planning to occur. Reforms over the last two decades promoting mission support "chiefs" in each federal agency (e.g., chief financial officers, chief information officers, chief human capital officers, chief data officers), for example, elevate such a cadre and structure their efforts in initiatives that run across agencies. The likes of the Volcker Alliance and the Senior Executive Association also sustain creative networks to promote resilience within the ranks of administrative leaders and develop pathways for talent to get into government as it struggles with waves of retirement and a broken image. Because these communities consist of veteran managers and reformers, their proposals for improving administrative leadership are grounded on what the agencies confront in the trenches daily.

For instance, in *problem-solving* capacity building, these veterans emphasize organizational learning, distinguishing between insight and oversight, and eschewing a compliance mentality or application of logic models that stifle understanding of the linkages between actions and results (S. Metzenbaum, personal communication, March 10, 2019). They recognize that OPM and OMB cannot keep playing their part as proxies in the battle to control the bureaucracy or as pawns in executive-legislative battles or partisan games. Experts know that the agencies' problems with the use of contracting, a staple of GAO's high-risk auditing activities, will persist until the civil service system itself is fixed (Verkuil, 2017, p. 14). They recognize the importance of developing executives' mental maps of administration. For example, Senators confirmed an administrative conservator's nomination because they believe that he could "unstick problems inside agencies and across agencies and, especially in an agency as large as VA." The conservator knew how the government worked, and he knew when it did not work (Katz, 2021). Such problem-solving ability was credited to his depth of experience in government, which would in turn help in rebuilding confidence and trust in and within the agency. Finally, administrative conservatorship should be not seen as the realm of senior executives alone. Middle managers and front liners may be counted on to sustain initiatives long after interest at the top level wanes. In Dan Chenok and John Kamensky's reflections on decades of government reform (2021, p. 11), they found that bottom-up engagement that taps creativity, such as the development of "playbooks" and "mythbusters" in the digital services, personnel, and acquisition communities – allows front line leaders to proactively continue those initiatives even if top leaders lose interest.

While experience, learning from past reforms, and analysis are important, according to Howard (2012), building problem-solving capacity in administration also requires political *courage*: courage to set aside rivalries to get work done; courage to confront the special interests that make money out of Washington incapacity, gridlock, or conflict; and courage to identify who has the responsibility for fixing a problem in government. As the pandemic and the Capitol riot proved, such solutions are not easy. And when administrative conservators are delegitimized in the eyes of the public and divided as they go about their work, they lose capacity even before a single cut is done to their budget or staffing.

In *engagement and communication*, the pandemic showed the importance of core problem-solving skills linked to knowledge, the formation of deliberative spaces, and investing in communication and engagement pathways between public agencies and citizens. The bureaucracy-bashing movement has been allowed to go on for as long as it had without requiring the debate about it to be responsible and capacity-centered, largely because many bashers get elected to Congress. That has clearly impaired capacity to coordinate services, communicate responses, and bridge the deep divisions that show up during crises. Making Congress spearhead resilience building will force them to confront this capacity-defeating phenomenon. They should also, in this age of political provocateurs, let bureaucracy "speak." Capacity rebuilding may require greater administrative skill building in attention channeling and belief making among bureaucrats as they engage policymakers and citizens. This is not about engaging with interest groups or the "iron triangles" of old but revisiting the educative facet of administration that was articulated in Woodrow Wilson's 1887 essay, and that retained some of its spirit in local participatory budgeting processes.

Federal administrative reforms have been built on a foundation that typically limits opportunities for these dimensions of capacity. That is not to say that administrative agencies cannot engage and communicate or to ignore the fact that reforms like the Administrative Procedure Act included new avenues for engagement and communication for processes like administrative rulemaking. However, reforms rarely publicize the achievements of federal administrators and too often restrict their opportunities to directly engage policymakers and the public. Many of these restrictions stem from public administration's notions of separating politics from administration. While such notions helped to prevent the abuses of the past, they also tend to constrict communication channels between administrators and policymakers and between administrators and citizens. The lack of public engagement in federal administration is even more alarming when considering the ease of online engagement and communication. Marketing the successes of administration is just as important as documenting its failures. If agencies invested smartly in communicating itself to the public and invested similarly in infrastructure for citizens to be able to communicate back, then greater interest in administration might result. It could even help end the vacuum of interest from Congress that has defined federal administration for at least a decade.

Engagement capacity should also be geared toward community building (see the last section). Crowdsourcing and rewarding ideas from the public and the private sector on how to improve government, as the GSA Centers of Excellence has done, promote pockets or communities of learning beyond government and academia that may contribute to a bigger reform movement. Finally, agencies must enhance their own communication capacity to stimulate the same repair in the polarized body politic. This would help address collective issues that require mutual problem-solving and less ideology.

8.4.3   An RX for the Reformer

The watchtower is a tough place to be – sounding frequent alarms that could go unheeded and watching reform proposals languish year in and year out amid tribal politics in Washington, DC. Emerging out of this pandemic, nostalgia in the field of public administration has a place. In the budding days of the administrative state, national reformers sought both business and academia for ideas. This partnership worked intermittently until the Great Society and then went downhill with fiscal conservatism and the anti-government movement. Flashy slogans from private think tanks instead influenced the last civil service reorganization and the reinvention movement. By the time Clinton and Gore celebrated the end of big government, public administration's influence was on its twilight (Ingraham, 2007, p. 83). This is a past from which we cannot avert our eyes.

Some lessons in reform may have to do with seeing the connection better between our meso-centered theories and macro-political desires and context, a connection that Alasdair Roberts suggested is necessary to make sense of administrative pasts and administrative futures. *Learning* being one of the elements of resilience, we can begin by evaluating the efficacy of our own prescriptions and strengthening the political system's *buy-in* of the same. As a discipline, public administration cannot be effective if our conversation is primarily among ourselves and bemoaning how our subject matter, government itself is shrinking. And each year that administrative capacity is neglected in the manner we have observed, there may be fewer and fewer ways to rebuild it. So, how do we drive the car differently from here on? How do we *move* the ground and not just the timing of the waves? This requires more political awareness in public administration, first, and, second, a higher regard for the power of belief systems.

A more politically aware administrative theory must eschew administrative precepts that presuppose a balance of Constitutional powers and civic support for a functional democratic administration. Those may not be true anymore and instead prove academic warnings on federal administration to be an exercise in futility, part of a long-standing reform theater that does little to alter the balance (or imbalance) of power or long-term administrative capacity. Reforms need to resonate among politicians whose currency is power and among a public mistrustful of expertise, academic or not. We need to adapt to the political incentives existing within this technologically abetted, polarized environment. We need to quickly grasp the philosophy of those who capture the levers of power every 4 or 8 years and to make our reform theories of relevance to them. What leaders conceive of as the biggest challenges facing the nation and what their strategies and priorities are must be built into the strategies we advocate for capacity building. Refusing to anchor in that manner might relegate us to even more irrelevance.

This is not to say that good government proposals must be politicized. It means they should be geared toward adoption or implementation by politicians whose incentives, in history, were often to *control, first, and capacitate bureaucracy, second*. To be heard effectively, the community must improve its own engagement capacity at the macro level. Post-truth era reform advocacy requires being tactical, rather than academic, using the appeal of frameshifts in changing government and leaders' mindsets. Paradoxical as this may sound, we must engage politicians with ideas that go beyond Weberian notions of performance improvement. The appeal to frameshifting may be done by grounding reforms and couching them in the language of *beliefs, values, and movements*. Buy-in must be developed among administrators to develop "champions…with an immense ability to use symbolism to convey a compelling" reform agenda (Chenok & Kamensky, 2021, pp. 8–9). Larry Lane (1992, p. 108) observed that during last reform of federal personnel administration, the reformers were satisfied with being influenced by theory alone, but in the implementation phase, they needed true believers, and that was where things got difficult. The result was the weakness of OPM as a central agency, out of the gate, and look how the entire merit system crashed in 2020, as a consequence.

Symbolism and beliefs have proved their potency in recent years. What citizens are made to believe is an important thing to keep a close watch on, as an almost altered sense of reality has pervaded a sizeable segment of the population. For so long, many people have delegated to politicians and factions the job of framing the relevant questions of the state, but it is time for administrators to speak up. We must complement our community's political reorientation by cultivating interest and belief in the *grand design* of administration, embedding those elements of resilience and trade-offs we discussed above. One of the biggest lessons of this era may involve embracing the importance of communication and signaling, a skill the 45th president displayed masterfully in the technological age. Before a backdrop of populism, Trump's disinvestment, delegitimization, and bifurcation of governmental capacities did not seem to bother the 70 million who chose him in the last election. It seemed the more he broke things in Washington, the more they supported this unitary executive, because the symbols he cultivated in their minds were not about reconciling any two liberal ideas together. They were straight and singular: it's identity, not unity; politics, not administration; control, not capacity. We have to match that skill for the values and institutions we cherish.

As we have just seen, anti-intellectualism and mistrust of expertise have reached new heights. When politicians themselves encourage those tendencies, some lessons are meant for those of us who keep advancing the same medicine for transformation. Prescriptions that promote capacity building are of little use to a unitary executive intent on weakening government if it gets in the way of his politics and belief-making enterprise. Reports advancing clear, actionable ways of modernizing government may also not get traction in a deinstitutionalized Congress.

We probably have reached that point in history at which politically correct sounding agendas would only flounder in this new ecology of disinformation and polarization. The best way to call attention is by being bold and adjusting our theories and practice in path-breaking ways, with the citizens behind us in fashioning change on a larger scale. It would at least match the tempo of the Biden administration, which frames its governing challenge as aspiring to, or even eclipsing that of, New Deal reforms (Debenedetti, 2020). As those who have been on the trenches of administrative reform for a long time have recognized:

> Being bold is hard these days; there's no magic wand. The fundamental observation regarding government reorganization is that it requires both branches and bipartisan agreement. And, that it is more likely to successfully promote a reorganization in response to an urgent problem than to advocate reorganization for reasons of greater efficiency or effectiveness. (Chenok & Kamensky, 2021, p. 25)

We need to ponder such sentiments as the stakes are so much higher now and the country no longer possesses the luxury that reformers of old enjoyed at the dawn of American state building. Reformers who have seen pendulum swings, reinventions, and deconstructions know that a storm gathers quickly in the political sphere, and even though they may dissipate as quickly, the disruption they leave in their wake for bureaucrats could be inimical to continuing innovations, problem-solving, or engagement efforts. But the starting point always matters in the evolution of bureaucracy. We are in the aftermath of deconstruction: take stock. Sometimes reform markers move capacity forward, as desired, and sometimes they conceal the cracks in capacity. With politics contributing to uncertainty, resilient administrators and their brethren in good government are the only ones who could help find and fix those gaps.

8.4.4 Renewing the Democratic Bargain and Citizens' Sense of a Shared Fate

At some point, we have to find a way to address the notion that only crises should wake people up, that only by becoming a failed state would people appreciate the collective spirit and work that goes into maintaining democratic and administrative institutions. Because by then, it would be too late.

If, across American government history, power has been accomplished through the administrative mechanism, there is likewise no way to go around political parties and citizens in rebuilding administrative capacity. In the beginning, partisan influence and the role of citizens were fundamental questions in the forging of the administrative state. We can only move forward by getting those questions back into our national conversations. Ultimately, a capacity-centered approach links bureaucratic resilience with democratic resilience in reseeding capacity. Stakeholders in good government – political parties and their support base, especially – need to renew the democratic bargain and develop a greater awareness of how much the battle for political control injures capacity building. With militant, white extremism capturing the base of the Republican Party and voting rights in great peril in many states, the social contract is fraying. No capacity rebuilding effort would last long without everyone's explicit assent to democracy and the legitimacy of its instruments. The nation barely passed the recent test of democratic resilience. There is now no time to wait to fix the elements that had led to those vulnerabilities. Certain things can be reformed by legislation, and certain things can only be repaired by rebuilding trust. Agility in national problem-solving during a pandemic might have been enhanced, for instance, via reform of the presidential transition rules and processes. The 2020 election saga showed that capacity could be held hostage in the long interregnum between the departure of the defeated incumbent and the inauguration of his rival.

As Congress deals with the political parties, administrators must be enabled to rebuild citizen trust. The public administration community must reanchor its notions of reform around political development and craft a theory that places bureaucrats and citizens in an alliance for long-term capacity building. Civic participation theories of old must be geared to this strange new reality in which a president could divide from within and laws work with such excruciating slowness that much capacity may be destroyed by the time they take effect.

Many questions need to be answered around capacity's decline, decay, and resilience in view of the recent threats to public health and democratic norms. It would be interesting to see what any commission-style inquiries into the handling of the pandemic (Govtrack, n.d.) and the Capitol assault, for example, would discover. Surely they could lead to greater enhancements in intelligence and management capacities in heading off cyberattacks, epidemics, or extremism in law enforcement. But Congress could also direct those investigations to focus on resilience – how it is lost, regained, and enhanced – with the added perspective of citizens. Congress may find that these mass traumas have profoundly changed people's perceptions of governmental risks and their appreciation for professional bureaucracy.

Decades before the coronavirus pandemic, a former leader of the West, Margaret Thatcher, declared, "there is no such thing as society. There are individual men and women, and there are families, and no government can do anything except through people, and people must look to themselves first" (*BBC News, 2017*). The practical consequences of such a philosophy were seen in conservative programs that did not bet on society, but placed their faith on the private sector. Now that the privatization revolution has almost completed its run, we are confronted with wicked problems that neither markets nor individualism could fix. The former absorbs shock by passing the burden to the least sophisticated actor, while the latter is vulnerable to elements that benefit from cultural wars and government paralysis.

Public servants and the public must re-engage each other and materialize that idea of mutual promising (Stivers, 2008), somehow. The dynamics that have recently brought the country to the edge of the cliff show we must conscript citizens in capacity building and renew the sense of a shared fate they used to have with government in the post-War era. In the mid-1960s, the public's trust in the federal government reached a high of almost 80 percent. But by 2020, the public's trust routinely hovered near 20 percent (Pew Research Center, 2017). Without public support, administrative capacity always tends to decline and decay. Past reformers recognized this fact, but many of today's reformers do not emphasize it enough. Our zone of resilience lies among professional public servants and the people who believe in them and their complementary strengths. There is nothing like an appreciation for the nuances of administration, not just policymaking, to underscore the need for the soul and the apparatus of public service to be made accessible to the public and, when those two things need fixing, for the same public to ensure that their representatives do the necessary work of rebuilding. In the long term, we must find a way to elect reformers and those who would promote a sense of shared ownership of good government. Ways must be found to get such reform candidates a constituency. They are out there, particularly among the youth who have, during the pandemic, gotten to know government up close and discovered new ways of public service. Many powerful forces benefit from the brokenness of the status quo; the only countervailing force is citizen muscle behind a reform movement, outside of the Beltway.

It is said that the pandemic has damaged the economy in irreparable ways, that any financial infusions might never bring back the conditions that the world enjoyed before 2020. Are democracy and public administration also weakened in long-lasting ways? The hit that America's democratic reputation took as a result of the Capitol assault gave ammunition to those who believe that power must never be shared and good government should not be allowed to stand in their way. As some of the destruction and deconstruction of 2020–2021 move to our rearview mirror, we must take the time to reflect. We fear that the scarring of American administrative capacity must be addressed promptly. Right when new threats are forming on the nation's horizon, the hour is already late. To cope, patchwork changes may have to happen at the street-level administration, but those who command the macro-political levers will have to steer a new direction, fast. To shift the path of capacity, Congress ought to lead in the work of reconstitution, a more politically aware public administration community must supply its intellectual foundation, and administrative conservators, in lockstep with citizens, should serve as the legs of a resilience movement. The dream of a vibrant and equitable democracy is at stake. – EJ/TG.

References

Ackerman, B. (2016). What is to be done? In S. Skowronek, S. M. Engel, & B. Ackerman (Eds.), *The progressives' century: Political reform, constitutional government, and the modern American state* (pp. 478–494). Yale University Press.

Beitsch, R. (2021, March 14). Biden struggles to unravel web of Trump immigration rules. *The Hill.* https://thehill.com/homenews/administration/543041-biden-officials-struggle-to-unravel-web-of-trump-immigration-rules. Accessed 19 Mar 2021.

BBC News. (2017, January 9). *Society and the Conservative Party.* https://www.bbc.com/news/uk-politics-38553797. Accessed 29 Apr 2021.

Borger, J. (2021, April 30). 'We no longer fear the tweet': Biden brings US back to world stage in first 100 days. *The Guardian.* https://www.theguardian.com/us-news/2021/apr/30/joe-biden-foreign-policy-first-100-days. Accessed 30 Apr 2021.

Chenok, D. & Kamensky, J. (2021). *Government reform: Lessons from the past for actions in the future* (Special Report). IBM Center for the Business of Government. http://www.businessofgovernment.org/sites/default/files/Government%20Reform-Lessons%20from%20the%20Past%20for%20Actions%20in%20the%20Future.pdf. Accessed 17 Mar 2021.

Comfort, L. K., Boin, A., & Demchak, C. C. (2010). Resilience revisited: An action agenda for managing extreme events. In L. K. Comfort, A. Boin, & C. C. Demchak (Eds.), *Designing resilience: Preparing for extreme events* (pp. 272–284). University of Pittsburgh Press.

Debenedetti, G. (2020, May 11). Biden is planning an FDR-size presidency. *Intelligencer.* https://nymag.com/intelligencer/2020/05/joe-biden-presidential-plans.html. Accessed 1 June 2020.

Durant, R. F. (2010). Herbert Hoover's revenge: Politics, policy, and administrative reform movements. In R. F. Durant (Ed.), *The Oxford handbook of American bureaucracy* (pp. 153–178). Oxford University Press.

Friedman, U. (2020, November 15). The pandemic is revealing a new form of national power. *The Atlantic.* https://www.theatlantic.com/ideas/archive/2020/11/pandemic-revealing-new-form-national-power/616944/. Accessed 21 Nov 2020.

Frum, D. (2020, November). Last exit from autocracy. *The Atlantic.* https://www.theatlantic.com/magazine/archive/2020/11/last-exit-trump-autocracy/616466/. Accessed 1 Dec 2020.

Govtrack. (n.d.). *S. 4132 (116th): National Commission on the COVID–19 Pandemic in the United States Act.* https://www.govtrack.us/congress/bills/116/s4132. Accessed 21 Mar 2021.

Howard, P. K. (2012, August 3). Reform is not enough: The federal government needs a complete makeover. *The Atlantic.* https://www.theatlantic.com/politics/archive/2012/08/reform-is-not-enough-the-federal-government-needs-a-complete-makeover/260669/. Accessed 6 Aug 2020.

Ingraham, P. W. (2007). Who should rule? In D. Rosenbloom & H. E. McCurdy (Eds.), *Revisiting Waldo's administrative state: Constancy and change in public administration* (pp. 71–85). Georgetown University Press.

Katz, E. (2021, January 27). Biden's VA pick says he can 'unstick problems' within the bureaucracy. *Government Executive.* https://www.govexec.com/management/2021/01/bidens-va-pick-says-he-can-unstick-problems-within-bureaucracy/171689/. Accessed 30 Jan 2021.

Kettl, D. F. (2020). *The divided states of America: Why federalism doesn't work.* Princeton University Press.

Lane, L. M. (1992). The Office of Personnel Management: Values, policies, and consequences. In P. W. Ingraham & D. H. Rosenbloom (Eds.), *The promise and paradox of civil service reform* (pp. 97–120). University of Pittsburgh.

Lewis, M. (2018). *The fifth risk.* W.W. New York.

Mashaw, J. L. (2009, January 13). Government practice and presidential direction: Lessons from the antebellum republic. *Willamette Law Review, 45*(3). https://ssrn.com/abstract=1327056. Accessed 18 Dec 2020.

Michaels, J. D. (2017). *Constitutional coup: Privatization's threat to the American republic.* Harvard University Press.

National Academy of Public Administration (NAPA)National Academy of Public Administration (NAPA). (2017, July). *No time to wait: Building a public service for the 21st century.*

Partnership for Public Service (PPS)Partnership for Public Service (PPS). (2020, November 20). Coalition letter on Schedule F. https://cdn.govexec.com/media/gbc/docs/pdfs_edit/112320ew1.pdf. Accessed 7 Dec 2020.

Perrow, C. (2011). *The next catastrophe: Reducing our vulnerability to natural, industrial, and terrorist disasters* (Revised ed). Princeton University Press.

Pew Research Center. (2017, May 3). *Public trust in government remains near historic lows as partisan attitudes shift.* Pew Research Center. https://www.pewresearch.org/politics/2017/05/03/public-trust-in-government-remains-near-historic-lows-as-partisan-attitudes-shift/. Accessed 11 June 2019.

Skowronek, S., Dearborn, J. A., & King, D. (2021). *Phantoms of a beleaguered republic. The deep state and the unitary executive.* Oxford University Press.

Stivers, C. (2008). *Governance in dark times: Practical philosophy for public service.* Georgetown University Press.

U.S. House. (1868). *Civil service of the United States.* H.R. Rep. No. 40-47. Government Printing Office.

Verkuil, P. R. (2017). *Valuing bureaucracy: The case for professional government.* Cambridge University Press.

Index

© Springer Nature Switzerland AG 2021
M. E. Joaquin, T. J. Greitens, *American Administrative Capacity*,
https://doi.org/10.1007/978-3-030-80564-7

CPSIA information can be obtained
at www.ICGtesting.com
Printed in the USA
LVHW021937101121
702935LV00003B/216